Living
Smart—
New York City®

Living Smart—
New York City®

**THE ULTIMATE
INSIDER'S GUIDE
FOR THE
BUDGET SAVVY**

Craig Wroe

First Limelight Edition December 2004

© 2004 Craig Wroe

Published by:
Limelight Editions (an imprint of Amadeus Press)
512 Newark Pompton Turnpike
Pompton Plains, New Jersey 07444, USA
www.limelighteditions.com

For sales, please contact:
Limelight Editions
c/o Hal Leonard Corporation
7777 West Bluemound Road
Milwaukee, Wisconsin 53213, USA
Tel. 800-637-2852
Fax 414-774-3259

Book interior design and typesetting by Rachel Reiss

Printed in the United States of America

LIBRARY OF CONGRESS CATALOGING-IN-PUBLICATION DATA
Wroe, Craig.
  Living smart--New York City : the ultimate insider's guide for the budget
savvy / Craig Wroe.-- 1st Limelight ed.
     p. cm.
  ISBN 0-87910-308-6 (pbk.)
  1. New York (N.Y.)--Guidebooks. 2. New York (N.Y.)--Hand-
books, manuals, etc. 3. Finance, Personal--New York (State)--New
York--Handbooks, manuals, etc. I. Title.
F128.18.W76 2004
917.47'10444--dc22
                                          2004024268

For
John Ryan
and
Frank Rizzo

"On any person who desires such queer prizes, New York will bestow the gift of loneliness and the gift of privacy. It is this largess that accounts for the presence within the city's walls of a considerable section of the population; for the residents of Manhattan are to a large extent strangers who have pulled up stakes somewhere and come to town, seeking sanctuary or fulfillment or some greater or lesser grail. The capacity to make such dubious gifts is a mysterious quality of New York. It can destroy an individual, or it can fulfill him, depending on a good deal of luck. No one should come to New York to live unless he is willing to be lucky."

—E.B. WHITE, *HERE IS NEW YORK*

"If I can make it there, I'll make it anywhere."

—KANDER AND EBB

Acknowledgments

I would like to thank John Ryan, who years ago suggested that I put all of the following into a book and encouraged me throughout the writing process. Thanks, too, to Frank Rizzo who provided constant crucial guidance and inspiration.

I offer my deepest appreciation and thanks to the many friends and colleagues who offered their invaluable suggestions and contributions. Special thanks to Nina Maynard, Jacqueline Farrington, Carol Schultz, Rob Birnbaum, Laurine Towler, Lisa Tatham, Bill Clarke, Michael Chaban, Don Bayley, Gina Daniels, Dennis Delaney, Shelley Delaney, Jay Patterson, Bill Kux, Andrea Cirie, Dave Ciliberto, Chris Downey, Pamela Nyberg, Eve Eaton, Paul Gamner, Stefano Imbert, Larry Gershberg, Glenn Teller, John Sullivan, Jim Duncan, Charles Karchmer, David Kennedy, Henny Russell, William Gibson, Sharon Washington, Michael Feingold, Reno Roop, Marjorie Murray Roop, Patricia S. Schwadron, Patrick Frederic, Maggie Frederic, Sybil Lines, Todd Phillips, Ellen Ferris, Valerie Coates, Sarah Stasaitis, Heather Muhleman, Matthew Floyd Miller, Todd Hunter, Blake Barlow, Carla Capone, Bob Sacheli, Jim Poles, Matt Loney, Mauricio Alexander and Dea Lawrence.

Infinite thanks to Paul Reisman at Abrams Artists for his encouragement. Special kudos to my literary agent Maura Teitelbaum, the best agent a writer could ask for.

My heartfelt gratitude goes out to my legit agents Mary Harden, Nancy Curtis, Michael Kirsten, Scott Edwards, Nancy Clarkin and Diane Riley for their years of support and friendship. Ditto that sentiment to Tracy Goldblum, Genine Esposito, Alison Quartin and the entire crew in the Commercial Department at Abrams Artists.

Heaps of praise goes out to my publisher John Cerullo, Jenna Young and the entire crew at Amadeus Press/Limelight Editions.

Thanks to the Metropolitan Transit Authority for their $21 unlimited weekly "Metropass," which made it possible for me to haul my butt all over the city to research this book.

Contents

All Work and No Play   263

Foreword

Every New Yorker, whether born-and-bred or yesterday's emigrant, knows or quickly learns that the only constant about life here in Gotham is that nothing is constant. All is in flux; nothing stays the same. It should come as no surprise then that much has changed in the Big Apple in the two years since I completed the first edition of this book (originally titled, *An Actor Prepares... to Live in New York City*). Countless services, institutions, organizations and retailers have sprouted up and shut down, and keeping up has been a challenge—nearly a full-time job.

Every chapter has been updated, revised and expanded, with myriad additions and, sad to say, several deletions (R.I.P.: Guggenheim Museum Soho, Today's Man, The Wiz, Ninth Avenue Cheese, Healthy Pleasures, Dances for Wave Hill, Gryphon Bookstore, Urban Leather Outlet, Tower Records Clearance Outlet, Godmother's League Thrift Store, Void Lounge, Elbow Room, Crocodile Computers, Nice Price Women's Clothing, Mainly Manhattan Walking Tours, Norman's #2 New and Used CDs and DVDs, Props For Today's retail store, Theodore Roosevelt Birthplace $2 piano concerts, Tompkins Square Studio, HMV Records' "CD Club" card, American Value Centers, Sugar Hill Thrift Shop, the volunteer usher programs at Primary Stages and Union Square Theatre, and the free or "Pay-as-you-Wish" admissions to the New York Historical Society, Skyscraper Museum, Isamu Noguchi Garden Museum, Brooklyn Historical Society, China Institute and Cooper-Hewitt National Museum of Design). New information, as well as several listings and chapters, have been added on such subjects as New York real estate terms, "frugal living" websites, union only discount programs, the recycling phenomenon "freecycling," important/emergency phone numbers, low-cost veterinary services and clinics, how to avoid health insurance scams, inexpensive yoga and meditation classes, free Alexander Technique lessons, cheap party supply and DVD/video retailers, and much, much more. Web addresses have been added for almost every business, service and organization listed.

I have made every effort to ensure that all material in this book is current as of the time of this writing. But, as Alexander Pope once said, "to err is human" ("and to forgive, divine!"). All information included herein, such as addresses, telephone numbers, prices, hours, conditions, services and facilities, is subject to change.

Welcome to New York

Introduction

Welcome to New York—capital of the arts, finance, fashion, commerce, communications and conflict—the greatest city in the world.

Great as it is, living here can be demanding. For those without drive and a strong constitution, New York can chew them up and spit them out—or at the very least, put them on the next bus out of town. Why? Well, it's dirty, edgy and congested. It's fast-paced, raucous and curt. It's glacial in the winter and a hothouse runamok in the summer. Oh, and did I mention expensive?

Believe it or not, it's all those things and more that ultimately endear New York to most of its inhabitants. And truth be told, expensive as it may appear, you'd be hard pressed to find a major urban center that offers more free or cheap resources than the Big Apple. You just have to know where to look...

During the twenty years I've resided here, I have become the master of *living* above my means without *paying* above my means. Unwilling to sacrifice quality of life to my tight actor's budget, I've devoted a large amount of time, effort and energy to getting superior products and services for less. Blessed with a photographic memory, a network of friends and colleagues whom I continually poll for tips on the best and least expensive that New York has to offer, and compulsive organizational skills, I have accumulated mountains of information on everything: affordable apartments, inexpensive shopping outlets, quality products and services at bargain prices, financial institutions, discounts for union members, free or cheap entertainment, and low-cost medical and legal providers. After years of living well on an actor's salary, I turned my knowledge and burgeoning files into a resource for all.

My design is to provide readers with the information they'll need to survive and thrive here as comfortably and as inexpensively as possible. Anyone on a budget who wants to take full advantage of all the city has to offer can benefit from the information. No matter what your profession, no matter if you're a newcomer, a life-long resident or simply passing through, this book offers a comprehensive and detailed guide to the city's inexpensive resources, shopping venues and services. And the chapters on New York's free and cheap sites, landmarks, parks, institutions, museums and cultural events are ideal for anyone wanting to partake in the city's best—for less.

Now, go out and start living smart!

Getting Settled

Finding a Home

The horror stories are true: apartment hunting in New York is a nightmare for everyone except the very wealthy. Rents are obscenely high, broker and/or "key" fees are exorbitant, and most landlords will not rent without a guarantor on the lease. Also, there are too few apartments, and a lot of those that do exist are uninhabitable hovels in "iffy" buildings, or smaller than most suburban closets. Welcome to New York.

Forget completely about finding a cheap place to live—it doesn't exist. You swear you know a friend of a friend of a friend who found a rent-stabilized studio in *The New York Times* for only $400 a month? Yeah, and I swear that after a blind date I woke up in a bathtub full of ice to discover that one of my kidneys was missing. It's an urban legend, a lie, or the "friend of a friend of a friend" found his apartment in 1961.

A burgeoning Wall Street and Silicon Alley have altered, irreversibly it seems, the Manhattan real estate market. Stockbrokers and dot-commers who make buckets of money have flooded this tiny island and are willing to pay whatever price a landlord sets for the convenience of city living. Studios now start at about $1,800 a month, and it's not unheard of for two-bedrooms to go for $4,500. The junior millionaires have priced those of us on a budget right out of the city. We're now lucky if we can find affordable housing in Newark, Jersey City or the outlying hinterland areas of Brooklyn and Queens.

About right now you're thinking, "This guy promised that he was going to show me how to live here cheaply. Now—in chapter one, no less!—he says that there are no cheap apartments. Why the hell did I buy this book?"

Don't shoot me—I'm just the messenger. I don't pretend to know the sure-fire way to find a cheap place to live. What I am able to do is offer some suggestions on how you can go about looking for your New York City home. I've drawn on my own experiences as well as those of several friends and colleagues who have had success tackling this most difficult task. A word of advice: Apartments being as hard to come by as they are, if you find something that is even remotely suitable, take it immediately. If you don't, someone else will. That doesn't mean you should rush into a decision. Examine the apartment, the building, the neighborhood and the commute to midtown thoroughly to determine whether you would feel safe and content living there.

Before You Start

Before beginning your apartment search, you should have an understanding of a few real estate terms that are pertinent to the New York City market. Knowing the definition of each and being educated as to how this market works will give you the edge in finding a home that best fits your budget and aesthetic:

Broker's Fee: This is a fee you pay to the real estate broker who helped you find your apartment. It's usually a percentage of your total first year's rent, which can range anywhere from a couple to several thousands of dollars.

First and last month's rent: Most landlords require this at the time you sign your lease. Paying the last month's rent up front is a landlord's insurance that you won't skip out without paying before your lease is expired.

Guarantor: An individual (often a parent) who is willing to take on all of the financial responsibilities associated with renting an apartment in case the renter defaults on paying the rent.

Key Fee: Basically, a tip required by the superintendent of a building before he or she will hand over the keys to your apartment to you... a shady practice but one that occurs a lot nonetheless.

Lease: A legal contract between you and the landlord binding you to renting a particular apartment for a specific period of time (one year, two years, etc.).

Lessee: You; the person to whom property is rented under a lease, otherwise known as a tenant.

Rental Application: A basic application form that lets the landlord collect information about the applicant. In it, the applicant agrees to bind himself/herself to the apartment and to be responsible for its entire financial and other obligations stated in the lease.

Rent Control: Limits the rent an owner may charge for an apartment and restricts the rights of an owner to evict tenants. As the New York City Rent Guidelines Board website states, "Rent control generally applies to residential buildings constructed before February 1947. For an apartment to be under rent control, the tenant must have been living there continuously since before July 1, 1971, or for less time as a successor to a rent controlled tenant. When a rent controlled apartment becomes vacant, it either becomes rent stabilized or is removed from regulation."

Rent Stabilized: This lease specifically states by how much the rent can be increased by the landlord if the renter chooses to re-rent the same apartment (standard leases have no restrictions on rent increases). A landlord is only obliged to offer a first-time tenant a one-year lease; at renewal time, however, the landlord must offer tenants either a one- or two-year lease. According to the New York City Rent Guidelines Board website, rent stabilized apartments are "generally apartments in buildings of six or more units built between February 1, 1947, and January 1, 1974. Tenants in buildings built before February 1, 1947, are also covered by rent stabilized."

Security Deposit: This is a deposit (usually equivalent to one month's rent) required by a landlord to insure that you will leave the apartment in approximately the same condition as you received it. If you've damaged or broken anything, the landlord can legally keep all or part of the security deposit to make repairs and/or to return it to a habitable space.

Subletting: Taking over somebody else's lease, either permanently or temporarily.

For an extensive glossary of New York City real estate terms, visit the New York City Rent Guidelines Board website at www.housingnyc.com.

Where to Look

Bulletin boards can be a real help in the elusive apartment search. Check the boards at your job, union, gym, church or synagogue, as well as social organizations, clubs, bookstores and grocery stores.

If you've exhausted all your networking connections and contacts (see below) and still come up empty-handed; the next best way to find an apartment is through the wonderful community-based website **Craigslist** (www.newyork.craigslist.org), which features several low-cost housing options, including thousands of apartments for rent, broker and agent listed apartments, rooms for rent, shares, sublets and temporary accommodations. It lists housing swaps as well as sections for home-hunters to itemize what they are looking for. On a recent surf through the site, searching for apartments under $800, I came up with hundreds of listings (granted, most were in the outer boroughs and New Jersey) and almost all were fee-free. (For more on Craigslist, see the chapter on "Shopping.")

Even if you have your heart set on residing in Manhattan, unless you are willing to pay an outrageous sum in rent, you should think seriously about living outside of Manhattan: in the upper reaches of the island, in one of the boroughs or just across the Hudson River in New Jersey. Finding an apartment in Washington Heights, Inwood, the Bronx, Brooklyn, Queens, Staten Island, Hoboken or Weehawken will be much less expensive and competitive than Manhattan. To find a place in one of these areas, choose a neighborhood where you might like to live and wander through it. Go up and down the blocks looking for "For Rent" signs. Talk to the people on the street or those sitting on their stoops. Don't be afraid to ask if they know of any vacant apartments. Be nice. Be warm. Smile. Ring the superintendent's buzzer (the person who oversees the complex is almost always listed on the buzzer) of any building you particularly like and ask about vacancies. Be nicer, be warmer and smile bigger. Give the super and anyone else you meet your contact information, ask them to please call if they hear of anything, and consider offering a reward of $100 or more if they connect you to a place. By doing this, you avoid a steep broker's fee and you are not competing with others. The rents on these apartments are often lower than those that are advertised and shown through agents. Remember though, be nice—and smile. Make them want you to live there.

Created in 1955 to provide affordable housing for low- to moderate-income residents, the **Mitchell-Lama Program** offers those who are eligible (and steadfast—the wait for a Mitchell-Lama apartment can be quite long) very low rents in a number of residences. As there are several buildings under the program, you must apply to each. Detailed information, eligibility requirements and an up to date list of Mitchell-Lama buildings is maintained by the New York City Department of Housing and Preservation Development, as well as the New York State Department of Housing and Community Renewal. Eligibility and income requirements (income must not exceed a prescribed maximum) vary from building to building, and rent is based on annual income; therefore, those under the Mitchell-Lama Program must submit income tax forms every year. If your income exceeds low-income standards, you will not be kicked out of the program, but your rent will be marked up to "fair market," a rate based on apartment size and location.

- **New York City Department of Housing and Preservation Development**, 100 Gold Street between Frankfurt and Spruce Streets—212-863-6500, www.nyc.gov/html/hpd/html/for-apartment-seekers/mitchell-lama.html

- **New York State Department of Housing and Community Renewal**, 25 Beaver Street between Broad and New Streets—212-480-7343, www.dhcr.state.ny.us/ohm/progs/mitchlam/ohmprgmi.htm

Having thoroughly spooked you about New York apartments, let me say that I have occasionally heard stories with happy endings.

Most of the people I know who have been successful at finding affordable housing have done it by networking with their friends and colleagues. Inform everyone you know who lives here that you are looking for an apartment. I mean EVERYONE—friends, relatives, acquaintances, colleagues, friends of friends, friends of friends of friends. Write, call or e-mail and ask them to contact you immediately if they hear of a vacancy. New Yorkers are always hearing about someone who is subletting a place for a few months, a colleague who is looking for a roommate, or an apartment that is about to go on the market. I hear about vacant apartments all the time, and on average hook people up with a place two or three times a year.

BEST BET

Consider becoming a **roommate** to someone who already has a place rather than trying to secure your own lease. Ask your friends (the ones you trust and like) if they or someone they know needs a roommate. If no one is looking to share, check for roommate postings on bulletin boards, Craigslist and newspaper classifieds.

While there are **roommate-pairing services** listed in the *Yellow Pages* and on the internet (type in "New York Apartment Roommate"), if you try one of these agencies you will pay a fee. They ask you to fill out forms about the type of apartment and roommate you are seeking, your living habits, and the amount you can spend on rent. Do proceed cautiously, as I don't know of anyone who has had success with these services. One friend discovered, *after* he moved into his new digs, that his roommate was a drug addict and very violent; the situation got so dire that my friend did a stealth escape one afternoon while his roommate was at work. The service I used paired me with a guy who advertised "two-bedrooms" in Chelsea; one of the two bedrooms, *my* room, was a closet—literally a closet, with a cot placed under *his* hanging clothes. Needless to say, I did not take the room and subsequently cancelled my membership with the service.

Subletting an apartment can be advantageous. It allows you to get semi-settled in the city and have a place to lay your head while you are searching for your permanent home. Again, bulletin boards, Craigslist and newspapers with apartment listings are a good bet for finding sublets.

One way of beating the hassle and expense of finding your own lease that lots of New Yorkers swear by is **sublet hopping**. This entails putting all your worldly possessions into storage except clothing, some books, maybe, and a few creature comforts, and living from one sublet to another. By stringing sublets together you may never have to be burdened with finding your own place. This is much too transient for me, but it works for a lot of people. A guy I met at a party recently told me he has been living this way for fourteen years. He claims it has saved him thousands of dollars in broker's fees, furniture, towels, bed linens, decorating costs, kitchen utensils—even telephone and cable installation charges. As he said, "It's helped me remain true to myself and live a purer, simpler life."

I asked him if it didn't make him crazy to always live with other people's stuff. "No. You see, I just visualize that all that stuff is mine. I pretend it's all mine and make up a scenario in my head why I would own it." My kingdom for a lease . . . and my own sofa, and my own tchotchkes!

The "Apts for Rent" section of the ***Village Voice*** is still considered a pretty good way of finding a place. When I came to New York in 1984, I spent several late Tuesday evenings lining up with hordes of others at the Astor Place newsstand, the first place in the city to receive that week's edition. As the papers came off the truck, I would hurriedly grab a copy, throw down some change (it wasn't free back then like it is now) and dash to a nearby coffee shop to scour the apartment ads, circling those that looked interesting or affordable. The objective of all of us in Astor Place at two in the morning was to hightail it to as many landlords as we could early the next day and beat out the descending hordes. It took a few weeks, but I did eventually find a place on Amsterdam and 85th. Luckily, it was Thanksgiving weekend and I was the first to reach the landlord. It was also fortuitous that I chose to tell the landlord I was in a different profession. I'd heard most were reluctant to rent to actors, so I created a job for myself (fund-raiser) and gave him the phone number of a friend who I claimed was my employer. My friend vouched for me, the landlord bought it, and the apartment was mine. At the lease signing he snickered, "At first I thought maybe you were an actor. Well, good thing you're not, 'cause I never rent to actors!"

Times have changed. Besides now being free, the *Voice* also has a website (www.villagevoice.com) with a full classifieds section that is posted early Tuesday evenings. You still have to get to the landlord as early as possible the next day—and go with a certified check for the amount of the rent, the deposit and the fee when you actually view the apartment. Do yourself a favor: have a good "backup" profession to present if you get even an inkling that the landlord has an aversion to what you do for a living. The *Village Voice* is available from newsstands and distribution boxes around the city.

More and more high price, high-rise apartment complexes are going up all over Manhattan. As the price of real estate here escalates, so do property taxes. Many building owners offer an **80/20 Lottery** to obtain a tax break from the city. This system allows the owners to designate 20 percent of their building's units for low-

and moderate-income recipients, giving these renters a generous rent break in exchange for a sizable tax reduction. A prescribed earnings ceiling per year that varies from building to building determines low-income eligibility. The good news is that once you're in an 80/20 building, you don't need to maintain a low income to stay in. An up to date list of 80/20 buildings is maintained on the New York City Department of Housing and Preservation Development website (www.nyc.gov/html/hpd/html/for-apartment-seekers/apt-listings), as well as the New York City Housing Development Corporation site (www.nychdc.com). (Note: As this is a very popular program, applicants are chosen by lottery and waiting lists are generally long.)

If you find yourself at the point of homelessness, the following are a few of the **low-cost hotels, hostels and dorms** that can provide life-saving, temporary accommodations while you're looking for a permanent home:

- **Aladdin Hotel**, 317 West 45th Street—212-246-8580

- **Big Apple Hostel**, 119 West 45th Street—212-302-2603

- **Chelsea Center Hostel**, 313 West 29th Street—212-643-0214

- **Chelsea International Hostel**, 251 West 20th Street— 212-647-0010

- **DeHirsch Residence** at the 92nd Street "Y," 1395 Lexington Avenue—212-415-5650

- **International Student Center**, 38 West 88th Street— 212-787-7706

- **Jazz on the Park**, 36 West 106th Street—212-932-1600

- **New York International Hostel**, 891 Amsterdam Avenue at 103rd Street—212-932-2300

- **Sugar Hill International House**, 722 Saint Nicholas Avenue—212-926-7030

- **YMCA Flushing**, 138-46 Northern Boulevard, Queens—718-961-6880

- **YMCA Vanderbilt**, 224 East 47th Street—212-756-9600

- **YMCA West Side**, 5 West 63rd Street—212-875-4100

Tenant Information and Support Organizations

The **New York City Department of Housing Preservation and Development** answers myriad queries you may have regarding 80/20 and Mitchell-Lama buildings, as well as questions about your rights as a renter. To lodge housing complaints or report maintenance code problems or violations, call 311, the city's non-emergency government services information line.

100 Gold Street between Frankfurt and Spruce Streets—212-863-8000/212-863-5610, www.nyc.gov/html/hpd/home.html

The **New York City Rent Guidelines Board** maintains a website (www.housingnyc.com) that addresses almost every question you may have regarding leases, rent control, rent stabilization, subleasing, lease renewals, subsidized housing, tenants' rights, fees, apartment hunting, occupancy standards, maintenance and services, building codes, housing, small claims court and more.

Tenants with questions regarding rent regulation rights and responsibilities may call the **New York State Division of Housing and Community Renewal** general information numbers at 212-480-7200 or 718-739-6400, or visit their website (www.dhcr.state.ny.us). The Division of Housing and Community

Renewal also has rental offices in each of the five boroughs that you may visit or contact:

- **Manhattan**

  (north side of 110th Street and above) 163 West 125th Street—212-442-1999

  (south side of 110th Street and below) 25 Beaver Street—212-480-7200

- **Brooklyn,** 55 Hanson Place—718-722-4778

- **Bronx,** 1 Fordham Plaza—718-563-5678

- **Queens,** 92-31 Union Hall Street—718-739-6400

- **Staten Island,** 60 Bay Street—718-816-0278

For questions regarding tenants' rights under rent stabilization leases, contact the **Rent Stabilization Association** at 212-214-9200.

Banking and Credit Cards

Boasting Wall Street, the New York Stock Exchange, the NASDAQ, as well as headquarters or offices of most of the world's leading monetary institutions, New York is truly the financial center of the universe. As a result of mega-mergers and hubris ("We are the Financial Capital of the Universe"), New York's brick and mortar banks are ubiquitous throughout the city. There are branch offices on practically every corner, vying with Starbucks and The Gap for total domination. Unfortunately, the larger these institutions have become, the less user-friendly they are to us poor schmoes who just want plain, everyday checking and savings accounts.

For those dealing with small balances, gone are the days of free monthly checking and excellent customer service (and forget about the free toaster you'd get for opening a new account!). Although many banks offer free ATM withdrawals, this is where their generosity ends; they more than make up for this benefit with astronomical monthly checking fees, high penalties and impersonal service.

Fortunately, there are some great banking options.

Credit Unions

For my money, the better alternative to commercial banks is credit unions. A credit union is a member owned and controlled nonprofit financial cooperative serving its constituent members. Most offer similar services to banks, including free or low-cost checking, competitive interest and dividend rates, federally insured deposits up to $100,000, overdraft protection, online banking, ATM cards, credit cards, investment counseling, touchtone teller services from your phone, loans and mortgages (often at lower rates), Individual Retirement Accounts, Savings and Money Market accounts, Certificates of Deposit, and more. To join a credit union, you usually need to be a union, employee group or community member, or a parishioner of a participating church. If you don't fit into any of these categories, don't worry: credit union eligibility rules have relaxed of late making it easier to join. If you are related to a member or, as in some cases, you live or work in a community which a particular credit union serves, you may sign up. Ask those you know who are members to sponsor you.

For years I resisted the exhortations of friends and colleagues to join a credit union (I now belong to the Actors Federal Credit Union). Not that I'm stubborn, but it was hard for me to comprehend that it could be as safe and dependable as a commercial bank. It was only after wretched experiences at three of the New York banking behemoths that I decided to give the AFCU a try. I still kick myself for the years I wasted and the money I lost banking with the big boys. With enormous benefits, competitive interest rates and excellent service (not to mention your money stays in the "family," so to speak), there is no better place to bank.

Alternative Banking Institutions

If you don't qualify for membership at a credit union, below you'll find a list of some of New York's smaller banking institutions. Although they have less of an ATM presence than the financial giants (Chase/Citibank/Bank of New York), they don't gouge you as terribly with penalties and monthly fees. Call each, ask about locations, interest rates and fees, and do some comparative shopping.

- **Amalgamated Bank of New York**—212-255-6200, www.amalgamatedbank.com

- **Apple Bank for Savings**—914-902-2775, www.theapplebank.com

- **Carver Federal Savings**—212-876-4747, www.carverbank.com

- **Commerce Bank**—888-751-9000, www.commerceonline.com

- **Doral Bank**—877-313-6725, www.doralbankny.com

- **Emigrant Savings Bank**—212-850-4000, www.ebcc.net

- **Fleet Bank**—800-841-4000, www.fleet.com

- **First Republic Bank**—800-392-1400, www.firstrepublic.com

- **Greenpoint Bank**—212-681-8470, www.greenpoint.com

- **HSBC**—800-975-4722, www.hsbc.com

- **North Fork Bank**– 877-694-9111, www.northforkbank.com

- **Sterling National Bank**—212-935-1440, www.sterlingbancorp.com

- **Wachovia**—800-275-3862, www.wachovia.com

- **Washington Mutual**—800-788-7000, www.washingtonmutual.com. This bank advertises "Free Checking that's actually free," with no monthly fees (no matter what your balance), no fee to return cancelled checks, and free standard online banking. Definitely worth looking into.

Beating High Credit Card Interest Rates

Do you feel like you're paying too much interest on your credit cards? Does a large chunk of what you pay on your monthly bill go to paying only the interest? Do you find it hard to get out of credit card debt because of the accrual of high monthly interest charges? Do you feel helpless to change your rates? If you answered yes to these questions, I'll bet that you, like most credit card holders, are paying anywhere from 17 to 23 percent interest. It doesn't take Sherlock Holmes to deduce that you should not be paying that much.

"Okay," you say, "but I can't do anything about it." Not true. You can have the rate lowered. That's right—you can have the rate lowered. Here's how...

Call your credit card company and tell them that you feel you are paying too much interest. Mention that you have recently been offered a credit card from another bank at a lower rate and that you want to cancel your existing card. The bank representative will almost immediately offer you a rate slightly lower than the one you are paying. The negotiations have begun! Ask for a few points more; even suggest the rate you'd like to pay to stay with this bank. There will be some hemming and hawing on their part—something along the lines of, "I have to speak to my supervisor..."—but they will almost inevitably give you what you want. They want to keep your business.

I have done this with every credit card I've owned, and it has always worked. With one simple phone call and about six minutes of your time, you can have your interest rate reduced substantially.

Avoid Paying ATM Charges

There is a way to avoid paying huge ATM charges (ranging from $1 to $3) every time you withdraw cash from a bank machine not linked to your card. Stop using those ATM machines! Instead, make purchases using your ATM/debit card, and then when the cashier asks you if you want cash back, say yes and request the amount you need (most places have a ceiling of between $50 and $100). Because you used your card to make a purchase, no added fee or charge is deducted from your account. You can easily save $200 to $300 a year doing this.

Getting Around

Getting around the city can be costly. To ride the subway and bus system, you have to fork over a hefty $2 for each trip, regardless of whether it's ten blocks or to another borough. Those $2 fares add up quickly. Fortunately, the **Metropolitan Transit Authority's Unlimited MetroCard** provides a potent reprieve from the high cost of transportation. For $21 per week, or $70 per month, this MetroCard gives you unlimited use of the subway and bus systems, including transfers. If you ride the subway infrequently, you can still save money: every $10 MetroCard you purchase gives you an extra free trip ($20 buys two extra rides, $50 buys five extra rides, etc.). MetroCards may be purchased at all subway stations and newsstands, the Visitor's Center in Times Square, and pharmacies and grocery stores displaying a MetroCard sticker. (Note: Bus and subway maps to help you plan your route are available on all buses, at train stations, public libraries, hotel lobbies and visitor centers.)

Need to get to a city destination by subway but don't know which train or combination of trains to take? **Hotstop.com** will figure it out for you. Simply go to this website and enter your starting address and destination address. In a matter of seconds Hotstop.com will find the best subway(s) to get you where you want to go. And—believe it or not—walking directions from the station to your destination are also included.

Public Transportation Information Telephone Numbers and Web Addresses

- **Amtrak**—212-630-6400, www.amtrak.com

- **John F. Kennedy International Airport**—718-244-4444, www.panynj.gov/aviation/jfkframe

- **LaGuardia Airport**—718-533-3400, www.panynj.gov/aviation/lgaframe

- **Long Island Railroad**—718-217-5477, www.mta.nyc.ny.us/lirr

- **Metro North Commuter Railroad**—212-532-4900, www.mta.nyc.ny.us/mnr

- **Metropolitan Transit Authority Bus and Subway Information**—718-330-1234, www.mta.nyc.ny.us

- **Newark International Airport**—973-961-6000, www.panynj.gov/aviation/ewrframe

- **New Jersey Transit**—973-762-5100, www.njtransit.com/sf_tr.shtml

- **Port Authority Bus Terminal**—212-564-8484, www.panynj.gov/tbt/pabframe

- **Port Authority Trans-Hudson Corporation (PATH)**— 800-234-7284, www.panynj.gov/path

- **Staten Island Ferry**—718-727-2508, www.nyc.gov/html/dot/html/masstran/ferries/statfery

Street and Avenue Address Locator

Native New Yorkers and newcomers alike are occasionally stumped when trying to **find an address on the avenues in Manhattan**. There seems to be no rhyme or reason to how buildings are numbered. It may then come as a surprise to know that there actually is a handy formula, undoubtedly devised by some algorithm expert with a lot of time on his hands. I won't attempt to explain how it works (as if I know—I'm an actor for God's sake!), but it does. Use the calculator below and you'll arrive within a block or two of where you need to go.

INVALUABLE RESOURCE

To **locate avenue addresses**:
> Take the address,
> Drop the last digit,
> Divide by 2,
> Then add or subtract the number in the second column.
> The result will be the nearest numbered cross street.

(Note: Do not apply this guide to Broadway below Eighth Street, because many of the cross streets are named rather than numbered; for those addresses, you're on your own!)

Avenues A, B, C and D . . . . Add 3
First and Second Avenues . . . . Add 3
Third Avenue . . . . Add 10
Fourth Avenue . . . . Add 8
Fifth Avenue up to 200 . . . . Add 13
Fifth Avenue up to 400 . . . . Add 16
Fifth Avenue up to 600 . . . . Add 18
Fifth Avenue up to 775 . . . . Add 20
Fifth Avenue 776 to 1286 . . . . Subtract 18
Fifth Avenue 1287 to 1500 . . . . Add 45

Fifth Avenue 1501 to 2000 .... Add 24
Sixth Avenue/Avenue of the Americas .... Subtract 12
Seventh Avenue below 110th Street .... Add 12
Seventh Avenue above 110th Street .... Add 20
Eighth Avenue .... Add 10
Ninth Avenue .... Add 13
Tenth Avenue .... Add 14
Amsterdam Avenue .... Add 60
Audubon Avenue .... Add 165
Broadway (754 to 858) .... Subtract 29
Broadway (858 to 958) .... Subtract 25
Broadway (1000 and above) .... Subtract 30
Columbus Avenue .... Add 60
Convent Avenue .... Add 127
Central Park West .... Divide address
                                        by 10, add 60
Edgecombe Avenue .... Add 134
Fort Washington Avenue .... Add 158
Lenox Avenue .... Add 110
Lexington Avenue .... Add 22
Madison Avenue .... Add 26
Manhattan Avenue .... Add 100
Park Avenue .... Add 35
Pleasant Avenue .... Add 101
Riverside Drive (to 165th Street) .... Divide address
                                        by 10, add 72
St. Nicholas Avenue .... Add 110
Wadsworth Avenue .... Add 173
West End Avenue .... Add 60
York Avenue .... Add 4

Finding an address on a numbered street is a lot less compli-
cated. Follow the charts below and it'll be a breeze. (Note: All even

addresses are on the south side of the street; odd addresses on the north side.)

For the West Side above 59th Street:

ADDRESS	LOCATED BETWEEN:
1–99	Central Park West and Columbus Avenue
100–199	Columbus and Amsterdam Avenues
200–299	Amsterdam and West End Avenues
300–399	West End Avenue and Riverside Drive

For the West Side below 59th Street:

ADDRESS	LOCATED BETWEEN:
1–99	Fifth and Sixth Avenues
100–199	Sixth and Seventh Avenues
200–299	Seventh and Eighth Avenues
300–399	Eighth and Ninth Avenues
400–499	Ninth and Tenth Avenues
500–599	Tenth and Eleventh Avenues

For East Side addresses:

ADDRESS	LOCATED BETWEEN:
1–49	Fifth and Madison Avenues
50-99	Madison and Park Avenues (Park becomes Fourth Avenue below 14th Street)
100–149	Park and Lexington Avenues
150–299	Lexington and Third Avenues
200–299	Third and Second Avenues
300–399	Second and First Avenues
400-499	First and York Avenues (York becomes Avenue A below 14th Street)
500–599	Avenue A and Avenue B

Telephone Service

Believe it or not, there are many lower-priced alternatives to the phone giants (e.g., Verizon) for both home and cellular service. The best way to find one of these discount alternatives is to first visit the websites **www.discounttelephonerates.com** and **www.thelowestphonerates.com**. These great sites offer information and assistance in selecting the service that best meets your calling needs and budget by letting you compare plans and rates with literally dozens of phone carriers. Whether you want local, long distance or cellular service, both sites will point you in the right direction.

Other telephone options include:

Local

RCN Cable's "Power CPI+" package (800-RING-RCN, www.rcn.com) is the best deal out there for combined cable TV, local and long distance telephone and high-speed internet access. Telephone services include unlimited local, regional, and long distance calling; Caller ID Deluxe, 3-Way Calling, Call Waiting ID Deluxe and basic voicemail. The price tag for all this may sound high, but it's really not when you factor in that you are getting cable TV (with expanded HBO and Cinemax channels, access to Pay-Per-View events, Video on Demand and Digital Music channels) and ultra high-speed internet access. If you bought these services through Verizon or Time Warner, you'd

BEST BET

pay substantially more. (For a more detailed description, see chapter on "Cable Television.")

Long Distance

If you opt not to use RCN Cable's "Power CPI+" as your phone/cable/internet access provider, there are other low-cost carriers to help you cut down on your long-distance bills:

United Carriers Network (800-UCN-5050) offers discounted local and long-distance service in New York state. There is no monthly fee charge; you will be billed $2.50 if your monthly usage falls below $25, which is typical of most long-distance providers. With UCN you get low international rates, a discounted calling card rate (with no surcharge), and a low-priced domestic 800 number rate for an additional $1 per month. Billing is in sixty-second increments; you can pay either online with a credit card or by mail with a check. In addition, by turning other people on to this service, you can earn monthly cash rebates of $10 per referral.

CallingCard.com offers a standard prepaid calling card that can be used from home, work or when traveling, with what has to be one of the lowest long-distance rates around (quotes on rates can be found on the website). International rates are only slightly higher. Signing up for this plan is incredibly easy: just go to their website at www.callingcard.com with a credit card handy and open an account. You charge as much as you'd like to your card. You can recharge your card online at any time. There are no access fees, no fees for universal use, no weekly surcharges and no startup fees, and billing is in full one-minute increments. Moreover, you can view your call records and account information and manage your account online. Twenty-four-hour customer support is provided.

With **OneSuite.com's** prepaid long-distance phone plan, you can call anywhere in the forty-eight contiguous United States for just 2.9¢ per minute with their toll-free service, or use one of their local access numbers for an even lower rate of 2.5¢ per minute. Their international rates are equally as impressive (rates vary from country to country, so consult their website for an exact quote). You get all this and live customer support twenty-four hours a day, seven days a week; no plan is required to join, no monthly fees, and no hidden charges. Additionally, for just a dollar a month, you can get OneSuite.com's MessageOne, a feature that lets you receive fax and voicemail service in one e-mail account, allowing you to access all your messages in one place, with one number, from anywhere you connect to the Web. (The dollar fee is waived if you make $20 or more in long-distance calls per month.) To join, simply go to www.onesuite.com, fill out the sign-up form and create an account by choosing an amount of instant long-distance credit. (As this is a "prepaid" plan, you'll have to pay up front, but think of it this way: if you pay $10 per month, you get approximately 345 minutes of long distance.) The only rub is that OneSuite.com will charge you 55¢ for each call made from a pay phone.

Opex "Value-Plus" long distance provides quality, inexpensive domestic and international phone service with no monthly fees, billing that is in one-minute increments with a one-minute minimum call length. Opex also offers low-rate inbound toll-free calls for $2 a month. They have several payment options: pay online with a credit card; pay monthly by check; prepay several months with a credit card (which gives you an additional 8 percent savings off your monthly bill); or use auto-pay, which will automatically deduct your monthly balance from either your checking account or any major credit card. Other benefits of the Opex plan include up to 100 free state-to-state minutes and 24/7 online customer service. (Note: There is a $2 fee if your monthly usage is less than $20.)

Cellular

Of the hundreds of cellular phone plans out there—and I've polled friends and colleagues and have researched each and every one for quality of service, access, minutes, availability and roaming charges—the following companies offer the best service and most cost-effective plans. (Please note that in competing for customers, cellular plans change almost daily.) Each company has several store locations throughout the city.

- **Cingular Wireless's** (866-CINGULAR, www.cingular.com) main advantage is that it allows you to roll over unused anytime minutes from month to month.

- **Sprint**—888-253-1315, www.sprintpcs.com

- **T-Mobile**—800-T-MOBILE, www.t-mobile.com

- **VoiceStream Wireless**—888-787-3267, www.voicestream.com

Saving Money on Cell Phone Calls

It's real easy to use up all your monthly cell phone minutes. The cell phone companies are hoping that that's exactly what you're going to do, because once you've exceeded those minutes, your phone rates jump drastically, and that's when they make the big bucks—your big bucks. To avoid this, don't use your cell phone when you're at home. When someone calls your cell, ask that person if you can call them right back, then return the call from your home phone. Accordingly, when you are home and need to check cell phone messages, do so through your land line.

Working Out

Membership in most of New York's gyms is prohibitive for those on a budget. There are, mercifully, inexpensive alternatives.

Until recently, one of the arguments a lot of people I know had against living in Washington Heights was that there was no gym in the area. None of them wanted to travel the half hour south on the subway to work out. Now that **Big Gym** has moved into the neighborhood, that argument is no longer valid. Though this gym, like its name, is big (three floors in which to sweat: a large area for classes, a coed machine and free weights training gym, and a gym for women only), membership rates are small: only $279 (plus tax) per year. If you're an infrequent user, pay $99 up front and then just $3 per visit. Big Gym's free classes include aerobics, kickboxing, step, merengue, and belly dancing. There's also a juice bar and steam rooms; free day care is provided to look after the kiddies while you pump.

625 West 181st Street—212-568-2444

Dolphin Fitness Clubs advertise that they "provide an affordable refuge from the overpriced pickup bars often disguised as fitness clubs." I'm not sure that the pickup bar/fitness club analogy applies anymore, but if they think that's how they are going to sell their clubs, who am I to say they're not? They are, however, one of the lowest priced health club chains in the city, with memberships starting as low as $499 for sixteen months that allow you access to all of Dolphin facilities citywide. Dolphin Fitness gyms are equipped with state-of-the-art machines, comparable to the machines and free weights you'd find at higher-end clubs. Dolphin also offers numerous classes, including yoga and martial arts. There are eighteen Dolphin Fitness Clubs in the New York City area and continued expansion is planned. Consult your phone book for the nearest Dolphin Fitness Club location or visit www.dolphinfitnessclubs.com.

The **Fitness Point Health Club**, a full-service gym in Astoria, offers yearly memberships for just under $250. Yep, you heard right—under $250 ($249 to be exact, and $300 for a two-year membership). Membership includes access to all weights and machines, guest passes, a free session with a trainer, and all the aerobic/cardio/yoga/boxing classes that your heart and body can take.

2514 34th Avenue, Queens—718-609-0670

Conveniently located in the heart of the theater district, the moderately priced **Gold's Gym** has 40,000 square feet of free weights, and weight training and cardio machines on three levels. Membership per year is advertised at $998, but don't let that scare you—no one I know who is a member has paid that. Go in, take a tour and then haggle over the rate; depending upon your tenacity, you can bargain your way to a substantial discount of between $200 and $300 off the advertised price. If you are opposed to haggling and are a member of one of the performing unions, Gold's Gym will give you a discount of about $200. Membership includes use of all exercise equipment, sundeck, and unlimited free classes like rebounding, tribal dance, hiphop, spin, abs of steel, step, body sculpture, Hatha and Jivamukti yoga, cardio Thai boxing, kickboxing and belly dancing. Onsite medical and chiropractic care and massage therapy is available at an extra cost.

250 West 54th Street—212-307-7760, www.goldsgym.com

Lucille Roberts Fitness for Women (sorry guys, this gym is strictly for women only), delivers on its promise of being "more gym, less money." For a very low rate, members receive such amenities as the latest cardio and weight training equipment, a free weight loss plan, babysitting, events and workshops, affordable personal training, and an array of movement, toning, fatburning, aerobic, ab, kickboxing, pilates and yoga classes. Throughout the year, Lucille Roberts offers numerous discount joining specials. (Recently, the cost to sign up was only $5, with a monthly rate that was under $35; and, if you joined with a friend, you would both receive a 15 percent discount.) There are several Lucille Roberts Fitness for Women clubs in Manhattan and the Bronx; visit www.lucilleroberts.com or call 800-USA-LUCILLE.

The **New York City Parks and Recreation Centers** (main number—212-360-8222; Manhattan borough office—212-408-0243, www.nycgovparks.org) feature almost everything you'd find at the upscale gyms, including weight lifting equipment, cardio machines, classes, swimming pools, running tracks, handball/racquetball courts, and climbing walls (the types of things offered at the Centers varies depending upon location). You get all this for an unbelievable $75 per year; $10 per year if you are fifty-five or older. There are thirty-six NYC Recreation Centers throughout the city. Manhattan locations include:

- **Asser Levy Center**, East 23rd Street between First Avenue and the FDR Drive—212-447-2020

- **Carmine Center**, Seventh Avenue South at Clarkson Street—212-242-5228

- **54 East Street Center**, 348 East 54th Street between First and Second Avenues—212-408-0243

- **Hamilton Fish Center**, 127 Pitt Street at Houston Street—212-387-7688

- **Hansborough Center**, 35 West 134th Street near Fifth Avenue—212-234-9603

- **Thomas Jefferson Center**, 2180 First Avenue at 112th Street—212-860-1383

- **North Meadow Center**, Central Park, mid-park, at 97th Street—212-348-4867

- **Pelham Fritz Center**, 18 Mount Morris Park West at 122nd Street—212-860-1380

- **Recreation Center 59**, 533 West 59th Street between Tenth and Eleventh Avenues—212-397-3159

- **Jackie Robinson Center**, 89 Bradhurst Avenue at 146th Street—212-324-9608

- **Alfred E. Smith Center**, 80 Catherine Street between Madison and South Streets—212-285-0300

- **West 59th Street Center**, Tenth Avenue and 59th Street—212-397-3166

- **J. Hood Wright Center**, 351 Fort Washington Avenue at 174th Street—212-927-1563

For information regarding centers in the outer boroughs, consult the Parks and Recreation website or call the local borough office:

- **Queens**—718-520-5916

- **Bronx**—718-430-1825

- **Brooklyn**—718-965-8938

- Staten Island—718-390-8020

The clean and friendly **Synergy Fitness Clubs** (www.synergyfit-clubs.com), with several Manhattan locations, has some of the cheapest membership rates I've heard of. Synergy has compara-ble amenities and classes to the more expensive clubs, like New York Sports Club and Equinox, but charges only half to a third what the super clubs do, sometimes even less when they are fea-turing a special. Synergy also offers savings bonuses for students, civil service members and members of other health clubs. A friend of mine who is a member told me, "Don't hesitate to bargain with them; after a bit of haggling, my membership costs me only $360 a year." At each Synergy location (most of which are open twenty-four hours) there is a good selection of machines, free weights and lots of cardio. Consult your phone book or the website for the Syn-ergy Fitness Club nearest you.

The "Ys," as in **YMCA, YWCA and YM-YWHAs** are an inexpen-sive alternative to the city's pricey boutique gyms. Most "Y" facil-ities have a good selection of free weights, cardio, Universal, Nautilus (and the like) machines, as well as handball/racquetball courts, basketball courts, swimming pools, running tracks, steam rooms, saunas, and numerous classes. The selection does vary at each location. Call the "Y" in your area for more information and membership rates.

- **Vanderbilt YMCA**, 224 East 47th Street—212-756-9600

- **West Side YMCA**, 5 West 63rd Street—212-875-4100

- **McBurney YMCA**, 125 West 14th Street—212-741-9210

- **92nd Street YM-YWHA**, 1395 Lexington Avenue at 92nd Street—212-415-5729

- **Manhattan YWCA,** 610 Lexington Avenue at East 63rd Street—
  212-755-4500

- **Chinatown YMCA,** 100 Hester Street—212-219-8393

- **Harlem YMCA,** 180 West 135th Street—212-281-4100

- **Bronx YMCA,** 2 Castle Hill Avenue, Bronx—718-792-9736

- **Greenpoint YMCA,** 99 Meserole Avenue, Brooklyn—
  718-389-3700

- **Flatbush YMCA,** 1401 Flatbush Avenue, Brooklyn—
  718-469-8100

- **North Brooklyn YMCA,** 570 Jamaica Avenue, Brooklyn—
  718-277-1600

- **Bedford-Stuyvesant,** 1121 Bedford Avenue, Brooklyn—
  718-789-1497

- **Prospect Park YMCA,** 357 9th Street, Brooklyn—718-768-7100

- **Long Island City YMCA,** 32-23 Queens Boulevard–
  718-392-7932

- **Flushing YMCA,** 138-46 Northern Boulevard, Queens—
  718-961-6880

- **Brooklyn YWCA,** 30 Third Avenue—718-875-1193

Recently, **24/7 Fitness Club** offered yearly memberships for just $352 at their West 14th Street location, or an unbelievably low $211 at the Chambers Street club. Besides access to its fully equipped facilities, a 24/7 membership includes classes (e.g., yoga, Afro aerobics, Pilates, toning and abs, kickboxing, urban rebounding and boxing), a free personal training session, free body fat analysis and free nutritional information. This club's biggest plus? It never closes.

47 West 14th Street between Fifth and Sixth Avenues—212-206-1504

107 Chambers Street at Church Street—212-267-7949

Personal Appearance

The *Village Voice's* 2002 issue devoted to Shopping in New York crowned **Aminova Barber Shop at the Essex Street Market** the city's "Best Barber." With such a glowing title, I trundled off to check it out. After passing fish and fruit stands, I found the gruff and imposing owner, Yacha, in a small, no-frills space. He's popular, so I had to wait. I told him what I wanted; he grumbled something back in an accent so thick it was completely incomprehensible to me. I nodded, pretending to have understood, and he began to cut. Twenty minutes later, he finished: the cut wasn't what I wanted at all, but it was great. The biggest surprise was the price—just $7. If I wasn't loyal to my barber, and if the Essex Street Market was more convenient for me, I'd be a regular.

BEST BARGAIN FOR MEN'S CUTS

120 Essex Street—212-388-0449

Astor Place Hairstylists used to be *the* place for the terminally hip to get a haircut. In the '80s, this salon was so popular you would have to wait an hour or more on the sidewalk outside until a guy who was perched on a ladder high above the throng would call your number. Over blaring music, barbers named Nick or Tony would ask in Brooklynese, "Whadja wanna do widja haih?" In the chair next to you, someone would be having his (or her) blue Mohawk reshaped; and on the other side of you, someone would be having a map of the subway system buzzed into the back of his head. When finished, you would walk out content with your cut, feeling slightly cocky that, for the half hour or so that you sat there, you were part of Manhattan's ultra-cool underworld. Best of all, the cut, "local color" and feeling of community cost only a few dollars.

Times have changed and Astor Place Hairstylists has mellowed. The music still blares and the atmosphere is still funky and fun, but you see less "out-there" cuts and the SRO crowds out front have diminished. And yet, this place is gigantic (three floors, 110 employees) and turns out plenty of satisfied customers. Best of all, they continue to charge very low prices: cuts start at $12, blowdrys at $15. "Quintessentially New York," says a friend of mine who has his hair cut here every three weeks.

2 Astor Place at Broadway—212-475-9854

The **Aveda Institute** offers a range of services, including cuts, coloring, facials and waxing that are performed by student practitioners utilizing Aveda's organic products at a little more than half of what you'd pay at an upscale salon. Cuts are $18; coloring starts at $35; facials are $45 for sixty minutes, $55 for ninety minutes. The Institute also occasionally offers free model cuts. Appointments are necessary: for cuts and color, call at least two weeks in advance; those who want waxing or facial services need only call one day in advance.

233 Spring Street near Varick Street—212-807-1492

"Barber Shop" is a tiny, subterranean, one-chair wonder. Proprietor Nick gives great cuts starting at $9 (long-haired cuts are a dollar or two more) and shaves for $8. Lots of people I know swear by this place, because, really, why pay $60 when you can pay $9?

349 West 44th Street, Basement

For years, the **Beauty and Youth Village Spa** was located directly across the street from the Randee Elaine Salon (see below), and seemed to be in an all out price battle with them for customers. Although they have recently moved, Beauty and Youth basically provides the same services as Randee Elaine for about the same prices, give or take a dollar. Competing for the gay dollar (of course you don't have to be gay to patronize), Beauty and Youth offers discount coupons that can be found in gay periodicals like *HX*, *MetroSourceNY* and *Next* magazines, which can be picked up at most newsstands, gay bars, restaurants and businesses, and on almost every corner in Chelsea. Their website, www.beautyandyouth.com, lists a complete menu of services, downloadable coupons for treatments, and special "Beauty Day" packages.

472 Sixth Avenue, between 11th and 12th Streets—212-463-0246

The **Clairol Product Evaluation Salon** provides services for both men and women and will color, perm, straighten, wash and set hair at no charge. Why, you may wonder? Clairol uses this salon to test its competitors' products in order to improve its own, and constantly needs guinea pigs. No need to worry, though—the services here are all done by professional stylists and your directions are followed with the utmost care and respect. You may use the Clairol Salon as often as you like, either as a walk-in or by appointment.

345 Park Avenue at 51st Street—646-885-4200

Two hair salon chains in the city that do very good work and charge reasonable prices for their services are:

Dramatics NYC has nine shops around town that offer a menu of salon services at moderate prices: from haircutting, to having a deep pore oxygen complex facial, to eyebrow shaping, paraffin hand treatment, manicure and underarm waxing. Their press materials promise that "entertainment" is always a feature of their services. I've never patronized this chain, but it's nice to know that there is a salon with a sense of humor. Wash and cuts start at $18.95. Check your phone book for the nearest Dramatics location, or visit the website at www.dramaticsnyc.com.

The chain that is most popular and has the largest presence in New York is **Jean Louis David**. These ultra-hip European-style salons are all over Manhattan and are always bustling and packed with clients wearing the salon's signature white smocks. The work is very stylish and satisfying to a loyal and discriminating clientele: shampoo, massage and cut for $23.43; shampoo, massage, dry set for $26.00; shampoo, massage, cut and dry set for $36.96; shampoo, massage, cut, dry set and either perm, gloss, color or contrast for $88.49. Customers twenty and under get a 10 percent discount. The salons accept "walk-ins." Consult your telephone listings for one of the eleven Manhattan Jean Louis David salons nearest you.

A friend of mine has been going to Limitone Hair Salon in the West Village for years and loves it. She is always very pleased with the work they do and can't believe (neither can her friends) that she pays just $25. Wash and cuts for both men and women start at $22 for walk-ins; $25 if you request a particular stylist. Single process color starts at $50; highlights at $75.00.

162 Seventh Avenue South, between Perry and Charles Streets— 212-675-3865, www.limitonesalon.com

My personal favorite is **Marella's Unisex**, located inside the south annex of the Port Authority Bus Terminal. Even though Marella's has lots of chairs and barbers, there is almost always a wait of a few minutes, a testimony to this salon's popularity, service and customer satisfaction.

I happened upon Marella's by accident a few years ago as I was coming out of the 42nd Street subway under the Port Authority.

Seeing the sign for an $11 haircut and needing a trim, I ventured in. I was handed over to Jairo, who asked me what I wanted. "A little cleaned off the sides," I said. He started buzzing me quite close—a lot more hair than I desired was falling all over the brown smock I was wearing. It was too late by the time I protested; most of my hair was gone. I was very angry and voiced my dismay quite loudly. Jairo, one of the mellowest human beings I have ever met, very gently assured me that this was the best cut for my face (and receding hairline). Although he didn't say it, his whole demeanor oozed, "Trust me." I grumpily assented and slouched in the chair, but couldn't watch him finish the job. I decided I definitely would not be coming back and that there was no way I was going to tip the son-of-a-bitch!

When he was done, I looked up poutily, ready to hate what I saw. I didn't. The cut was very different from how I normally wore my hair, but it wasn't bad. "Okay," I thought, "I'll give him a tip, but I'm still not coming back." Then during the day several friends complimented me on my new haircut. Strangers on the street and in the subway stopped me. It continued all week—and for the next few weeks. You know the ending of this story: I went back to Jairo and have become a loyal customer.

Cuts at Marella's start at $12 (they've gone up a buck since my first visit) for men, $13 for women; shampoo and blow dry is $8 for men, $16 for women; a shave is $12; color, $23; color and set, $39; perms are $60.

625 Eighth Avenue at 42nd Street—212-868-0127

The **Mayfair Beauty Shop** on the Upper East Side looks like the kind of place where your mother would have had her hair done when you were a kid. The prices here are about what she would have paid as well: a shampoo and cut is an unbelievable $14 and up, blowdrys are $18 and up, color is $20 and up, and a manicure and pedicure is $25. The friend who recommended Mayfair feels she gets a better cut here than at other salons in the neighborhood that charge more than ten times the price. Walk-ins only.

> 252 East 73rd Street between Second and Third Avenues—
> 212-535-7038

Seek out some of the city's more upscale salons that constantly need models for student classes. As a model for these beauticians-in-training, you are charged nothing or next to nothing for a haircut and/or coloring. The tradeoff is you are literally in the hands of students—and at their disposal. Not to worry, they are always overseen by a professional. (Note: Most salons will only accept cash for model cuts.)

Leading salons that offer model cuts include:

Bumble and Bumble Model University offers FREE model cuts by professional stylists who work in the Bumble and Bumble network of salons throughout the country. These stylists come to New York to refine their technique at this "graduate school for the top hairdressers." To schedule an appointment, you must stop by the Model University on Mondays, between 5:30 P.M. and 6:30 P.M. At that time, an assessment will be made of your hair and you will be asked about the kind of cut you'd like. A final consultation will be made as to the style you'll be receiving and you will then be given an appointment.

> 415 West 13th Street between Ninth Avenue and
> Washington Street—866-7-BUMBLE,
> www.bumbleandbumble.com/modelcall

Frederic Fekkai Beaute de Provence does model cuts or coloring for $40 on Tuesdays, beginning at 6:30 P.M. Call in advance for an appointment.

15 East 57th Street off Fifth Avenue—212-753-9500

John Sahag Salon offers model cuts for $40, single process color for $30, and highlights for $60 on Tuesdays, beginning at 6:30 P.M. As space is limited, call 212-826-3305 on Mondays, between 8:30 A.M. and 9 A.M., to reserve a chair.

425 Madison Avenue at East 49th Street—212-750-7772

Louis Licari Salon does model cuts on Wednesday evenings for $30, single process hair color for $40 and highlights for $60. Call for an appointment.

693 Fifth Avenue, 15th Floor, between 54th and 55th Streets—212-758-2090

Oscar Blandi gives model $40 cuts and $60 color processes on Wednesdays at 7 P.M. Call Wednesday afternoons to schedule an appointment.

The Plaza Hotel, 768 Fifth Avenue at 59th Street—212-593-7930

Oscar Bond Salon Spa gives FREE model haircuts or coloring two to three times a week. Due to the overwhelming popularity of the price (free!), they are backed up for eons, so don't be surprised when they tell you the next opening will be in four months.

42 Wooster Street between Broome and Grand Streets—212-334-3777

Vidal Sassoon for Men & Women's two locations have model cuts from $20 to $40. You must stop in on Wednesdays at 6:15 P.M. to make an appointment, as the staff needs to see the cut you want before scheduling you.

> 730 Fifth Avenue, between 56th and 57th Streets, 2nd Floor—212-535-9200
>
> 90 Fifth Avenue, between 14th and 15th Streets— 212-229-2200)

Don't let the downscale surroundings of the **Randee Elaine Salon for Men and Women** dissuade you from using their services. This decidedly unglamorous place in the West Village can make you gorgeous for very little money. Overall, for some services I don't think there is another salon in the city that comes close to the low prices Randee Elaine charges. Where else can you get a one-hour full-body massage for $45, a manicure *and* pedicure for $20 and a one-hour facial for $45? Other low-priced services include: haircuts starting at $18, hair coloring starting at $35, "painless" full-leg and bikini wax for $30, "painless" chest or back wax for $20, butt wax for $15, eyelash and brow tint for $15, Parafango body wrap for $45, and acne back treatments for $30. You can find discount coupons to the Randee Elaine Salon in *HX*, *MetroSourceNY* and *Next* magazines.

> 180 Seventh Avenue near Perry Street—212-229-0399

BEST BARGAIN FOR MANICURE

Of all the women I polled about their favorite inexpensive nail salon, most named **Shanel Nails** as their top pick. The consensus is that this tiny salon in Hell's Kitchen is clean, does great work and charges very low prices. Manicures here are just $7 (the cheapest in New York, according to my research) and pedicures, $17. This full-service nail salon also offers a complete menu of waxing treatments at very reasonable prices.

748 Ninth Avenue, between 50th and 51st Streets—212-397-5078

The **Shiseido Studio** in Soho has one of the city's best bargains: beauty treatments at no cost. This store, which proudly proclaims, "No cash registers," offers a choice of free private makeovers, facial treatments, facial massages and product samples as a marketing tool to introduce the Shiseido line to the public. As great as this offer sounds, you can only take advantage of it once a year by appointment (which isn't that easy to get; the wait can be as long as six weeks). The Studio does offer a free weekly series of skincare and makeup classes that you may attend as many times as you like, and a free computerized virtual makeover, the "Beauty Navigator," which demonstrates what you would look like with different makeup applications.

155 Spring Street between West Broadway and Wooster Street—212-625-8820, www.shiseidostudio.com/studio.cfm

The **Christine Valmy International School for Esthetics** has a number of programs and curriculums geared to helping aspiring estheticians and nail specialists become licensed professionals. The school offers a slew of low-cost services to the public (including skin-care treatments, makeup application, waxing, hair services and chemical and nail processes), performed by soon-to-graduate students and supervised by licensed instructors. These services are popular and inexpensive, so call a month in advance to make an appointment.

437 Fifth Avenue at 39th Street—212-779-7800, www.christinevalmy.com

Legal Services

A time may come when you will need a lawyer, but you won't be able to afford exorbitant legal fees. A few alternatives offer legal assistance either at no cost or at greatly reduced rates:

Established for the exclusive use of members of participating AFL-CIO unions and their families, **Union Plus Legal Services** (www.unionpriv.org/benefits/legal) provides free or low-cost legal assistance. Benefits through Union Plus include:

Free thirty-minute consultation by phone or at the attorney's office on any personal legal matter you choose. There is no limit to the number of consultations, provided each is about a separate matter.

Free review of important documents such as leases, insurance policies, etc., followed by an oral explanation of the terms of these documents. (Note: Written evaluations are *not* part of this service, nor are documents written by you or for use in a business capacity.

Free follow-up services by phone or letter to help you resolve a problem or dispute you may have.

Confidentiality—only your attorney knows you are using the program.

Thirty percent discount on more complex legal matters. In a contingency fee case (where the lawyer's fee comes out of any recovery or award you obtain), or business matter, a smaller discount may apply; otherwise, flat fees usually apply to commonly needed services.

Written agreement on all fees to prevent any financial surprises.

All lawyers participating in the Union Plus program are selected for their involvement in the labor movement and their interest in serving union members. They have agreed to provide all program benefits (both free and discounted), to keep each member fully informed of the status of his or her case, and to abide by the administrative responsibilities required of them.

To insure your satisfaction with the program and the quality of its participating attorneys, Union Plus asks you to evaluate the services of your lawyer. Should you disagree with your lawyer regarding fees or other matters, Union Plus tries to resolve the dispute through informal mediation, or, if necessary, arbitration. (Note: Because this is a union program, matters involving any union-related organization or official are not included. Furthermore, a Union Plus attorney may refuse to take any case as he or she so chooses. For more information or to utilize these services, you must first enroll in the Union Plus program at www.unionplus.org.)

Each year, **Volunteer Lawyers for the Arts (VLA)** provides pro bono and low-cost legal services to over 5,000 members of the creative community in the greater New York Metropolitan area. Since 1969, the group has assisted artists with mediation services, educational programs and publications, advocacy, legal advice, professional business counseling, and representation. Included in VLA's many services are:

Art Law Line—a free legal hotline

Pro bono placements for low-income artists and nonprofit arts organizations with volunteer attorneys from the area's finest law firms

Low-cost membership ($50 for full-time students; $100 for individuals; $200 for nonprofit arts organizations) entitling members to half-hour appointments with highly qualified volunteer attorneys to address arts-related legal issues at the group's bimonthly clinics. Membership also covers discounts on seminars, workshops, publications and MediateArt Services; invitations to all Member Events; VLA Newsletter; access to the Speaker's Bureau and VLA's Board Bank; and discounts on pro bono consultations for those who meet VLA's Financial Eligibility Guidelines.

Workshops on specific legal topics related to the arts, such as:
- Nonprofit Incorporation and Tax Exempt Status
- Artists Rights and New Technology
- Starting and Operating a For-Profit Business
- Starting and Operating an Independent Record Label
- Contract Basics for Arts and Entertainment Professionals
- Copyright Basics
- Mediation Training

Assistance with Nonprofit Incorporation

Call for more information on VLA's services and membership, or for a schedule of workshops.

1 East 53rd Street, 6th Floor—212-319-2787, www.vlany.org

If you have questions or need help with problems of discrimination in the workplace or housing due to sexual orientation or HIV/AIDS, contact the **Lambda Legal Help Line** (212-809-8585, www.lambdalegal.org) for free guidance on rights and recourse. Lambda's Help Line is open on weekdays from 9 A.M. to 5:30 P.M.

The **Metropolitan Council on Housing Help Line** (212-979-0611, www.metrocouncil.org/housing/housing) is set up to answer any questions you may have regarding apartments, leases, landlords, renter's rights, etc. This free service, staffed by legal professionals, can be accessed on Mondays, Wednesdays and Fridays from 1:30 P.M. to 5 P.M.

Internet Service Providers (ISPs)

RCN Cable's (866-603-4471, www.rcn.com) "Power CPI+" plan, in addition to its (already mentioned) incomparable deal on cable TV, local and long-distance service, offers high-speed internet access (featuring their "MegaModem Mach 7" at download speeds of 7 Mbps)—all for a reasonable monthly fee. The internet access portion of this "package" comprises unlimited, always-on access; four e-mail addresses that are accessible from anywhere; Web storage space (10 Mb); Pop-up stopper; and access speeds much faster than dial-up services, so that you can surf the net quickly and enjoy lightning-quick downloads. (For a more detailed description, see chapter on "Cable Television.")

GREAT RATE ON BUNDLED SERVICES

Some of the better-known ISPs, like AOL, MSN, Earthlink, AT&T, Prodigy and Compuserve, are all good and reliable, but their monthly charges for dial-up service range from $19.95 to $24.95 and can damage a tight budget. Fortunately, there are several **ISPs that offer low-priced, or totally free, access to the net**. The tradeoff for the freebies is the placement of an annoying banner ad on your screen while you are using them, and meager customer service. In addition, most of the free sites give you direct internet access for only forty hours per month and usually kick you off after about fifteen minutes per session. If you need to be online for any length of time, you will probably have to dial up several times. Low-priced Internet Service Providers (ranging between $8.95 and $15.95 per month) include:

www.juno.com

www.netscape.com

www.netzero.com—For the occasional internet user, Netzero offers free access for up to ten hours per month.

www.peoplepc.com

www.worldshare.com

Free ISPs include:

www.address.com

www.dotnow.com

www.nocharge.com

Need to receive faxes but don't want to splurge on a fax machine? On a computer with an ISP link, you can **receive faxes at no charge**. Go to either **www.efax.com** or **www.onebox.com** and download the fax application. Once installed, you will be given a free fax number that enables you to receive faxes via your e-mail address, which you can then print out if you need a hard copy. One caveat: Since these services are free, you will not be able to *send* faxes. To send as well as receive faxes, you must pay a fee to upgrade your service.

FREE
DEAL

Accessing the Internet
If You Don't Own a Computer

You don't own a computer but need to surf the web or check e-mail? Don't despair—there are ways to get online...

First, most **New York City libraries** offer free internet connection. Access is limited, however, to half-hour segments, and since it's first come/first served, there is almost always a wait for a terminal.

A good alternative, though it will cost you, is to visit a cyber café (see list below). Prices at each average around $10 to $12 an hour, with most serving food, beverages and even alcohol for an additional charge. The best bargain is **EasyInternetCafé** in the heart of Times Square, where you can go online twenty-four hours a day for only $1.

> 234 West 42nd Street between Seventh and Eighth Avenues—212-398-0724/ 212-398-0775

Other internet cafés:

- **Alt.Coffee**, 139 Avenue A, between St. Mark's Place and East 9th Street—212-529-2233

- **Cyber Café**, 250 West 49th Street between Broadway and Eighth Avenue—212-333-4109

- **Cyber Café**, 705 Eighth Avenue, between 44th and 45th Streets—212-245-3907

- **Cyberfelds**, 20 East 13th Street near Fifth Avenue—212-647-8830

- **Game Players Station Internet Café**, 28 Elizabeth Street at Canal Street, 2nd Floor—212-619-1019

- **Internet Café at the New York Computer Place**, 247 East 57th Street at Second Avenue—212-872-1709

- **Internet Café Centers**, 1476 Lexington Avenue at 95th Street—212-537-0437

- **Log-On Café**, 41 East 30th Street between Madison and Park Avenues—212-889-1555

- **NYI System Internet Café**, 3 East 33rd Street—212-679-6668

- **Whateverdot Internet Café**, 296 Atlantic Avenue, Brooklyn—718-596-4020

- **Web2Zone**, 54 Cooper Square at East 7th Street—212-614-7300

Cable Television

An incomparable deal on cable TV service is **RCN Cable's** "Power CPI+" package. The cable TV portion of this package (see "Local Telephone" and "Internet Service Providers" sections for additional information) includes over one hundred twenty-seven channels of basic digital cable TV programming, multiple HBO and Cinemax channels (including HBO and Cinemax "On Demand"), HDTV, thirty-one commercial-free CD-quality music channels, and numerous Pay-Per-View channels. RCN's price for all these services might seem high, but if you break it down by service, you'll realize that you would probably spend as much or more on the individual services. I paid an average of $173 a month (and that didn't include HBO!) for local and long-distance phone service, internet access and cable. With RCN's "Power CPI+," I now save about $55 per month. For more information and rates, call RCN at 866-603-4471 or visit their website at www.rcn.com. (Note: RCN wires haven't been laid in all city neighborhoods and some buildings may not have access yet, so when you call for information, verify that RCN is in your building.)

GREAT RATE ON BUNDLED SERVICES

Video and DVD Rental

In this arts and media capital, there are, as you would expect, a variety of outstanding places to rent DVDs and videos. We have everything from high-tech/low-charm mega-chains, to low-tech/high-expertise small specialty stores. Among the latter are even stores dedicated to a single genre such as Asian films or Indian "Bollywood" movies. Sure, the chains have put a lot of mom-and-pop shops out of business (a Blockbuster obliterated two of my neighborhood favorites several years ago), but others have not only survived, they are thriving. The following compilation, based on price and selection, showcases the city's better outlets for DVDs and videos:

With their huge selection of Shakespeare plays, live theater and BBC recordings, **Evergreen Video** is my favorite rental outlet. Evergreen has an immense selection, with specialized sections including cult trash, 1960s comedies, avant-garde special interest, musicals, film noir, fantasy, pre-1955 Afro-American, war, foreign, and dance. Daily rentals are $3.50 for the first night and $1.50 each night thereafter. Evergreen's best deal offers members four DVDs or videos for $14, plus tax, with up to three days to view them. Membership is free, but your credit card number is kept on file in case of lost, damaged or unreturned merchandise.

37 Carmine Street near Bedford Street—212-691-7362

Flik's Video (www.fliksvideo.com), in two city locations, offers several prepayment rental plans that provide good value to members:

Bronze Plan—10 DVD or videos, including 1 free video or DVD for $39.95, plus tax

Silver Plan—20 DVD or videos, including 2 free videos or DVDs for $74.95, plus tax

Gold Plan—40 DVD or videos, including 5 free videos or DVDs for $129.95, plus tax

Platinum Plan—100 DVD or videos, including 10 free videos or DVDs for $279.95, plus tax

Each plan includes a free catalog that lists Flik's inventory of over 25,000 films, fast free delivery to your door in fifty-eight minutes or less guaranteed, free pickup, two-day rentals, free next-day reservations, and free rental credits with early renewal. Tuesdays, get three rentals for the price of two; Wednesdays, get two rentals for the price of one. The scope of the selection here doesn't compare with places like TLA, World of Video and Movie Place, but there is something to be said for not having to leave your home to get a video or DVD.

175 West 72nd Street between, Broadway and Columbus Avenues—212-721-0500

1093 Second Avenue, between 57th and 58th Streets— 212-752-3456

Kim's Video (www.kimsvideo.com) in the East and West Villages and near Columbia University, have created an ultra-cool mini rental empire dealing in everything from alternative and independent, to rare and irreverent, film titles that cater to the tastes of urban hipsters. To appease the bourgeoisie (as well as the hipsters' occasional desire for the mundane), Kim's also shelves the requisite Hollywood hits. Categories include what you'd expect, as well as atypical genres like Blaxploitation, indie, queer, anime, avant-garde, shorts, and cult. VHS and DVD Catalog titles cost $1.25 same day (returned before midnight), $2.50 overnight, $3.75 for two nights or $5 for five nights; new releases cost $3.50 for one night, $5.00 for two. To save money, join "Kim-Money," their frequent renter's program: when you prepay for videos, you receive credit that is applied to future rentals (e.g. for every $20 you pre-pay, you are credited $25, for every $50 you pre-pay, you are credited $65, and so on.) Each branch requires a separate membership:

- **Mondo Kim's,** 6 St. Mark's Place near Third Avenue—212-505-0311

- **Kim's Avenue A**, 85 Avenue A, between 5th and 6th Streets—212-529-3410

- **Kim's Mediapolis**, 2906 Broadway at 113th Street—212-864-5321

- **Kim's Underground**, 144 Bleecker Street at LaGuardia Place—212-260-1010

The expert staff of cinephiles at **Movie Place** makes this rickety shop a "must" for serious film aficionados. Although their selection doesn't have the breadth of other independents (and heaven forbid that they should become computerized!), the knowledgeable and personable crew is unparalleled. No matter what you are looking for, they know whether they have it; name a film or genre you like, and they will rattle off a list of similar titles you are sure to enjoy. Movie Place has four very liberal prepayment plans: three DVDs or videos for $15, seven for $32, fifteen for $58 and thirty for $102. Better yet, plan members get a free film with each rental, every day. Other plan features include a two-day rental policy, Sunday through Thursday; rentals on Friday are due back by Monday closing; and free pick-up and delivery from 4 P.M. to 9 P.M., between 86th and 120th Streets on the Upper West Side.

> 237 West 105th Street near Broadway—212-864-4620, www.nycmovieplace.com

Many branches of the **New York Public Library** (www.nypl.org) have a wide assortment of videos that you may borrow for up to one week, with a limit of five at a time. As with books, there is no charge. The selection varies from branch to branch with the **Donnell** branch (West 53rd Street between Fifth and Sixth Avenues), having a tremendous choice of film categories, including documentaries, animated, foreign-language and television (look for the BBC's *Complete Works of William Shakespeare*). Other branches with well-stocked video sections are the **Mid-Manhattan** (Fifth Avenue at 43rd Street) and the **Library for the Performing Arts** (Lincoln Center, 111 Amsterdam Avenue at 66th Street—212-870-1630), which focuses on videos related to the performing arts.

Too bad I don't live on the East Side. If I did, I'd be at **New York Video** all the time. This store has one of the city's best selections of DVDs and videos (only TLA's is bigger), and no place is better organized. Their entire inventory of titles is on convenient LP-sized cards in wooden bins, divided into categories and subcategories. Nowhere other than this store have I seen such specialized sections as monster, detective, Hammer horror, Russ Meyer, serial killer, courtroom, violence, mad scientists, Ed Wood and slasher flicks. Also, New York Video is the only store I'm aware of that organizes its classic film sections by actors and directors. All DVDs and videos are $4.25, plus tax, for two nights; children's titles under sixty minutes are $1.99, plus tax. For a dollar more on any Friday rental, you can keep the film until the following Monday.

949 First Avenue at 52nd Street—212-888-4545

TLA Video in the West Village is a godsend for film buffs. One step inside and you'll agree that this store has the city's largest selection of DVDs and videos. And, the quality of the selection is substantial. There are Hollywood blockbusters and new releases, but TLA focuses on unconventional titles, and there are tons of them, representing every genre of celluloid ever conceived. I'd venture to say that almost any domestic and foreign title you are looking for is carried by this wonderful store. If not, the knowledgeable and dedicated staff will know how to find it. New releases are $4.50 for two nights, $2.50 each additional night; general releases are $3.75 the first three nights, $1.75 each day thereafter. TLA offers two ways to view films economically: a 3-for-2 Special—when you rent any three films and return them all together on time, you will be charged only for two; and a pre-paid discount card allows ten rentals for $35, twenty for $65 and fifty for $150.

BEST OVERALL SELECTION

52 West 8th Street between Fifth and Sixth Avenues—
212-228-8282, www.tlavideo.com

The bulk of the enormous inventory at the large **Tower Record and Video** (www.towerrecords.com) stores is general interest and Hollywood titles and sticks to the usual genres: television, comedy, drama, foreign, etc. Tower has little in the way of cutting-edge or avant-garde films, and instead relies on offering safe and dependable titles like Blockbuster. However, one can't

BEST BARGAIN

quibble with the prices, which are some of the best in the city: new DVD or video releases are $2.99 per night, while catalog titles are only $1.49 for VHS tapes and $1.99 for DVDs for three nights.

383 Lafayette Street—212-228-5100

1961 Broadway at 66th Street—212-799-2500

725 Fifth Avenue in Trump Tower—212-838-8110

Having survived both escalating real estate prices in its ever-gentrifying neighborhood and a bully Blockbuster that was for years located across the street, **Video Blitz** continues to faithfully serve the home viewing needs of Chelsea-ites. Its large selection consists of mostly mainstream titles from the usual genres, with few surprises. The exception is, its vast gay and lesbian section is probably the biggest in the city (no surprise there, given Video Blitz's location and demographics). In fact, the gay adult titles outnumber the straight ones three-to-one. New DVD and video releases are $4.30 per night; catalog titles are $4.30 for two nights. Video Blitz does have three low-priced rental specials: Tuesday and Wednesday rent any two movies for $5.40; Thursday rent any three movies for $8.60; on Friday, Saturday, Sunday and Monday, catalog titles are two-for-one.

267 West 17th Street, 2nd Floor—212-645-6410

Video Café offers free membership and a moderate $3.78 per night rental on new releases, $3.24 per three-night rental on catalog titles (which include any videos that are not "new releases"); and $2.16 per three-night rental on children's movies. To save big bucks, look into Video Café's discount specials: Tuesdays and Wednesdays, rent one movie and you get a second free; rent three movies in one day and you get a fourth one free; after every eleventh paid rental, the twelfth is free; prepay for ten video rentals, new or catalog titles, and it costs $32.58, including free delivery.

697 Ninth Avenue at 48th Street—212-765-6165, www.video-cafe.com

Along with Evergreen, TLA and the two Kim's locations on Bleecker Street (east and west), **World of Video** contributes mightily to making the West Village the city's best neighborhood for video rentals. This great store has one of the largest selections of general-purpose videos and DVDs, drawn from just about every genre imaginable including documentaries, dance, opera, horror, western, PBS/A&E, musicals, classics, TV, stand-up comedy, comedy classics, gay and lesbian, cult, adult, and Shakespeare. The store requires you to buy a membership, but as the saying goes, membership does have its privileges: $21.70 per year gets you three free rentals plus special rental savings, sale discounts and other club extras. Members choose their price: movies for three days/two nights are $4.55; tapes returned early receive $1-off coupons good towards the next rental; pay for twenty-five videos or DVDs in advance at only $2.20 for each three day/two night rental; pay cash on Tuesdays and receive a second tape free.

51 Greenwich Avenue—212-691-1281, www.worldofvideo.com

Discount Service Providers via the Internet

There are two outstanding websites that help consumers comparison-shop for a variety of vital services ranging from cell phone to long distance, credit cards, home and auto insurance, utilities and much more. I have used these sites to research all kinds of services, and through them found both my cellular phone and renter's insurance plans, getting exactly what I was looking for at the lowest possible price:

The mission of **MyRatePlan** (www.myrateplan.com) is to ensure that users of their website get the best value for the services they use every day. MyRatePlan provides a comprehensive, unbiased online information resource to help consumers "cut through the fine print" and locate the lowest price for the services they need. MyRatePlan, launched in 1999 as a comparison-shopping site for wireless phone plans, has since added several other services, such as long distance, travel, satellite TV, credit cards, package delivery, insurance, internet access, online stock brokers, mortgages and auto loans. The site's consumers are able to evaluate and select plans among a number of providers. When a plan is located that fits an individual's needs, MyRatePlan opens the necessary links to complete the purchase online.

The **LowerMyBills** (www.lowermybills.com) press release states that its website aims "simply to help every American household save money for the important things in life," and it indeed does a very good job of fulfilling that goal. To comparison-shop at LowerMyBills enter your zip code, e-mail address and monthly bill information. The site assesses your current services, reviews others in your area and searches for the cheapest price on everything from phone and utilities, to insurance, mortgages, internet access, debt relief and home and auto loans. Once the site's calculators have finished searching the net, a list of offers pops up in order of cheapest to most expensive, based on your personal criteria. If it finds alternative providers that can give you a better deal, LowerMyBills will assist you in switching. Best of all, LowerMyBills is completely free to use.

Union Members Only Discount Programs

There are three outstanding programs for which deep discounts are given on a variety of goods and services to union members only:

Union Members Discount Network, a free discount program offering savings at local and national businesses to all union members. UMDN has put together a "Local Network" of businesses (or "Preferred Providers") in New York that guarantee to give members discounts on goods and services. Preferred Providers include chiropractors, auto rentals, restaurants, pharmacies, dentists, beauty salons, personal trainers, legal services, tickets for concerts and sporting events, hotels, retail outlets, entertainment, opticians and more. To become a UMDN member, simply click on the "Register" button at the top of the Home Page of their website and fill out the form or register over the phone. To get your discount, just show the Preferred Provider your UMDN card (which will be sent to you within a few days of registering). You can obtain a list of Preferred Providers through their website or toll-free number. UMDN adds new Providers each week, and extends "Bonuses" and "Freebies" to members for using the network.

877-877-UMDN, www.umdn.com

Created in 1986 by the AFL-CIO, **Union Plus** (www.unionplus.org) provides union members and their families with valuable discounted consumer benefits. By using the collective purchasing power of more than thirteen million union members, Union Plus negotiates the best products and services at the lowest prices. Member benefits include discounts and deals on insurance, legal services, theme parks, movie tickets, cell phones, hotels, computers, vacation tours, car rentals, mortgages, credit cards, education services, entertainment and more. For information and to register to utilize its discount services, visit the Union Plus website.

The savings portal **Working Advantage** (www.workingadvantage.com), created for employees and members of thousands of companies, organizations and unions, offers discounts on myriad goods and services such as ski tickets, Broadway plays, movie tickets, video rentals, magazines, clothing, sporting events, theme parks, jewelry, household goods, gifts and gift certificates, online shopping, hotels, electronics, food and more. To become a member, go to the Working Advantage website, enter your union member ID number, contact information and e-mail address, and create a password for yourself. Once enrolled, you'll be eligible to access all of the Working Advantage deals and discounts. Working Advantage also maintains an incentive program in which, for registering and making purchases through the website, you are given "Advantage Points" that are redeemable for a variety of rewards.

"Frugal Living" Websites

The following websites have been devised to help you get the biggest bang for your buck. Each offers countless free money-saving tips for living well on a tight budget. Topics include everything from credit repair and budgeting, to coupons, inexpensive gift ideas, cost effective recipes, debt reduction, buying a car, decorating on a dime, homemade toiletries, lotions and household cleaners, low-cost funerals, do-it-yourself home repairs, and much more:

www.budget101.com

www.cheapskatemonthly.com

www.dealhunting.com

www.freakyfreddies.com

www.frugalcorner.com

www.frugalliving.about.com

www.frugalvillage.com

www.stretcher.com

www.thefrugalshopper.com

www.valupage.com

Important Municipal Phone Numbers

All Emergencies, Police, Fire, Ambulance—911

New York City Information (all non-emergency government services)—311

Directory Assistance—411

Abused, Abducted and Exploited Children—800-248-8020

American Society for the Prevention of Cruelty to Animals—212-876-7700

Battered Women Domestic Violence Hotline—800-621-4673

Better Business Bureau (complaints)—212-533-7500

Con Edison Customer Service—800-75-CON-ED

Con Edison Gas Leaks and Electrical Emergencies—212-683-8830

Consumer Fraud—212-416-8345

Cop-Shot—800-COP-SHOT

Crime Stoppers—800-577-TIPS

Crime Victims Report Line—212-577-7777

Daily Parking Regulations—311

Department of Health—311

Division of Motor Vehicles—212-645-5550

Housing Authority—212-306-3000

Lesbian/Gay Anti-Violence Project—212-714-1184

Mayor's Office—311

New York City Board of Elections—212-868-3692

New York City Buildings Department (complaints)—311

New York City Clerk (marriage licenses)—212-669-2400

New York City Commission on Human Rights (discrimination issues)—212-306-7450

New York City Department for the Aging—212-442-1000

New York City Department of Consumer Affairs—311

New York City Department of Education—718-935-2000

New York City Department of Health and Mental Hygiene—212-442-9666

New York City Department of Parks and Recreation—212-360-8222

New York City Department of Sanitation—212-219-8090

New York Convention and Visitors Bureau—212-484-1200

New York State Attorney General (information and complaints)—800-771-7755

Noise Complaints—311

Passport Office—212-206-3500

Poison Control Center—212-764-7667

Potholes—311

Sex Crimes Report Line—212-267-7273 (24 hours)

Streetlights—311

Taxi and Limousine Commission (questions, complaints and lost and found)—311

Time/Temperature—212-976-1616

Traffic Information—311

United States Passport Agency—212-206-3500

Water Mains and Sewers—311

Weather—212-976-1212

Restrooms

It was never my intention to include a chapter about bathrooms in New York, but as I shared my plans for this book with friends and colleagues, the overwhelming response was, "Tell us where there are toilets that are available to the public!"

As New York is bereft of this commodity—public toilets—you often have to be creative. Some simple planning and logical sleuthing, however, will keep bladders empty, hair neatly combed and makeup perfectly applied.

The golden rule for gaining access to restrooms in restaurants, hotels and stores is to never ask if you may use the facilities. Only tourists ask, and the answer is always "No." Pretend like you are a patron/guest—and go for it! (Warning: Don't do as a friend of mine did: pee against a tree in Central Park. As soon as his fly was zipped up, he was collared by two policemen, taken to jail and spent the next forty harrowing hours becoming acquainted with the city's netherworld.)

For me, the city's large **bookstores** have the best restrooms. In almost every part of Manhattan there is either a Barnes & Noble or Borders Books, and the facilities in each are usually clean and not far from the front door. Best yet, you don't need a key to access them, and no one knows if you are there solely to use the waterworks or to buy books:

- **Barnes & Noble:**
  4 Astor Place at Broadway
  396 Avenue of the Americas at 8th Street
  33 East 17th Street at Union Square

105 Fifth Avenue at 18th Street

675 Sixth Avenue at 21st Street

901 Sixth Avenue at 22nd Street

385 Fifth Avenue at 54th Street

750 Third Avenue at East 47th Street

600 Fifth Avenue at 48th Street

160 East 54th Street at Third Avenue

1972 Broadway at 66th Street

2289 Broadway at 82nd Street

1280 Lexington Avenue at 86th Street

240 East 86th Street between Second and Third Avenues

• **Borders Books:**

461 Park Avenue at 57th Street

550 Second Avenue at 30th Street

100 Broadway near Wall Street—212-964-1988

10 Columbus Circle

Most, if not all of the **fast food restaurants** like McDonald's, Burger King, Wendy's, Au Bon Pain, Ranch One, Boston Market and Popeye's have public facilities. Designated for "Customers Only," they often need a key to be opened. To gain entrance, act like a customer and pretend that you have just finished your Happy Meal. If it is obvious that you have not dined there and your need to go has reached emergency status, buy the cheapest thing on the menu and demand the damn key!

Bookstores and fast food chains aside, the first thing to do if you need to make a pit stop is look for a **hotel**. Almost all of Manhattan's neighborhoods have at least one medium to large hotel with public facilities located on or near the ground floor. None have a policing system to keep non-guests from using the facilities, so you won't be hassled. And most of these restrooms are impeccably clean.

Other **large retailers** like Kmart, Bed, Bath & Beyond, and Old Navy also have public restrooms...

- **Kmart:**

  One Pennsylvania Plaza on 34th Street at Seventh Avenue

  770 Broadway at Astor Place

- **Bed, Bath & Beyond:**

  620 Avenue of the Americas at 19th Street

  61st Street and First Avenue

- **Old Navy:**

  610 Avenue of the Americas at 18th Street

  300 West 125th Street

  150 West 34th Street between Sixth and Seventh Avenues

  503 Broadway between Spring and Broome Streets

Manhattan's three **main transportation hubs** (Grand Central Terminal, Penn Station and Port Authority Bus Terminal) all have bathroom facilities for the general public. The facilities at **Penn Station** (Seventh to Eighth Avenues, between 30th and 32nd Streets) and **Grand Central** (42nd Street and Park Avenue) are large, clean, safe and centrally located. All I can say about the bathrooms at the **Port Authority** (Eighth to Ninth Avenues at 41st Street) is "yikes!" But, if you gotta go, you gotta go.

In each of the **major department stores**, there are at least a couple of men's and women's restrooms located on different floors.

The larger the store, the more restrooms it has. These stores are scattered around three New York neighborhoods so that you are covered while you are in any of these areas:

- **Barney's**—Madison Avenue at 61st Street

- **Henri Bendel**—Fifth Avenue at 56th Street

- **Bergdorf Goodman**—Fifth Avenue at 58th Street

- **Bloomingdale's**—Lexington Avenue at 59th Street

- **Lord & Taylor**—Fifth Avenue between 38th and 39th Streets

- **Macy's**—34th Street between Sixth and Seventh Avenues

- **Saks Fifth Avenue**—Fifth Avenue between 49th and 50th Streets

- **Takashimaya**—Fifth Avenue between 49th and 50th Streets

In midtown there are lots of bathroom options, including the **Virgin Mega Store** on Broadway (between 46th and 47th Streets) in Times Square and several of the lower floors of the **Marriott Marquis Hotel** (across from the Virgin Mega Store). The beautiful and very trendy bathrooms at the **Paramount Hotel** (235 West 46th Street) are convenient at about 40 yards from the hotel's front door and are a narcissist's wet dream—all mirrors, reflecting surfaces and low, age-erasing lighting. **ESPN Zone** (4 Times Square, 42nd Street and Broadway—212-921-3776) is the only place where, while sitting on the john, you may watch your favorite sports game: ESPN TV is screened on monitors in each stall. There is even a public facility in the **Times Square Subway Station**. Located in the base of the Times Square Tower (42nd Street and Seventh Avenue) near the elevators and inside the turnstiles, this facility has four clean bathrooms equipped with aluminum-chrome toilets, mirrors and an intercom system (in case you need to call for assistance). An attendant buzzes users in one at a time and enforces a five-minute time limit and rules forbidding smoking, sleeping or gambling!

Four of the city's **parks** actually have public facilities, though none will ever win awards for cleanliness. They are, however, convenient, safe and handy in times of need.

- **Washington Square Park**—Thompson Street at Washington Square

- **Tompkins Park**—Avenue A at 9th Street

- **Bryant Park**—Sixth Avenue, between 41st and 42nd Streets

- **Central Park**—Near the Delacorte Theatre at the West 81st Street entrance

Public and government buildings such as libraries, courthouses, unemployment offices and the like all have restrooms that are available to the public.

Most New Yorkers' favorite pastime is to grumble over the obscene number of **Starbucks** there are in this city. But complain as we may, Starbucks offers one great service to all New Yorkers: public restrooms. Since Starbucks is everywhere, we need never worry about finding a place to go. The next time you need to use a facility and don't know where one is, stop anyone on the street and ask for the nearest Starbucks. Ten to one, one is within spitting distance. The restrooms, of course, are for "Patrons Only" and may require a key, so go in with the attitude that you will be dropping a couple of gold bricks for a cup of joe just as soon as you "wash your hands," and you won't be hassled.

Staying Healthy

Medical

It's hard to believe but a recent *New York Times* article estimated that as much as 40 percent of the city's population has no health coverage, or is underinsured. Premiums are becoming more and more exorbitant, many employers are limiting the coverage they provide or cutting it altogether, and insurance for minimum wage earners, freelancers and the self-employed is nearly impossible to come by.

Fortunately, the uninsured and underinsured do have access to several affordable health care providers in the city. These include:

The **Callen-Lord Community Health Center** has a sliding scale for the uninsured (office visits start as low as $30, depending on your income), without the third world feel of many public clinics. Though particularly interested in serving the gay and lesbian communities, the Center does not inquire as to sexual preference.

356 West 18th Street—212-271-7200, www.callen-lorde.org

D*O*C*S, which is affiliated with Beth Israel Medical Center, is both a "walk-in" and a "by appointment" health clinic that charges uninsured patients very modest rates. A typical office visit for the uninsured is around $100, with most D*O*C*S services ranging anywhere from $80 to $290. The great thing about this clinic is that before they treat you, they do a free evaluation and let you know exactly the amount the visit will cost, thus ensuring that there are no surprises waiting for you as you leave the offices. (For those with health insurance, D*O*C*S accepts most policies.) Open seven days a week and most evenings with extended hours.

55 East 34th Street between Madison and Park Avenues—
212-252-6000

1555 Third Avenue at 88th Street—212-828-2300

202 West 23rd Street at Seventh Avenue—212-352-2600

The **Gay Men's Health Crisis/Geffen Clinic** offering screenings for HIV and syphilis, charges on a sliding scale that ranges from $30 to $125. On Fridays and Saturdays, they have a "walk-in" program where screenings are only $15.

125 West 24th Street between Sixth and Seventh Avenues,
6th Floor—212-367-1100, www.gmhc.org

Established in 2003 by The Actors' Fund of America, **The Al Hirschfeld Free Health Clinic** is a free medical clinic providing quality health care for all uninsured and underinsured entertainment professionals in the New York City area. For continuity care, a full-time family physician is on-site at the clinic four days a week. The clinic also has a group of practitioners and specialists who volunteer their time to provide a variety of medical services. In cases where a specialty consultation is necessary, The Al Hirschfeld Free Health Clinic makes low-cost referrals to a wide range of clinics and practitioners throughout the region. Services include: ongoing information on wellness issues; laboratory testing; blood pressure and cholesterol screenings; gynecological examinations; prostate examinations; annual health fairs; vision screening; flu shots; women's health fair; mammograms; colon/rectal cancer screening; PSA blood levels; electrocardiograms; and an on-call physician after office hours. Who is eligible for clinic services? All documented entertainment professionals with a union card or other documentation (call for details) who have no health insurance or cannot afford their deductible or an indemnity plan. Those actors currently employed but in need of urgent care may also utilize the clinic. To make an appointment, call Monday to Friday, between 9:30 A.M. and 5 P.M.

The Aurora, 475 West 57th Street, 2nd Floor—212-489-1939, www.actorsfund.org

For almost twenty years **The Miller Health Care Institute** for the Performing Arts at St. Luke's/Roosevelt Hospital has been providing affordable general and specialized medical care for performing artists as well as those in allied professions such as teachers, coaches, designers, writers, directors and production crews. Designed for and dedicated to the specific health needs of performing artists, the Miller Institute is also sensitive to each performer's budgetary constrictions: uninsured and underinsured patients are offered quality care on a sliding scale. The Institute also accepts Medicare and has several grants to expand access to their specialty programs (for more information about grants, contact the Miller Institute or consult their website). Institute services encompass everything from routine checkups and diagnosis and treatment of acute and chronic medical problems, to specialized care like acupuncture, psychotherapy, dance medicine, speech therapy, physical rehabilitation, orthopedics, massage therapy and nutrition. Unique to the Institute are its voice laboratory for examining ailing vocal chords; a physical therapy gym with a sprung dance floor, ballet barres and mirrors; and a performance evaluation studio to examine musicians' performance problems and progress. Patients are seen by appointment only, but some slots are open every day for those with urgent medical problems.

425 West 59th Street between Ninth and Tenth Avenues, Suite 6—212-523-6200, www.millerinstitute.org

The **New York City Department of Health** (212-427-5120/
877-692-3647 or 311, www.nyc.gov/html/doh/html/std/std2.html)
offers free and confidential HIV and sexually transmitted disease
testing and treatment at several locations throughout the five boroughs. The Department of Health also sponsors free safe-sex seminars, and for those who test positive for HIV, free counseling and
doctor referrals. All clinic services are confidential and on a "first
come/first served" basis, so arrive early and expect a wait. For
hours of operation and other information, call the Department of
Health or consult its website. Clinic locations:

- **Central Harlem**, 2238 Fifth Avenue at 137th Street—
  212-690-1760

- **East Harlem**, 158 East 115th Street near Lexington Avenue—
  212-360-5962

- **West Harlem**, 21 Old Broadway at 126th Street, 2nd Floor—
  212-678- 6691

- **Chelsea**, 303 Ninth Avenue at 28th Street—212-239-1718

- **Riverside**, 160 West 100th Street between Columbus and
  Amsterdam Avenues—212-865-7757

- **Morrisania**, 1309 Fulton Avenue at 169th Street, Bronx—
  718-579-7714

- **Richmond**, 51 Stuyvesant Place at Wall Street, Staten Island—
  718-983-4515

- **Bedford-Stuyvesant**, 485 Throop Avenue, 1st Floor, Brooklyn—
  718-574-2482

- **Crown Heights**, 1218 Prospect Place at Troy Avenue, 2nd Floor,
  Brooklyn—718-735-0580

- **Fort Greene**, 295 Flatbush Avenue Extension, 5th Floor,
  Brooklyn—718-643-4143

- **Corona**, 34-33 Junction Boulevard, between Roosevelt and Northern Avenues, Jackson Heights, Queens—718-476-7626

- **Jamaica**, 90-37 Parsons Boulevard near Jamaica Avenue, 1st Floor, Queens—718-262-5572

- **Rockaway**, 67-10 Rockaway Boulevard at Beach 67th Street, Queens—718-945-7150

The **New York City Health and Hospitals Corporation (HHC)** (212-788-3321, www.nyc.gov/hhc) whose mission is, "to extend equally to all New Yorkers...comprehensive health services of the highest quality in an atmosphere of humane care, dignity and respect," sponsors several community healthcare programs and maintains numerous hospitals and treatment facilities throughout the five boroughs. All services are administered regardless of a patient's ability to pay and include primary, emergency room, walk-in and outpatient care; psychiatric, oral and home healthcare, free flu shots, asthma vans, women and child health clinics, the "Heartbeat Community Cardiology Initiative," and smoking cessation and colon cancer prevention programs. City HHC facilities include:

- **Bellevue Hospital Center**, 462 First Avenue at 27th Street—212-562-4141

- **Coler-Goldwater Specialty Hospital and Nursing Facility**, 900 Main Street, Roosevelt Island—212-318-8000

- **Gouverneur Healthcare Services**, 227 Madison Streets between Jefferson and Clinton Streets—212-238-7000

- **Harlem Hospital Center**, 506 Lenox Avenue at 137th Street—212-939-1000

- **Metropolitan Hospital Center**, 1901 First Avenue at 97th Street—212-423-6262

- **Renaissance Health Care Network Diagnostic and Treatment Center**, 215 West 125th Street between Seventh and Eighth Avenues—212-932-6500

- **Jacobi Medical Center**, 1400 Pelham Parkway South at Eastchester Road, Bronx—718-918-5000

- **Lincoln Medical and Mental Health Center**, 234 East 149th Street between Park and Morris Avenues, Bronx—718-579-5000

- **Morrisania Diagnostic and Treatment Center**, 1225 Gerard Avenue, between 167th and 168th Streets, Bronx—718-960-2777

- **North Central Bronx Hospital**, 3424 Kossuth Avenue at 210th Street, Bronx—718-579-4000

- **Segundo Ruiz Belvis Diagnostic and Treatment Center**, 545 East 142nd Street between Brock and St. Ann's Avenues, Bronx—718-579-4000

- **Coney Island Hospital**, 2601 Ocean Parkway, between Avenue Z and Shore Parkway, Brooklyn—718-616-3000

- **Cumberland Diagnostic and Treatment Center**, 100 North Portland Avenue, between Park and Myrtle Avenues, Brooklyn—718-260-7500

- **East New York Diagnostic and Treatment Center**, 2094 Pitkin Avenue, between Pennsylvania and New Jersey Avenues, Brooklyn—718-240-0400

- **Kings County Hospital Center**, 451 Clarkson Avenue between Albany and New York Avenues, Brooklyn—718-245-3131

- **Dr. Susan Smith McKinney Nursing and Rehabilitation Center**, 594 Albany Avenue at Rutland Road, Brooklyn—718-245-7000

- **Woodhull Medical and Mental Health Center,** 760 Broadway at Flushing Avenue, Brooklyn—718-963-8000

- **Elmhurst Hospital Center,** 79-01 Broadway at 79th Street, Queens—718-334-4000

- **Queens Hospital Center,** 82-70 164th Street at Grand Central Parkway, Queens—718-883-3000

- **Sea View Hospital Rehabilitation Center and Home,** 460 Brielle Avenue at Bradley Avenue, Staten Island—718-317-3000

The **Park Med Eastern Women's Center** offers free urine pregnancy tests from 11 A.M. to 4 P.M., Tuesday through Friday, and full OB-GYN examinations for $100. Appointments are necessary for examinations; however, you may "walk-in" for pregnancy test.

44 East 30th Street between Madison Avenue and Park Avenue South—212-686-6066, www.parkmedeastern.com

Planned Parenthood of New York City (www.ppnyc.org) offers family planning counseling and treatment of a wide array of gynecological needs, including abortion, contraception, HIV testing and STD detection and treatment. All Planned Parenthood services are inexpensively priced (HIV and STD testing and birth control is free to students under twenty, pregnancy testing is free to all) and discretion is assured.

Margaret Sanger Center, 26 Bleecker Street at Mott Street—212-274-7200

44 Court Street, Brooklyn—212-965-7000

349 East 149th Street between Morris and Courtlandt Streets, Bronx—212-965-7000

The **Ryan/Chelsea-Clinton Community Health Center**

(www.ryancenter.org/resources.htm) offers primary care physicians and a complete range of healthcare services to New Yorkers on a sliding scale. Those eligible for care at the Health Center include low-income, medically underserved and uninsured patients, as well as those who are covered by Medicare and Medicaid. The uninsured pay a minimum of $29 per visit; depending on income, the most a patient would be expected to pay is $90, which includes X-rays, tests and blood work. Patients able to pay on the day of services are given a 30 percent discount; and liberal payment plans are available for those who cannot pay on day of services. Uninsured patients are eligible for the Center's pharmacy plan, under which they may purchase medication with only a $5 co-payment. If, for any reason, the Center cannot treat a patient, they will refer the patient to one of their city affiliates. If hospital care is needed, the Center will refer the patient to St. Luke's/Roosevelt.

645 Tenth Avenue at 46th Street—212-265-4500

279 East 3rd Street—212-477-8500

110 West 97th Street—212-316-8367

160 West 100th Street—212-769-7200 (HIV Services)

Dental

The **Columbia University School of Dental and Oral Surgery Teaching Clinic** provides primary, emergency and specialty oral health care at reduced costs (between 40 and 50 percent below what you would pay at a dentist's office). Students and residents who work under the close supervision of Columbia University faculty perform all services. To qualify for care at the teaching clinic, you must first register (a fee of $75 is required); at that time, a medical and dental history will be taken; an examination will be made that includes a full set of X-rays; and you will be referred to one of the clinic's providers. The walk-in clinic sees patients on a first come/first served basis and is open weekdays from 8:30 A.M. to 2 P.M. Specialty care at the clinic includes endodontics, oral and maxillofacial surgery, orthodontics, pediatric dentistry, periodontics, prosthodontics, and advanced general dentistry. Treatment of dental emergencies is available Monday through Friday, 8:30 A.M. to 3:30 P.M. The fee for emergency care during normal business hours is $75; after hours, emergency care is available through the Columbia Presbyterian Medical Center Emergency Room, located on the first floor of Presbyterian Hospital, 622 West 168th Street (between Broadway and Fort Washington Avenues).

622 West 168th Street, 7th Floor—212-305-6726, www.dental.columbia.edu

The **New York University College of Dentistry** offers a full-service dental clinic and emergency dental care for those who are not covered by insurance or cannot afford private-practice dentist

fees. For an admission fee of $90, which includes X-rays, consulta-
tion and a treatment plan, an NYCD final-year student will examine your teeth and perform any work that is needed. Not to worry:
these students are expertly trained and are always overseen by an
experienced dental professional. As the clinic understandably gets
quite busy, it operates on a first come/first served basis, so be sure
to go early.

 345 East 24th Street between First and Second Avenues—
212-998-9872, www.nyu.edu/Dental

Chiropractic and Acupuncture

Dr. Craig Fishel at the **New York Chiropractic and Wellness Center** offers chiropractic care to uninsured patients on a sliding scale. The initial office visit, which includes consultation, examination, X-ray, diagnosis and treatment, is $100. Office visits after the initial visit start at just $25 and include a full body adjustment and other treatments as necessary. If you are in need of acute care, New York Chiropractic and Wellness will charge you $150 per month, no matter how many visits you need in a four-week cycle; e.g., you can go five times a week for a month and still only pay a total of $150.

> 115 East 57th Street at Lexington Avenue, 14th Floor—
> 212-980-5444,
> http://nychiro.chiroweb.com/recommendations.html

The **Pacific College of Oriental Medicine** instructs students in the healing art of acupuncture. To provide practical, hands-on training for its students, the College offers the general public an inexpensive acupuncture clinic. At $30 per visit (every fourth visit is free), Pacific College students, under faculty supervision, perform one-hour acupuncture sessions. If you are a little squeamish about a student sticking you (and you needn't be, as all students at the clinic are highly trained and have reached a level of qualification before they are allowed to treat patients), you may have treatments by one of the college's faculty-practitioners at $60 for the first visit and $40 for all follow-up visits.

> 915 Broadway, between 20th and 21st Streets—212-982-4600,
> www.pacificcollege.edu

The Yu Wen Center Acupuncture Clinic at the **Swedish Insti-tute School of Acupuncture and Oriental Studies** provides low-cost acupuncture treatments to the general public three trimesters per year. The clinic offers an initial consultation/intake and a twelve-treatment series with clinical interns who are super-vised by licensed acupuncture practitioners. The cost of the clinic is $300 (which works out to a little more than $23 per session); seniors pay only $100 for the series. For more informa-tion about the clinic or to request an application/registration form, contact the Swedish Institute. Due to the clinic's popularity, all applications are processed in the order that they are received; therefore, reply as soon as possible to insure clinic placement. (For more information about the Swedish Institute, see the chapter on "Massage.")

> 226 West 26th Street—212-924-5900, ext. 205,
> www.swedishinstitute.edu

Four days a week, the **Wellness Center at The Riverside Church** maintains a low-fee acupuncture clinic with supervised students and licensed acupuncturists. Rates for the clinic are be-tween $5 and $25, depending on ability to pay. Clinic times are Tuesdays noon to 4 P.M., Thursdays 4:00 P.M. to 7 P.M., Fridays 1:00 A.M. to 3 P.M., and Saturdays 10:00 a.m to 2 P.M. Prior to your ses-sion, a full medical history will be taken; preregistration is re-quired.

> 490 Riverside Drive—212-870-6758,
> www.theriversidechurchny.org

Prescription Drugs and Toiletries

For the uninsured in need of **prescription medication**, the best way I know of to save on the high cost of drugs is to shop at **www.drugstore.com**. Prescriptions at this site cost about half what you'd pay at a pharmacy, and there are no tax or shipping charges.

In all of New York City, there are no discount pharmacies or drugstores. Let me rephrase that: Although several drugstore and pharmacy chains like Duane Reade, Rite Aid and CVS would argue that they are indeed discount retailers, none really have everyday low prices. I'm not saying that they don't have discount prices; they all certainly have sales, specials and coupon offers to pull people into their stores. Almost everything these retailers sell, however, except of course prescription drugs, can be found at general merchandise discount stores like Kmart and Conway for less money. (For a list of these retailers, see chapter on "General Merchandise Stores.") Duane Reade and CVS, both of which have several locations throughout the city, exonerate themselves by offering free **"Club Card"** programs. These clubs offer members discounts on featured toiletries, sundries and other items each week, which can save you a good amount of money. Pick up the "Dollar Rewards Club Card" application at any Duane Reade store (www.duanereade.com), and the "Extra Care Card" at any CVS (www.cvs.com) store.

Therapy

New York is the greatest city in the world. It's also the toughest. The city is expensive, overcrowded, fast-paced, brusque...all the things that people who have lived here for any length of time ostensibly come to love. But it takes courage, tenacity, confidence, cunning and a bit of an edge to settle here comfortably. Often, city life reminds me of the lyrics from Boy George's song "Karma Chameleon"—"Every day is like survival."

So, how do we keep it together in this tough town? Therapy seems to help lots of New Yorkers. To some, therapy is ridiculous, unnecessary, inconceivable, even a dirty word. However, it can be a real boon for many of us. It can help us put our lives in perspective; it can give us an outlet to vent, cry, complain, meditate, ruminate, sort through the past, plan the future. Therapy is a way to unload without burdening (or revealing too much to) our friends and family. Probably most beneficial, it is a safe place where we can speak freely and candidly to a caring professional who can help us assess our lives and behavior, and hopefully point us in the right direction.

Therapy comes at a high price, though. New Yorkers all over the city are paying their "shrinks" anywhere from $90 to $200 dollars for a forty-five-minute session. For those of us on a budget, those sums are an impossibility, making therapy more a luxury than a necessity.

Fortunately, there are organizations that understand the importance of therapy for the entire New York community, not just the wealthy, and offer their services on a sliding scale to low- and moderate-income individuals. They are devoted to helping us survive, reach our potentials, and live freer, happier lives. Of the several organizations that charge on a sliding scale, the following are those that I have either had direct contact with, or have come highly recommended to me by friends and colleagues.

Community Guidance Services was founded in 1953 with the idea that fees for therapy should be set on a sliding scale, based on a patient's means and income. Your initial visit is with a Community Guidance Services intake worker, who asks you to discuss your background and the things you would like to work on. At this interview, you may request the kind of therapist you would like and your session rate is determined. Within a week or so, you are assigned to one of the group's therapists, all of whom are psychologists or certified social workers with advanced degrees. You meet the therapist in his or her private office. If at any time you feel the match is not a good one, you may request to be reassigned. Rates start at $35.

133 East 73rd Street between Park and Lexington Avenues—
212-988-4800

Identity House, a nonprofit organization of caring volunteers, provides counseling services and support to New York City's gay, lesbian, bisexual and transgendered communities. Founded as a safe place to explore issues of sexual identity and to help those who are struggling with sexuality, alienation, relationships and family, Identity House offers a wide range of services, including counseling by professional psychotherapists, therapy referrals, discussion groups, conferences and workshops, and non-clinical support services. The organization's walk-in center (open Monday, Tuesday and Friday from 6 P.M. to 9 P.M., and Sunday from 2 P.M. to 5 P.M.) provides peer counselors who themselves have confronted issues of personal identity, to discuss any concerns you may have; if necessary, they make referrals. No appointment is necessary; a $20 donation is requested at the time of services, but no one is turned away if they cannot make the contribution.

39 West 14th Street between Fifth and Sixth Avenues,
Suite 205—212-243-8181, www.identityhouse.org

The **National Institute for the Psychotherapies (NIP)** is a four-year post-graduate training facility for licensed mental health professionals. As part of their training, therapists are required to see patients under the auspices of the Institute. NIP offers the New York community the services of these professionals on a sliding scale based on income and expenses. Initially, the patient is required to do an intake screening at a cost of $50. After this initial consultation with a Ph.D. therapist, NIP will assign him/her to a therapist. If the client feels the match is not a good one, he/she can request to be reassigned. (A friend of mine, who found his therapist through NIP, says, "Therapy is more an art than a science, so if you smell shit, yell shit!") Sliding scale fees start at $50, although rates for full-time students and the unemployed start at $25. Therapeutic sessions may take place either at NIP's facilities or in the therapist's private office elsewhere in the metropolitan area, depending on the patient's needs and therapist availability.

330 West 58th Street between Eighth and Ninth Avenues—
212-582-1566, www.nipinst.org

The **Village Psychotherapy Referral Service** offers a wide array of psychotherapeutic, psychological and psychiatric services, including individual, couple and group psychotherapy. VPRS experts in child, adolescent and family therapy provide counseling as well as parenting and educational (e.g., psychological testing) services. All VPRS clinicians are certified, highly trained and experienced in working with a variety of populations, including fine and performing artists, gays and lesbians, children and young adults, and educators. All fees are based on a sliding scale.

80 East 11th Street at Broadway, Suite 643—212-842-0489

As a community mental health facility for over forty years, the **Washington Square Institute for Psychotherapy & Mental Health** provides psychological services to middle income individuals and families. Washington Square Institute emphasizes understanding patients' present difficulties in perspective of past personal history and helps them use this knowledge to achieve mastery over their lives. To enable their staff to arrive at the most appropriate plan of treatment for the patient, the Institute requires three intake sessions: an initial interview, a psychiatric evaluation and conference, and a treatment-planning interview, all of which are priced at around $50 for the first two sessions and $40 for the third. The patient is then matched with a therapist, assigned a specific forty-five-minute period for treatment, and informed what the subsequent session rates will be. These rates are determined on a sliding scale from $35 to $100. All therapeutic sessions are held at Washington Square Institute's East Village location. To ensure continued quality of care throughout treatment, Washington Square Institute's Treatment Center views all patients as patients of the entire Institute, not only of a particular therapist. Should a patient wish to change therapists, or if for any reason the patient's therapist leaves, the Institute finds another suitable and qualified staff member to continue treatment. Washington Square Institute also offers group therapy, couples counseling and medication services.

41–51 East 11th Street—212-477-2600, www.wsi.org

The **NYS Psychiatric Institute at Columbia Presbyterian Medical Center** provides therapy and treatment at free walk-in clinics for those who are unable to pay. The clinics are staffed by professional therapists and treat a variety of problems, including eating disorders, anxiety, depression and substance abuse. For more information and hours of operation, visit the institute or call:

Depression Evaluation—212-543-5734

Eating Disorders—212-543-5316

Substance Abuse—212-923-3031

1051 Riverside Drive at 168th Street

Help Lines

In an immediate crisis, there are several free **help lines** you can call. Most of those working the phone lines are trained in suicide prevention, as well as in counseling for sex and crime victims, depression and personal problems.

- **AIDS Hotline**—212-447-8200, ext. 6 / 212-807-6655

- **Alcohol & Substance Abuse Info Line**—800-274-2042, 24 hours

- **Mental Health Counseling Hotline**—212-734-5876, 24 hours

- **Crime Victims' Hotline**—212-577-7777, 24 hours

- **Help Line**—212-532-2400, 24 hours

- **The Samaritans Suicide Prevention**—212-673-3000, 24 hours

Established by the New York City Department of Health in conjunction with the Mental Health Association, **Lifenet** offers mental health counseling, information and a referral line in English, Spanish and Chinese to assist those who are experiencing emotional distress in the aftermath of the World Trade Center disaster. Twenty-four hours a day, seven days a week.

English Speakers—212-995-5824

Spanish Speakers—877-298-3373

Chinese Speakers—877-990-8585

Yoga and Meditation

To maintain mind, body and spirit harmony and balance, there's nothing better than yoga. Yoga tones and limbers the body while enhancing its elasticity and improving circulation. It alleviates aches and pains, cleanses toxins in the organs and can reduce the symptoms of many chronic diseases. Yoga also relieves stress and anxiety, centers the mind and helps us to think more clearly. It gives us both strength and inner peace to cope with city life and our careers. These many benefits, however, come with a price. At most yoga studios, a typical class (one to one and a half hours) costs between $15 and $30. There are, thankfully, a few places that are sympathetic to the budget conscious and offer free or discounted classes:

The four **Bikram Yoga NYC** (212-245-2525, www.bikramyoganyc.com) studios offer three savings options: First, for new students, they have an introductory special of $20 for one week of unlimited classes. Second, the midtown studio at 797 Eighth Avenue hosts a "Pay What You Can" class on Fridays at 11:30 A.M. with the proceeds benefiting Broadway Cares/Equity Fights AIDS. Third, all but the 72nd Street studio have an "Early Bird Special" in which all classes up to and including 12:00 noon are only $12. You should know, Bikram is different from other schools of yoga in that it is a twenty-six pose class, conducted in a heated room (about 110 degrees). The heat warms the entire body, which helps you to work deep into muscles, tendons, and ligaments. The classes are designed for all levels of experience, but the heat and poses can be demanding on beginners. Stick to it, though, and you'll find Bikram's rewards are many (it happens to be my favorite form of yoga).

797 Eighth Avenue, between 48th and 49th Streets

208 West 72nd Street at Broadway

182 Fifth Avenue, between 22nd and 23rd Streets

150 Spring Street at Wooster Street

For an unbelievable $5, you can take a hatha yoga class on Saturdays, from 12 P.M. to 1:30 P.M., through the **Central Park Conservancy** (212-348-4867, www.centralparknyc.org). Classes are held at the North Meadow Recreation Center located mid-park at 97th Street; ages 18 and up; no registration required.

Jivamukti Yoga Center (www.jivamuktiyoga.com), which is one of the city's most popular yoga studios, offers gratis introductory classes (a $20 value) on the last Sunday of every month. Jivamukti's downtown location gives you a second chance at a free class on the second Saturday of each month.

404 Lafayette Street between Astor Place and 4th Street, 3rd floor—212-353-0214

853 Lexington Avenue, between 64th and 65th Streets, 2nd floor—212-396-4200

Joyous Life Energy Center holds classes in hatha, Kripalu, restorative, vinyasa and yoga for weight loss, as well as Pilates, tai chi, chi kung and meditation, all for $10 each. For a bit more money, Joyous Life presents monthly workshops on topics such as Reiki, belly dancing, "Speaking your truth," and "Increasing your personal effectiveness." Call or visit the Joyous Life website for information and class schedule.

119 West 23rd Street between Sixth and Seventh Avenues—
212-352-9910, www.joyouslifeenergycenter.com

The **New York Open Center**, which is considered the largest holistic learning center in the U.S. (over 600 classes are offered), maintains a free meditation room that is accessible to everyone during operating hours. Also, the Open Center holds free introductory sessions to many of their classes and workshops. For hours and a schedule, contact the Center.

83 Spring Street between Broadway and Lafayette Street—
212≠219-2527, www.opencenter.org

The community arts and culture center **Office Ops** bills itself as a performance and production "office park" and is dedicated to providing "affordable space and services for progressive individuals and groups to pursue their ideas." One of the ways they fulfill this commitment is to offer hatha yoga classes on Tuesdays from 8:15 P.M. to 9:45 P.M. for an astounding $2. Call or reference their website for more information, as well as to learn about the other services they provide.

57 Thames Street, Williamsburg, Brooklyn—718-418-2509,
www.officeops.org

Although classes in kundalini, vinyasa, anusara and restorative yoga at **Prana Mandir** are $17, the studio offers introductory sessions of each for just $10 per class.

316 East 59th Street between First and Second Avenues—
212-803-5446, www.pranamandir.com

At **Sal Anthony's Movement Salon** there are myriad walk-in classes you can take for just $12 each. Class disciplines range from yoga to Pilates, tai chi, kickboxing, gyrotonic, Capoeira conditioning, anatomy for movers and chi gung.

> 190 Third Avenue, between 17th and 18th Streets—212-420-7242, www.movementsalon.com

Besides their main location, Sal Anthony's Movement Salon also holds classes at the following studios:

- **Exercise Anew Chelsea**, 175 Seventh Avenue near 20th Street— 212-414-1103

- **Exercise Anew East Village**, 247 10th Street at First Avenue— 212-375-0430

- **Body Evolution**, 221 Second Avenue between 13th and 14th Streets—212-228-4202

- **Studio 17**, 119 East 17th Street between Irving Place and Union Square—212-228-4478

At **Universal Force Healing Center**, for every two hours of volunteer work you do, you are rewarded with a free class. Volunteer duties include helping at the front desk, assisting with mailings and other public relations duties, and light cleaning.

> 7 West 24th Street—917-606-1730, www.universalforceyoga.com

The **Wellness Center at The Riverside Church**, which is committed to helping its congregation and community "attain and maintain a high level of wellness and explore the many dimensions of healing the body, mind and spirit," offers Hatha yoga classes, appropriate for all ages and abilities, on Saturdays from 10:00 A.M. to 11:30 A.M., Mondays from 6:30 P.M. to 8:00 P.M., and Wednesdays from 5:45 P.M. to 6:45 P.M. Cost is $10, but no one is turned away because of inability to pay. Also, scholarships and a work-exchange program are available for those who qualify (call for details). The center also offers several "by donation" meditation classes throughout the week; a schedule of all classes may be found on the Riverside Church website.

> 490 Riverside Drive—212-870-6758,
> www.theriversidechurchny.org

By far the best and least expensive way to take yoga classes in the city is to purchase a **Yoga Passbook from the American Health and Fitness Alliance**. The Fitness Alliance Passbook contains 250 passes for free admission to over seventy-five of New York's best yoga, dance and Pilates studios (with locations in each borough). Each pass is good for a minimum of two free visits per studio, with some good for one to two full weeks of classes. A few passes even allow you to bring a friend at no extra charge. The Passbook is redeemable until the end of the calendar year, so you can go when you want, where you want, among the participating studios. The best part of the Yoga Passbook is that it is only $65, with a money back guarantee if returned within ten days of purchase. You may order the Passbook through their website, by phone, or by sending a check or money order to the address above. (Note: For greater savings, enlist three friends to purchase Passbooks with you; with every three orders of the Passbook, you receive a fourth one free, which comes to $48.75 each.

> P.O. Box 843, New York, New York 10163—212-808-0765,
> www.health-fitness.org

Need to get centered and quiet but hate to sweat or bend your body? Consider doing a **guided meditation** at one of the city's low-cost meditation centers:

For a donation of $5, you may participate in a guided meditation that helps "to let go of stress, learn to get quiet and connect to the Spirit within" at the nonprofit **Center at Cosmos Tree**. Meditations take place on Monday, Wednesday and Thursday evenings at 6:10 P.M. and Sunday mornings at 11:30 A.M.

> 177 East 87th Street between Lexington and Third Avenues, Room 204—212-828-0464, www.cosmostree.org

The **Shambhala Meditation Center of New York** holds that through meditation, everyone has the ability to "cultivate the mind's inherent stability, clarity, and strength in order to be more awake and compassionate in everyday life." To that end, the Shambhala Center conducts daily group meditations on week-days from 6 P.M. to 7:30 P.M., and Sundays from 9 A.M. to noon. The Shambhala Center also offers basic meditation instruction for beginners as well as anyone who would like to refresh their understanding of the technique on Tuesdays at 7 P.M., Wednesdays at 6 P.M. and Sundays at noon. A $5 donation is suggested for the group meditation and $10 for the instruction session.

> 118 West 22nd Street between Sixth and Seventh Avenues, 6th Floor—212-675-6544, www.ny.shambhala.org

Tibet House offers "Pay What You Wish" sitting meditation classes on Tuesdays from 6:15 P.M. to 7:30 P.M. Instructors from diverse Buddhist traditions conduct the classes in which they present a range of techniques and methods. Each session begins with a brief explanation of the technique followed by the meditation and a brief question-and-answer period.

22 West 15th Street between Fifth and Sixth Avenues—
212-807-0563, www.tibethouse.org

On Sunday mornings, from 10 A.M. to 1 P.M., the **Zen Center of New York City** hosts a beginning instruction session, a Zen service, a zazen (guided meditation) and dharma talk, for a suggested donation of $5. Meditations are also held Tuesday through Friday evenings from 6:40 P.M. to 8 P.M., and Wednesday through Saturday mornings from 6:25 A.M. to 7:30 A.M., for a $3 suggested donation.

500 State Street at Third Avenue, Brooklyn—718-875-8229, www.mro.org/zcnyc

Massage

Founded in 1916, the **Swedish Institute School of Massage Therapy** is considered one of the preeminent massage therapy schools in the country and has graduated thousands of students. The Swedish Institute's mission is "to create a safe and challenging environment for training students in the most current, practical, theoretical, scientific and ethical foundations of Western and Eastern holistic health care so that graduates are able to find and perform therapeutic work in a variety of settings." To provide practical training for its students, the Institute offers the general public two different inexpensive massage clinics where students, under faculty supervision, perform one-hour massage sessions:

BEST BARGAIN

Stress Reduction Clinic—meets for a series of six weekend sessions and offers basic full-body massage utilizing Swedish and Shiatsu techniques. The cost for the clinic is $125 for six sessions, which works out at a little over $20 per session.

Therapeutic Massage Clinic—explores the application of both Eastern and Western techniques to treat a client's specific chief complaint. For this clinic, you must provide written approval from your doctor that you have no "contraindications for massage therapy." The twelve week series costs $225, $220 for seniors over 65.

226 West 26th Street between Seventh and Eighth Avenues—
212-924-5900, ext. 208, www.swedishinstitute.edu

Although the **Randee Elaine Salon** is a little on the dowdy side, the services are all very good and very cheap (see chapter on "Personal Appearance"). Their massage therapists are mostly hefty Russian men and women with very strong hands who can break up almost any knot you've got. You'll stay relaxed when you receive their bill: only $45 for a one-hour massage if you use a Randee Elaine Salon coupon, which can be found in most gay periodicals like *Metro Source*, *HX* and *Next* or through their website. You must make an appointment for massages.

180 Seventh Avenue South near Perry Street—212-229-0399, www.randeeelaine.com

Alexander Technique

Developed by the Australian actor F. Matthias Alexander at the end of the 19th century, the Alexander Technique is a practice that identifies and improves poor movement and posture habits that cause pain, stress and fatigue. The technique, conducted one-on-one with a trained practitioner, scrutinizes a student's movement patterns (such as walking, bending, sitting and lifting), and with light touch and verbal instructions guides the student to restore natural reflexes and balance by locating and releasing muscular tension. The result is greater flexibility and range of motion, increased energy and, in some circumstances, the alleviation of chronic pain. Moreover, Alexander aids in the treatment of a variety of conditions such as neck, back and hip disorders, arthritis, migraine, Lyme disease, chronic fatigue syndrome, lupus, and breathing, coordination, and stress related ailments.

To reap the full benefits of the Alexander Technique, several sessions (which last from thirty to sixty minutes) are recommended. This however, can be costly. Fortunately, the **American Center for the Alexander Technique**, considered one of the nation's best training institutions for Alexander practitioners, offers a couple of no- and low-cost ways to take lessons: First, it presents free demonstrations on the first Monday of each month from 7:00 P.M. to 8:30 P.M. (call to reserve a spot, as seating is limited). Second, the Center's Teacher Certification Program utilizes volunteers for its third-year trainees to practice on under faculty supervision. Volunteers in this program attend forty-five-minute sessions once a week for eight consecutive weeks (to be eligible, you must commit to all eight sessions). In order to serve as a volunteer, you must be an associate member of ACAT for which a one-time membership fee of $25 is required. Contact the Center for more information or to become a volunteer.

129 West 67th Street—212-633-2229, www.acatnyc.org

Opticians

White Cat Vision, (www.whitecatvision.com), probably the least expensive place in New York to buy eyeglasses, has two city locations. They stock a great selection of designer frames by Calvin Klein, Kenneth Cole, Fendi, Dior, and others, all starting at around $30. Most styles are very modern and fashion-forward. White Cat provides eye examinations, sells contact lenses, and has a doctor on the premises.

BEST BARGAIN

> 22 East 14th Street between Fifth Avenue and Broadway—646-336-9500
>
> 1475 Second Avenue at 77th Street—212-472-3030
>
> 103 Sullivan Street between Spring and Prince Streets—212-219-2300

For Eyes Optical Company carries inventory similar to chains like Cohen's Fashion Optical, Pearle Vision and Lenscrafters, but undersells its competitors by anywhere from 10 to 30 percent. If you see something you like elsewhere and can't find it at For Eyes, they can probably order it for you—and you'll still pay less.

> 420 Lexington Avenue—212-697-8888, www.foreyes.com

Health Insurance

Because many performers do not receive health insurance through employment and do not qualify for needs-based insurance, they frequently fall through the cracks. In response to this crisis, the National Endowment for the Arts, in partnership with The Actors' Fund of America, have established the **Artists' Health Insurance Resource Center**. The AHIRC assists the arts community nationwide in accessing information about health insurance options. Go to The Actors' Fund website (www.actorsfund.org/ahirc) to find information about several government-subsidized programs and consumer organizations that offer quality affordable healthcare coverage options. The information available includes guides to purchasing insurance, artists' groups offering health insurance, a list of free and sliding scale clinics, health care options for the uninsured and underinsured, sources of emergency financial aid for medical/hospital bills, plans for the self-employed, access to group health insurance, and guides to gaining disease-specific assistance. Individuals may also receive health insurance advice and counseling through The Actors' Fund offices (729 Seventh Avenue at 49th Street, 10th Floor—212-221-7300) or through the AHIRC toll free helpline (800-798-8447).

Community Premiere Plus (CPP) is a private, not-for-profit health plan providing for the needs of uninsured and underserved people in Manhattan and the Bronx. For those who qualify (eligibility requirements stipulate that members' incomes cannot exceed a very low monthly maximum; call for details), CPP connects members with quality health providers in their area. CPP's pri-

mary care base is comprised of over 250 doctors in settings ranging from private practices to health centers and clinics. Members
also have access to diagnostic and treatment centers, specialty
care, mental health and chemical dependency services. Through
the plan, CPP offers a variety of free or low-cost health insurance
options for those who are eligible, including Medicaid, Child
Health Plus, and Family Health Plus.

534 West 135th Street between Broadway and Amsterdam
Avenue—800-867-5885, www.cpphealth.org

Healthstat, administered by the Mayor's Office of Health Insurance Access (MOHIA), works to enroll those who are eligible
(yearly income may be no more than a prescribed maximum; call
for details) in one of several free public health insurance programs. To qualify, you must show documents that verify your financial status, such as pay stubs, bank statements, a copy of your
lease and other pertinent information. Healthstat also helps those
with low incomes, but who make too much to qualify for the free
insurance, to obtain low-cost coverage.

330 West 24th Street between Ninth and Tenth Avenues—
888-NYC-6116, www.ci.nyc.ny.us/html/hia/home

If you are uninsured and meet certain criteria, you may purchase
health coverage through **Working Today's Freelancer's Union**.
Working Today is a national organization that "represents the
needs and concerns of America's independent workforce through
advocacy, information and service." Working Today defines
independent workers as freelancers, consultants, independent
contractors, temps, part-timers, contingent employees and the
self-employed. For those who qualify, Working Today offers a
group-rate HMO plan through HIP Health Plan of New York.
With this plan, you designate one doctor to be your primary care

physician (there are over 20,000 in the network) who will oversee all medical care. Coverage includes doctor and specialist visits, preventive dental care, prescriptions, hospitalization and emergency room services. Monthly premium rates may sound high, but are actually competitive: for an individual, coverage is about $300 a month; an individual and child pays about $550; an individual and spouse pays close to $600; and a family pays around $900. There are also set-up charges: a one-time application fee and yearly membership dues ($25 each). Eligibility requires one of two things:

• That you are a skilled computer user who has worked 120 hours or billed $9,000 over three consecutive months within the last six months

• You are currently working at least twenty hours per week in one of the following industries: nonprofit, financial services, technology, media and advertising, or arts and entertainment

When applying for this plan, you must also complete a "Proof of Work" form, documenting that you meet the above eligibility requirements, and provide supporting documents, such as pay stubs, cancelled checks, bank statements, timesheets and/or invoices issued to clients. For a summary of benefits, full eligibility requirements, and information on enrollment, go to the Working Today website.

55 Washington Street, Suite 557, Brooklyn, New York, 11201— www.workingtoday.com

Avoid Health Insurance Scams

With the cost of health care and insurance premiums skyrocketing, many questionable plans are oozing out of the woodwork and into the wallets of unsuspecting consumers. To avoid becoming a victim of health insurance fraud, heed the following:

Not all programs are scams, but some may not provide adequate coverage. If a plan offers a premium that is significantly less than other companies, make sure you know exactly what you're getting for your money. Read the prospectus from beginning to end.

Avoid discount or Network Access card plans. Though these plans may give you discounts on prescriptions, laboratory work, hospitals and doctors, they are not health insurance and are of limited value. If you have a catastrophic illness or accident, a discount of up to even 40 percent (which is really rare with such plans; they usually pay only about 20 percent of medical expenses) would still leave you with insurmountable debt.

Steer clear of "Affinity Group Indemnity" or "Fee for Service" plans, as they offer only specific, limited benefits. They work this way: You pay a monthly premium, which makes you eligible for a certain dollar amount for hospitalization, surgery, doctor care and prescriptions. This may sound appealing, however once you've reached the cap for each, you should know that you are no longer eligible for further benefits. In the advent of an emergency or even chronic care, these plans would cover only a small fraction of your total medical bills.

Make sure that the insurance company that holds your policy is licensed. In this flagging economy, hundreds of thousands of people who thought they were getting affordable or even cheap medical coverage have been scammed by fake companies. If you're at all suspicious about an insurance company's legitimacy, query the New York State Insurance Department (212-480-6400, www.ins.state.ny.us/nyins.htm).

Veterinary Services and Clinics

Keeping a pet healthy in New York can be as costly as keeping ourselves healthy—and sometimes more. Addressing the needs and financial constraints of city pet owners on a budget, a handful of organizations provide no- and low-cost veterinary services. These include:

Spay and Neuter Services

The New York City **American Society for the Prevention of Cruelty to Animals**, through its "ASPCA Cares" program, provides free and low-cost spay and neuter services and rabies vaccinations via two fully equipped mobile veterinary clinics that travel to neighborhoods throughout the five boroughs. These mobile clinics operate on a first come/first served basis, but give priority to financially needy pet owners (proof of public assistance such as Medicaid, Medicare Disability, SSI, food stamp enrollments or public housing assistance is required). For all others, a donation of $25 is suggested. For more information and dates of mobile clinic services, contact the ASPCA or go to its website.

424 East 92nd Street between First and York Avenues—
212-876-7700, www.aspca.org

In keeping with its mission to "promote animal welfare," the **Bide-A-Wee Animal Shelter** in Manhattan offers a full range of affordable, subsidized care for pet owners on fixed incomes or in

117

financial need. Bide-A-Wee's veterinary clinic services, which include routine checkups, testing, vaccinations, treatment, spaying and preventive care, are provided by a staff of dedicated full- and part-time doctors and health technicians. Each summer Bide-A-Wee provides free neutering services for cats and dogs. Call or visit the Bide-A-Wee website for more information.

410 East 38th Street—212-532-5884, www.bide-a-wee.org

The organization Friends of Animals offers pet owners low cost certificates that can be redeemed for routine spay or neuter surgery at participating veterinary hospitals. Once you have ordered the certificates, Friends of Animals will provide you with a complete list of vets within a thirty-mile radius of your residence who accept the certificates. Certificates may be purchased online at www.friendsofanimals.org, or by calling 800-521-PETS.

Cremation Services

Animal Medical Center (AMC) provides free cremation services for pets that die at home. AMC's only stipulation is that you are required to transport the body to their facility.

510 East 62nd Street—212-838-8100, www.amcny.org

Important Animal Care Phone Numbers

Animal Bite Unit at the New York Department of Health—212-876-7700

Animal Medical Center, 510 East 62nd Street—212-838-8100, www.amcny.org

Bureau of Animal Affairs at the New York City Department of Health—311

New York Center for Animal Care and Control (pick up service for lost, stray or abandoned animals)—212-722-3620, www.nycacc.com

Shopping

Provisions

Although tiny in size, **Baldwin Fish Market** offers big savings on a variety of fresh seafood and fish. Some of the catch you can reel in at low prices at this Upper East Side emporium includes mussels for $2.50 per pound; cod for $5.99 per pound; squid for $4.99 per pound; Cherrystone or Little Neck clams for $7 per pound; and salmon steaks or Canadian salmon fillets for $7.99 per pound. If you have a yen for sushi, you can sate it at Baldwin's raw bar, located at the rear of the store. Baldwin Fish Market offers free delivery to area residents.

1584 First Avenue, between 82nd and 83rd Streets—
212-737-4100

Bell Bates Natural Food Market, which has been serving Tribeca since 1885, carries a hefty variety of provisions and products at discounted prices. The aisles of this pristine, well-stocked store are brimming with inexpensive vitamins, homeopathic remedies, protein powders, organic household cleaners, natural cosmetics, herbal and sports supplements, organic produce, gourmet teas and coffees, natural foods and bulk items (see chapter on "Vitamins and Supplements"). Some of the impressive deals I found on a recent visit include three packages of De Boles organic pasta for $4.19; two Genisoy Protein Bars for $2; a 32-ounce carton of Rice Dream for $1.79; and Lightlife Smart Bacon for $2.69. Bell Bates also prepares delicious, healthy foods in its deli and has a juice bar and all-natural salad bar.

97 Reade Street—212-267-4300

Although fresh ravioli is the house specialty at **Bruno The King of Ravioli**, Bruno also makes and sells a wide variety of other pastas, delicacies and sweets. The prices at this purveyor of all things Italian are affordable, with a box of 40 ricotta-filled ravioli (a meal for three people) starting at just $3.99. And twice each week, Bruno's discounts selected ravioli for a savings of a dollar or more. Their many Ravioli choices include seafood, Tex Mex, smoked salmon and cheese, pumpkin, artichoke, shitake mushroom with Marsala wine, and lobster. Other homemade pastas include manicotti, fettuccini, linguine, taglierini, gnocchi, cannelloni, stuffed shells, cavatelli (my favorite) and tortellini. For those who are watching their weight or cholesterol, Bruno's makes several pastas that have no eggs, no cheese, and are low in fat. Bruno's also features several "Heat 'N Eat" take-home dinners, sold by the pound starting at $2.89, as well as salads, olives, cheeses, gelato, fresh sausage, bread, specialty meats, a large selection of their own sauces (starting at $3.99 a pint, $4.99 a quart), and much more.

2204 Broadway, between 78th and 79th Streets—212-580-8150

249 Eighth Avenue, between 22nd and 23rd Streets—212-627-0767

387 Second Avenue, between 22nd and 23rd Street—212-685-7666

East Village Cheese Store has tremendously low prices—perhaps the city's lowest—on an abundance of imported and domestic cheeses. To insure their low-price-leader status, East Village Cheese has weekly "Superspecials," in which up to fifteen cheeses sell for only $2.99 a pound. Havarti, smoked Gouda, English Five County cheddar, ricotta salata and Israeli yogurt cheese were among those recently designated as "Superspecials." This shop also carries lots of meats, breads, sweets, savories, pâtés, crackers, coffees, teas, pastas, olives, jams and beverages at nadir prices.

40 Third Avenue between 9th and 10th Streets—212-477-2601

Ask just about any New Yorker to name their favorite supermarket and nine times out of ten you'll hear **Fairway Fruits and Vegetables**. For good reason... For freshness, variety and price, no other grocery store in the city comes close. Fairway has everyday low prices and special sales on unparalleled selections in every one of its huge departments: produce, bread, dairy, prepared foods, baked goods, beverages, cheese, olives, condiments, water, canned goods, fish and seafood, meat, coffee, tea, bulk food, olive oil and sushi. In an enormous space upstairs, Fairway sells reasonably priced vitamins, supplements and organic and health foods. Caution: this popular store is not for the claustrophobic or those who can't endure aggressive crowds. Although Fairway is a big place, its maze-like aisles are cramped with goods, forcing the pushy masses to constantly jockey for position. Be especially aware of seemingly sweet little old ladies who wield shopping carts as if they were lethal weapons. If you want to avoid huge crowds and long checkout lines, don't even think about shopping at Fairway on weekends or after work. Open 24 hours, 7 days a week. (Note: A Fairway store is expected to open in the Red Hook section of Brooklyn in late 2004.)

2127 Broadway at 74th Street—212-595-1888

For value and selection, the city's number one food retailer is **Fairway's Outlet**. Housed in a huge, dilapidated building on the Hudson River in Harlem, this warehouse store is literally packed to the rafters with an awesome array of provisions; the produce and refrigerated sections alone are larger than most Manhattan supermarkets. For those who have been to the Upper Westside Fairway, it's hard to imagine that this outpost store could stock a larger inventory (or that any place could, for that matter), but it does. And no market has better prices. Fairway Outlet's

BEST BARGAIN ON FOOD

motto is, "Wholesale prices for the retail customer." The tradeoff (there's always a tradeoff) is that this market is not easy to get to or leave from, located several blocks from the 1 and 9 subway in an area by where few cabs pass. It is therefore imperative that you have a car. Fortunately, Fairway provides free parking.

2328 Twelfth Avenue at 133rd Street—212-234-3883

Though not expressly an inexpensive market, the **Food Emporium** (www.thefoodemporium.com) chain offers shoppers several ways to save money on their grocery bills. Food Emporium features two different "house brands"—America's Choice and Master's Choice, which are basically generic versions of name brand grocery items—for about a third less. It has several weekly sales on a vast array of items and additional reductions for members in its Gold Points Reward Network. There is no charge to sign up for a member card. Gold Point sale items change weekly and can save you hundreds of dollars each year. Often, the only things I will put in my shopping cart are those that are on sale through the Gold Points card. Food Emporium has a huge presence throughout the city. All stores are clean, well-stocked and feature lots of specialty foods like coffee, cheese and caviar. Each store also has a fresh fish and seafood section, salad bar, deli, bakery, and heaving produce section. Check your phone book for the closest to you of its twenty-three New York locations.

Sure, you know you can buy just about anything over the internet, from books, CDs, and DVDs, to clothing, computers and porn. But did you know that you could also do all of your grocery shopping over the World Wide Web as well? Including perishables and frozen foods? And have them delivered directly to your front door? Well, you can, through the portal **FreshDirect.com** (www.freshdirect.com, 866-2UFRESH). FreshDirect carries just about any grocery item you desire, including popular brands and household items, and they guarantee that their fruits, vegetables, meats, baked goods, coffees, seafood and dairy items are the freshest you can find anywhere. (Their food comes directly from farms, dairies, and fisheries, so none of the freshness is wasted sitting around on a shelf.) Better yet, most everything is between ten and 35 percent less than you'd pay at your local supermarket, and everything is backed by a 100 percent satisfaction guarantee. If that's not enough of an incentive, FreshDirect also has a great enticement for first-time users: If you spend $100 or more on your first order, they will treat you to $50 worth of free fresh foods (anything that is perishable). Delivery couldn't be easier: just tell them where and when you want your groceries delivered by choosing a convenient two-hour window, morning, noon or night, seven days a week. With FreshDirect's prices and convenience, you'll never have to leave your apartment to go grocery shopping again! (Note: There is a $40 minimum per order; delivery costs $3.95 in Manhattan and $4.95 in Brooklyn.)

All five metropolitan area **The Health Nuts** stores have competitive pricing and monthly sales on all kinds of healthy, organic and natural foods, products and cosmetics, as well as a large variety of vitamins, supplements and herbal and homeopathic remedies. Seen recently: Boca Veggie Burgers for $2.99 (regularly $4.29); Westsoy Organic Soy Beverage for 99¢ (regularly $1.99); Old Wessex Instant Oatmeal for 99¢ (regularly $1.99); Westbrae organic beans for 99¢ (regularly $1.59); Muir Glen organic pasta sauce for $2.69 (regularly $3.99); and Santa Cruz organic applesauce for $1.99 (regularly $3.59). If you need an immediate boost, The Health Nuts has a juice bar where they will make your favorite fruit and vegetable concoctions.

1208 Second Avenue at 63rd Street—212-593-0116

835 Second Avenue at 45th Street—212-490-2979

2141 Broadway at 75th Street—212-724-1972

2611 Broadway at 99th Street—212-678-0054

Bay Terrace Shopping Center, 211-35 26th Avenue, Bayside,
Queens—718-225-8164

Who would've thought that in the very expensive Chelsea Market
(where a cookie goes for as much as $12; a loaf of bread can be $6;
a quart of "designer" milk sells for $2.75; and 16 ounces of juice—
albeit fresh squeezed—is $3.50), you can actually find unfath-
omably cheap produce? Well, you can at **Manhattan Fruit
Exchange**. This retailer charges fair prices (barely above wholesale) for a cornucopia of beautiful, fresh fruits and vegetables.
Some examples: grape tomatoes, 89¢ a pint (usually $2.50 in most
supermarkets); red potatoes, 2 pounds for $2; mesclun salad, $3.99
a pound (usually $7.99); greenleaf lettuce, 99¢ a head; and a 6-
ounce carton of mushrooms, $1. Manhattan Fruit Exchange has
great prices on milk, cheese, juice, gourmet-flavored coffees (at a
very low $4.59 a pound), bulk nuts, dried fruits and candies, and
many more.

448 West 16th Street at Ninth Avenue—212-989-2444,
www.manhattanfruitexchange.com

The venerable (and venerated) **Murray's Cheese Shop** in the
West Village has excellent prices and weekly sales on a staggering
variety of domestic and imported cheeses. Besides the stuff that
clogs arteries and increases cholesterol, look for Murray's good selection of affordable breads, crackers, olives (ranging from $4.99
to $7.99 per pound), pastas, vinegars and olive oils (a 1-liter bottle
of Murray's "Private Stock" Extra Virgin is $8.99). Recent deals on
cheeses included domestic feta and pecorino romano at $4.99 per
pound; homemade mozzarella, which they boast is the best in the

city, at $5.99 a pound; Brie 60% at $3.99 a pound; Cupid's Choice camembert (in honor of Valentine's Day) at $4.99 each; and a goat's milk Coeur du Gilbert cheese for $5.99.

> 254 Bleecker Street near Seventh Avenue– 212-243-3289, www.murrayscheese.com

Although not a food store per se, **National Wholesale Liquidators** (www.nationalwholesaleliquidators.com), sells brand-name manufacturer's overstocks and seconds, and carries nonperishable food items at very low prices. You can find candy, dried fruits, nuts, preserves, canned, packaged and jarred goods, spices, tea and coffee, all at about 40 percent less than you'd pay at your neighborhood grocery store. On a recent tour, I found 2-liter bottles of soda for 50¢; 2-pound tubs of dried apricots for $1.88; 16-ounce jars of honey for $1.59; 1-liter bottles of mountain spring water for 44¢ and 6-ounce jars of marinated artichoke hearts for 79¢. Best yet, unlike most other closeout stores, all National Wholesale Liquidators' products are in pristine condition and don't have dubious expiration dates. (See chapter on "General Merchandise Stores.")

> 632 Broadway, between Bleecker and Houston Streets— 212-979-2400

> 71-01 Kissena Boulevard, Flushing, Queens—718-591-3900

Along a twenty-block stretch of Ninth Avenue, **between 37th and 57th Streets**, are a number of low-priced grocery stores, butchers, fish and seafood merchants, specialty food shops and produce dealers. This agglomeration of provisions purveyors—probably the city's largest—is a blessing to those who live in the neighborhood (like me), but also draws tightwad gourmands from five boroughs for its quality foods and low prices. Based on inventory and savings, the following are my picks for the Ninth Avenue/Hell's Kitchen area's best and least expensive food retailers:

Bereft of charm (this place is a dive), the **Big Apple Meat Market** has unbelievably cheap prices on a variety of fresh meats, groceries and household goods. Some great savings include USDA prime boneless beef pot roast, $1.78 a pound; leg of lamb, $1.98 a pound; sirloin steak, $2.18 a pound; veal shoulder cutlets, $4.98 a pound; fresh Perdue seasoned roasting chickens, 58¢ a pound; 6-ounce container of Axelrod yogurt—45¢; White Rose bath tissue, 50¢. For a real *The Cook, The Thief, His Wife and Her Lover* kind of experience (or to cool off in the summer), be sure to go into the meat section, a huge walk-through refrigerated area where butchers, bundled in several layers of clothing and covered by blood-soaked aprons, are carving up giant slabs of beef.

573 Ninth Avenue, between 41st and 42nd Streets—
212-563-2555

Central Fish Company and **Sea Breeze Seafood**, a block apart, are two of the best and least expensive places in the city to buy just about anything that lives in water. "Fresh" doesn't begin to describe the quality of goods at either store; the fish are so fresh, they're practically flapping. Both have titanic selections and minisubmarine-sized prices. Last time I looked at Central, salmon fillets were $3.99 a pound; sea bass, $2.99 a pound; tilapia, $1.99 a pound; red snapper, $4.99 a pound and bay scallops were $3.99 a pound. Sea Breeze had mackerel at 99¢ a pound; sea scallops at $5.49 a pound, sea trout at $1.99 a pound; and catfish at $1.49 a pound. The unique feature at Central is its huge tanks that hold an orgy of lobsters ($6.99 a pound, "special" lobsters are 3 pounds for $14.99). Sea Breeze specializes in a huge assortment of sea creatures: clams, mussels, oysters, and even sea urchins. If you don't find what you want at one place, you're sure to find it at the other.

Central Fish Company, 527 Ninth Avenue, between 39th and 40th Streets—212-279-2317

Sea Breeze Seafood, 541 Ninth Avenue at 40th Street— 212-563-7537

Almost a century before Starbucks besieged our fair city, **Empire Coffee and Tea** was vending caffeine to the residents of Hell's Kitchen. Still going strong, Empire is a great alternative to the slick atmosphere and high prices of the leviathan megachain. This laid-back, friendly neighborhood shop has an abundance of aromatic, flavorful and fresh teas and coffees at reasonable prices: their stock of custom-roasted coffees, from light and dark roasts, special blends, flavored to decaffeinated, range between $7 and $9 per pound. A large selection of loose and bag teas includes Pin Head Gun Powder Green, Pan Fried Green, Kenya Black, Chunmee Green, Lapsang Souchong and Licorice Spice. If you need coffee/tea paraphernalia such as mugs, teapots, coffee makers, filters, canisters and grinders, Empire carries a small supply. Why not try a cup of java while you're there? Empire has several flavors brewing.

568 Ninth Avenue, between 41st and 42nd Street— 212-586-1717, www.empirecoffeetea.com

International Grocery is beloved by professional and amateur chefs alike for its giveaway prices on a vast selection of bulk foods. This unique food store, which specializes in Greek, Italian and Spanish products, has dozens of bins filled to overflowing with the freshest of items, including a variety of rices, flour, grains, pastas, couscous, dried fruits, beans, condiments, nuts, olives, spices and herbs. International Grocery discounts a large array of olive oils, coffees ($5 a pound for regular, $6 for water process decaf), cheeses, specialty meats, Middle Eastern delicacies like hummus and baba ganoush, and canned and packaged goods. Halvah lovers rejoice: International Grocery sells myriad flavors of what one friend calls, "the best and freshest in the city."

543 Ninth Avenue, between 40th and 41st Streets—
212-279-5514

Kashkaval has low prices on a mouthwatering selection of cheeses from around the world, as well as a host of other rations like bulk items, prepared foods, sauces, spreads, breads, candies, condiments, olives and olive oils. They also carry lots of teas and a large array of flavored coffee beans (which they will grind to your specifications) for just $5.99 a pound. Kashkaval makes the city's most delicious gourmet sandwiches stuffed with the likes of smoked mozzarella and eggplant, chicken tarragon, brie and sun dried tomatoes, grilled vegetables and turkey pastrami, for an amazing $3.99 each. Not in the mood for a sandwich? Try their homemade soup bar ($1.99 for a quart container) or salad bar ($4.95 with a choice of fresh greens and four vegetable toppings). Besides their everyday low prices, Kashkaval has frequent sales and specials.

856 Ninth Avenue, between 55th and 56th Streets—
212-581-8282

The year-round **Ninth Avenue Farmer's Market at 57th Street** is minuscule—seven or eight vendors in the spring/summer/fall, and only a couple in the winter—but you can buy a variety of goods at very low prices. Besides seasonal fruits, vegetables, herbs and plants that are grown at metro-area farms, the market features homemade baked goods like breads, pies and cookies, as well as locally-made cheeses and honey. The Ninth

Avenue Farmer's Market operates on Wednesdays and Saturdays from 8 A.M. to 6 P.M.

The intoxicating, sweet aromas wafting from the **Pozzo Pastry Shop** lure even the most calorie-conscious passersby to partake of the their fresh baked goods. Unlike most "baked on the premises" bakeries, Pozzo is incredibly cheap. Nowhere else that I'm aware of can you buy fresh made 10-inch pies (apple, lemon meringue, pecan throughout the year, pumpkin and mince during the holidays) for only $8, 6-inch cheesecakes for $6.50, and 9-inch cheesecakes for $9.50. Pozzo makes delicious 7-inch pound cakes and flavored loaf cakes (chocolate chip, black forest, banana nut, cranberry walnut and cinnamon pecan) for a whopping $3. Need a cake for a special occasion? Pozzo does custom orders with a variety of flavors and icings starting at just $15.50.

690 Ninth Avenue, between 47th and 48th Streets—
212-265-7530

By far the cheapest places in all New York to buy fruits and vegetables are the **Stiles Farmer's Markets**. Both Hell's Kitchen markets are set in small circus-tent structures (one across from the Port Authority at the entrance to the Lincoln Tunnel; the other beside a parking lot on 52nd Street). Both operate year-round (the tents are heated in winter) and have unbelievable prices on a fairly standard array of items; the prices are so good that I have friends who live as far away as Inwood who come to Midtown twice a week specifically to shop at Stiles. You'll encounter bananas for 39¢ a pound; five ears of corn for $1; asparagus for $1.50 a pound; 2 pounds of Anjou pears for $1.50; New onions as well as red and Idaho potatoes

BEST BARGAIN ON PRODUCE

all at 99¢ for 3 pounds; mesclun greens for an astounding $3.99 a pound (compare that with $7.99 at Whole Foods!); gourmet coffee beans you grind yourself for $3.99 a pound; romaine lettuce 75¢ a head; and celery 50¢ a bunch. Stiles carries a good selection of bread, pasta and eggs that are often fresher than those in supermarkets. I always walk out of Stiles Market with two large grocery bags heaping with produce, for which I never spend more than $10.

> Across from the Port Authority at the entrance to the Lincoln Tunnel, between 41st and 42nd Street—212-502-4918
>
> Parking lot on 52nd Street between Eighth and Ninth Avenues—212-582-3088

For Brooklyn's tree-hugging, crunchy-granola lefties on a budget, **Park Slope Food Coop** is a "must-join" organization. This member-owned and operated market offers a diverse assortment of products, with an emphasis on organic, minimally processed and healthful foods, and household supplies that are marked only slightly higher than wholesale. Environmentally conscious, the store obtains most of its goods from local, "earth-friendly" producers, avoids products "that depend on the exploitation of others," promotes recycling, and supports nontoxic, sustainable agriculture. Throughout the year, the Coop sponsors several events, including vegan and vegetarian dinners, free workshops, lectures and seminars on everything from healthful foods to holistic healing, astrology and aromatherapy. Only members may shop here, but membership is open to all: pay a $25 joining fee; commit to working at the coop two hours and forty-five minutes per month; pay a $100 investment fee (payment plans are available) that is returned when a member leaves the coop; and attend a new member orientation meeting (held every Monday and Wednesday at 7:30 P.M. and the second Sunday of each month at 4 P.M.). The

Park Slope Food Coop provides free childcare during shopping/working hours.

782 Union Street, Brooklyn—718-622-0560, www.foodcoop.com

How has the unglamorous **Pioneer Supermarket** (289 Columbus Avenue at 75th Street—212-874-9506, www.pioneerspmkt.com) managed to stay afloat amidst the proliferation of self-consciously trendy shops, boites and boutiques on Columbus Avenue? Undoubtedly Pioneer has an ironclad lease that locks them to this location 'til the end of time. A good thing for their customers; this bastion of old New York (well, 1960s New York) looks like it hasn't been renovated in forty years (one glance at the linoleum floors and you will see what I mean) and has prices on several items that don't seem to have changed much in forty years either. Recent Pioneer bargains included Just Pik't premium orange juice (half gallon) for $2.50; 3 pounds of bananas for $1; boneless sirloin steak for $2.99 a pound; a pint of Häagen Dazs ice cream or sorbet for $1.99; Perdue whole chicken legs for 69¢ a pound; 12-pack of Amstel or Heineken beer for $10.99; whole pork loin for $1.99 a pound; 10 Temple oranges for $1; a 32-ounce jar of White Rose mayonnaise for 99¢; and 2 1-pound packages of San Giorgio pastas for $1. The Columbus Avenue store isn't the only Pioneer in the city; check your phone book for the nearest location.

Porto Rico Importing Company (201 Bleecker Street between Sixth Avenue and McDougal Street—212-477-5421, www.portorico.com) has been buzzing the city since 1907 and is a coffee and tea drinker's paradise. This West Village emporium offers its customers over one hundred kinds of coffee beans (which they will grind to specification) from the world over, in a variety of blends, roasts, shades and flavors. To insure the highest quality and freshness, and to make good on their promise that their joe is

BEST
COFFEE
SELECTION

"the best that money can buy," Porto Rico does its own roasting. The results: a flavorful and aromatic product that is far superior to Starbucks and the other chains, and with prices that range from $5.99 to $7.99 a pound, also cheaper. For added savings, Porto Rico places a different coffee on special each week, and two times yearly (October 22–31 and April 15–30) drastically reduces its most popular beans. Porto Rico has what seems like endless rows of canisters of loose teas from exotic locales, all at excellent prices.

107 Thompson Street between Spring and Prince Streets—212-966-5758

40½ St. Mark's Place near Second Avenue—212-533-1982

Since the first edition of this book hit the market, I've received countless recommendations of discount shopping venues that friends, colleagues and readers feel should be included in subsequent editions (like this one). The best of these suggestions has been the specialty purveyor and Middle Eastern food importer **Sahadi's**. This medium-sized mom and pop shop has an amazing array of delicacies, almost all at rock bottom prices. At Sahadi's you'll find a wide selection of international foods, including coffees (starting as low as $3.75 a pound), teas, nuts, spices, pastas (fresh and dried), cheeses (over 200 American and European varieties), pâtés, crackers, bulk candies, cookies, jams and preserves. If olives are your thing, look no further: Sahadi's has a remarkable diversity of olive oils and a choice of twenty-eight different types of olives from around the world. Don't feel like cooking? Sahadi's also has many delicious and inexpensive prepared items like salads, spanakopita, filo wraps and leek pies. Customer service here is great—the staff really know the inventory, are helpful, and seem to love their jobs.

187-189 Atlantic Avenue, Brooklyn—718-624-4550

New York's biggest, best and oldest farmer's market is the **Union**

Square Greenmarket. At this bustling market with its carnival-like atmosphere, you will find reasonably priced just-picked produce, as well as bargains on quality fish, baked goods, home-jarred preserves and honey, and plants and flowers. At the end of each market day, many vendors discount their goods by as much as 50 percent so they won't have to cart them home. Market hours are Mondays, Wednesdays, Fridays and Saturdays from 8 A.M. to 6 P.M.

Union Square at 17th Street between Broadway and Park Avenue South—212-477-3220, www.cenyc.org

People in the know come from all over New York to buy their groceries at the **Westerly Natural Market**. This cramped store is packed to the ceiling, literally, with brand-name natural foods at the city's lowest prices. In addition to its everyday discounts, Westerly also has monthly sales where items are so drastically reduced that it seems the store is practically paying you to shop there. It is not uncommon to find Health Valley and Barbara's brand natural cereals for as low as $1.29; 6-ounce Fantastic brand Chicken Flavor Rice Pilaf, two for $1; or Newman's Own Chocolate Chip Cookies for $1.89. Beware: fresh produce and meat are not inexpensive, though I'm sure that if and when the store expands, those prices will come down too. The Westerly prides itself on offering its customers huge discounts on a vast selection of vitamins, herbs and homeopathic remedies, as well as nutritional and sports supplements. Many, if not most, of the vitamins are "Buy One, Get One Free;" protein bars cost almost half what you would pay at other places; and supplements sell at rock-bottom prices. The staff is always friendly and helpful, and those overseeing the vitamin and supplement areas are definitely experts in their field.

BEST BARGAINS ON HEALTH FOOD

911 Eighth Avenue on the northwest corner of 54th Street—212-586-5262

Unless you live in the Meatpacking District, **Western Beef**'s main Manhattan outlet on the far reaches of West 14th Street is quite a schlep. Not a problem. With the money you'll save shopping at this large warehouse-like store, you can afford a cab to get you home; hell, you can afford a car service! As you'd expect from the store's name and location, this place specializes in meat; what you might not expect is how cheap the prices are—practically wholesale. For example, recently whole fresh hams, split chicken breasts and boneless beef briskets were $1 a pound; combination end and center cut pork chops were $1.65 a pound; boneless beef eye round or bottom round steaks were $2.99 a pound; store-made ground turkey was 99¢ a pound; beef rib steak was $4.99 a pound; rib or loin lamb chops were $2.99; and London Broil was $1.69 a pound. I could go on and on listing the savings here, but you get the point. If I've left you with the impression that Western Beef is strictly a butcher, my mistake. This is a full-service supermarket whose aisles are heaving with produce, frozen foods, canned goods, household products, you name it—everything and more to stock the pantry and fridge. And the prices on non-meat items are just as low, like plum tomatoes for 69¢ a pound; a 6-ounce can of Star-Kist Tuna for 60¢; and four 16-ounce packages of Barilla pasta for $3. Hail a cab and get thee to Western Beef! Residents of the Upper West Side and the boroughs will be happy to know that Western Beef has stores in their areas; consult your phone book for the nearest location.

403 West 14th Street at Ninth Avenue—212-989-6572, www.westernbeef.com

Whenever I tell anyone that I am including **Whole Foods Market** (www.wholefoods.com) in my discussion of inexpensively priced grocery stores, they almost always look at me as if I have lost my mind. Most everyone agrees that Whole Foods is the finest and most beautiful market in New York. All also agree that it is one of the city's most expensive. I cannot argue with the NY's "finest" assessment, for it is indeed a pleasure dome of a super-market: the aisles are artistically stacked and stocked with "healthy," "all-natural," "clean," "free range," "fresh" and "pure" foods, and the store is bright and accessible. The employees are all cheerful, helpful and knowledgeable, and the attractive patrons look as if they were hand-picked by Central Casting to enhance the store's already ideal ambience. It makes me happy to shop at Whole Foods; I've cured a case of the blues more than once by me-andering up and down the glistening aisles. As for being one of the city's most expensive markets, I don't necessarily agree. Yeah, most items can be purchased elsewhere for less, but Whole Foods redeems itself with its many weekly sales and promotions. In ad-dition, Whole Foods markets its own brands at everyday discount prices, like its "365" brand soups for only $1.19, salad dressings for $1.79, cereals and peanut butter both always $1.99. This chain packages its own protein bars, "Verve" and "Everyday," which are comparable to "Cliff Bars" and "Powerbars" and priced at only 99¢ each. Whole Foods has an expansive prepared foods section, the most aesthetically pleasing produce section you've ever seen, an exquisite cheese section, fresh baked breads and desserts, envi-ronment friendly cleaning products, luxurious natural toiletries, and a separate store next door devoted to vitamins, supplements, scents, aromatherapy, personal hygiene products and a plethora of products that other stores don't carry. (Note: Whole Foods ex-pects to open a store in the Gowanus Section of Brooklyn in 2005.)

250 Seventh Avenue, between 24th and 25th Streets—
212-924-5969

The Shops at Time Warner Center, Columbus Circle (Broadway between 58th & 60th Streets), Concourse Level—212.823.9600

For years, Healthy Pleasures was the only large market in the NYU/Washington Square Park area that specialized in health

foods. Being the only kid on the block, most of the Healthy Pleasures inventory was downright pricey, with protein bars priced
higher than almost anywhere in the city and a salad bar that was
a real wallet buster. Recently renamed **Wholesome Market**, this
new store has very competitive prices on myriad provisions, as
well as frequent promotions and sales (be sure to pick up their
monthly sale circular at the front door). A second Wholesome
Market is located at 489 Broome Street—212-431-7434. (For a further discussion of Wholesome Market, refer to the chapter on "Vitamins and Supplements.")

93 University Place—212-353-3663

To many a city dweller, especially those who love to cook, **Zabar's**
is as synonymous with New York as the Empire State Building
and the Statue of Liberty. A city icon, Zabar's is a veritable monument to great food and good dining and carries an awesome selection of the crème de la crème (as well as crème anglaise and crème
fraîche) of imported and domestic food items. Whether you desire
coffee, cheese, charcuterie, olives, smoked fish, candy, Jewish delicacies, baked goods or prepared foods, Zabar's has the very best.
Labeled by such superlatives, you'd think that the store would be
expensive; for the quality and variety of its gourmet goods,
Zabar's is actually relatively inexpensive.

2245 Broadway at 80th Street—212-787-2000, www.zabars.com

Spirits, Beverages and Brews

For Brooklynites, or those who are willing to make the trip out to Cobble Hill, **American Beer Distributing Company** offers outstanding selection, savings and service on beer, soda, water, sport drinks, and other beverages. This superstore stocks one of the area's largest assortments of beers, including domestic ales, lagers, microbrews, hard ciders, malt beverages, bocks, stouts, porters, wheat beers and barley wines. It also carries a huge variety of imported brews such as doppelbacks, amber and dark lagers, British ales, smoked beers, festival beers and malt liquors. Even teetotalers will want to shop here, because they stock almost every soda imaginable, as well as a wide range of carbonated and noncarbonated bottled waters, "New Age" beverages, syrups, teas and juices. Best of all, American Beer offers incredible daily discounts and weekly Super Sales and coupons.

256 Court Street at Butler Street—718-875-0226, www.americanbeerbuzz.com

B & E Quality Beverage is a discount retailer of almost every liquid consumable except wine and liquor. They carry a full compliment of sodas, waters, sports drinks, juices, and teas, plus their wide selection of American microbrews and international beers from Europe, Russia, Brazil, India, Korea, China, Thailand and Argentina. B & E specializes in inexpensively-priced Belgian beers, and there are a lot to choose from. You'll also find a smattering of "seasonal" brews: on one December visit I discovered featured beers with names like "Winter Warmer," "Christmas Ale," "Winter Welcome" and "Delirium Noel." Speaking of novelty beers, B & E is one of the few stores I've seen that carries the 14 percent alcohol content "Samichlaus Bier," termed the "strongest beer in the world" by the Guinness Book of World Records ($4.50 for a 12-ounce bottle). Great beer deals include a 6-pack of Tsingtao for $6.95, a 6-pack of Sam Adams for $6.50, a case of Saranac for $19.95 and a 6-pack of the New Orleans brewed Abita Ale for $7.95.

511 West 23rd Street between Tenth and Eleventh Avenues—212-243-6559

For price, selection and service, wine retailer **Best Cellars** is my favorite. I'm completely ignorant about wines, so selecting a suitable bottle is a grueling chore for me, however Best Cellars takes the drudgery out of wine shopping by organizing its inventory by category, color and flavor. Whether I'm in the mood for a sparkling wine, a light red, a heavy white, a dessert wine, or anything in between, I go to the respective section and take my pick. Moreover, the staff is extremely knowledgeable and ready to offer insight and guidance in the selection process . . . not something you'd expect from a store where all bottles are under $10. That's right, *all* wines are priced under $10. Free tastings are held daily, except Sunday, from 5 P.M. to 8 P.M.

1291 Lexington Avenue at 87th Street—212-426-4200, www.bestcellars.com

In Chelsea, the small shop **Crossroads** is stacked from floor to ceiling with wine and liquor from all over the world. Crossroads cannot be categorized as a "cheap" liquor and wine outlet, but it does carry several good, inexpensive wines, such as Bogle Chardonnay, $8.99; Preece Sauvignon Blanc, $4.99; Livio Felluga Pinot Grigio, $14.99; and Rabbit Ridge Zinfandel; $8.79. On multiple purchases you find bargains: buy any six bottles that are tagged with an orange price sticker and you will receive a 10 percent discount; buy any twelve bottles for a 20 percent discount. There are occasional liquor bargains. On a recent price-sniffing expedition, a "Magnum Madness" sale had Cutty Sark Whisky for $25.99, Jim Beam Bourbon for $18.99, Ron Rico Rum for $16.99, Georgi Vodka for $10.99 and Gilbey's Gin for $14.99. One visit and you'll understand why both *New York Magazine* and *New York Press* have in the past named Crossroads the city's "Best Wine Shop."

55 West 14th Street at Sixth Avenue—212-924-3060

Garnet Wines & Liquors discounts wines from around the world and has something for every taste and budget. For frugal imbibers, Garnet has hundreds of excellent vintages from Chile, Australia, California, Spain, New Zealand, New York, France, Italy and elsewhere, at remarkably low prices. Among Garnet's bargains, I found Yellow Tail Shiraz for $5.49, Macon-Villages Chardonnay for $6.49, Hardys Nottage Hill Merlot for $7.99, Orvieto Classico for $6.49, Baron Herzog Chenin Blanc for $6.99 and Beringer White Zinfandel for $6.99. If you favor champagne, Garnet carries several inexpensively priced brands like Chandon Brut for $12.99, Freixenet for $7.99, Charles Lafitte for $15.99 and Piper Sonoma for $11.99.

929 Lexington Avenue at 68th Street—212-772-3211,
www.garnetwine.com

The expert staff at **Nancy's Wines for Food** is trained to assist consumers in making informed decisions about what to serve with any type of meal. Nancy's specializes in small batch wines and imports from Germany (with over one hundred Rieslings), but features an impressive selection of international, sparkling, dessert and "weird and wondrous" wines—and over one hundred eighty different bottles of wine for under $10.

313 Columbus Avenue at 75th Street—212-877-4040,
www.nancyswines.com

New York Beverage's remarkable inventory of almost every beverage imaginable (except wine and liquor) includes a full range of domestic and imported beers and microbrews, sodas, waters (sparkling and non-sparkling), mixers, juices and ciders. Since New York Beverage, located in Harlem, is a warehouse, you'll pay warehouse prices, which means huge savings over your supermarket or deli. Don't worry about how to transport your potables home: the company offers reliable home and office delivery for a nominal price. Too lazy to make the trip uptown? No problem. Phone orders are also available. Check the website (www.newyorkbeverage.com) for a complete list of products.

207 East 123rd Street between 2nd and 3rd Avenues—
212-831-4000

Slope Cellars in Brooklyn has a great marketing gimmick that means savings for you: with their "Slope Cellars Wine Club Card," every thirteenth bottle of wine you buy is only 99¢.

436 Seventh Avenue, between 14th and 15th Streets, Park
Slope—718-369-7307, www.slopecellars.com

BEST
BARGAIN

The lowest prices in town on wine and liquor are at **Warehouse Wine and Spirits**. This megastore stocks its shelves with almost every kind of wine and brand of liquor imaginable, and at prices that no other retailer in the city can beat. For inexpensive, quality wines, they have a huge selection for under $10; a good clearance section with wines starting at $4.99 a bottle; and by the case there is always a 10 percent discount. If you want the hard stuff, a wide range of liquors, from "call" to premium brands, are sold here at bargain prices. Once you've entered Warehouse Wine and Spirits and seen their discounts, you will want to snap up all you can carry. But don't go crazy—remember bottles are heavy and you have to get them home! Okay, go crazy, because if you spend $100 or more and live below 86th Street, Warehouse will deliver at no charge.

735 Broadway between Waverly and 8th Street—212-982-7770

Vitamins and Supplements

Bell Bates Natural Food Market, serving Tribeca for one hundred years, carries a plentiful selection of vitamins, minerals, homeopathic remedies, protein powders, and herbal and sports supplements, in addition to its discounted provisions. Recently, all Bell Bates brand vitamins were 30 percent off, and all Twinlab, Nature's Answers and Nature's Herbs vitamins and supplements were 25 percent off. Natrol Ester-C (500 mg.) with Bioflavanoids, regularly $41.59, was $24.95; a 36-pack of Alacer Emergen-C, regularly $14.95, were $8.97; Twinlab Daily One Caps, regularly $43.95, were $21.97; and Boericke and Tafel Echina-Spray, regularly $9.49, was $5.69.

97 Reade Street—212-267-4300

General Nutrition Center (GNC) Stores (www.gnc.com), which carry most major brands of vitamins, performance supplements, diet pills, herbs, fat-burners, etc., is by no means cheap. At best, this natural health chain can be considered moderately priced. What they have going for them, besides locations in all five boroughs (twernty-nine stores in Manhattan, alone), is their "GNC Gold Card." Using the Gold Card, which costs $15 per year, 20 percent is deducted from any purchase you make in the first week of each month. GNC has weekly promotional sales on various items; EAS products are always discounted 20 percent; and all GNC brand products are always "Buy One, Get the Second One at 50% Off."

The Health Nuts stores price competitively and set monthly sales on their large variety of vitamins, supplements and herbal and homeopathic remedies. Recent bargains included 30 percent off the entire lines of vitamins by Twinlab, Natrol, The Health Nuts, Schiff, Nature's Answers and Nature's Herbs. A 36-pack of Alacer Emergen-C was $8.97 (regularly $14.95); 60 Oreganol gel caps were $19.97 (regularly $33.29); and 32 ounces of Naturade Aloe Vera gel was $10.47 (regularly $17.45). Monthly specials include protein bars and powders, sports and nutrition supplements, and diet aids.

1208 Second Avenue at 63rd Street—212-593-0116

835 Second Avenue at 45th Street—212-490-2979

2141 Broadway at 75th Street—212-724-1972

2611 Broadway at 99th Street—212-678-0054

Bay Terrace Shopping Center, Bayside, Queens—718-225-8164

The Vitamin Shoppe always discounts name brand and its own brand products 20–40 percent off suggested retail prices. The store's selection of health products is huge and includes vitamins (of course), supplements, herbs, teas, alternative and homeopathic remedies, nutrition and sports bars, bodybuilding supplements, books, personal care products and appliances. In addition to shopping at its twenty-seven stores citywide, you can also order by phone (1-800-223-1216), by fax (1-800-852-7153), by mail, or on the web (www.vitaminshoppe.com). Its monthly catalog is chock-full of discounts and specials. On top of their everyday low prices, The Vitamin Shoppe maintains a "Frequent Buyer" program that rewards customers with points (one point for every dollar that you spend) to be used for credit toward future purchases. Check your local listings for the nearest Vitamin Shoppe location.

Go to the **Westerly Natural Market** for its huge discounts on a vast selection of vitamins, herbs and homeopathic remedies, as well as nutritional and sports supplements. Many, if not most, of the vitamins are "Buy One, Get One Free;" protein bars cost almost half what you would pay at most other places; and supplements sell at rock-bottom prices. (For more information, see chapter on "Provisions.")

BEST BARGAIN
ON VITAMINS &
SUPPLEMENTS

911 Eighth Avenue at 54th Street—212-586-5262

At **Wholesome Market** in the East Village, the shelves of vitamins and nutritional supplements are stocked so high with the many formulations, brands, types and sizes, library ladders are in place to help you get to the hard-to-reach products. The enormity of the inventory can be a little daunting. I often stand agape in the aisles, puzzling over (among other things) what the real benefit of "time-release" over "non-time-release" is. My choice is based ultimately on which products are on sale. Fortunately, Wholesome Market is always having a 2-for-1 special on one or another of its brands of vitamins, herbs and supplements. (See my discussion of Wholesome Market in the chapter on "Provisions.") The staff here knows their products, and if you are afraid of heights, they will climb the ladders for you.

93 University Place—212-353-3663

489 Broome Street—212-431-7434

Willner Chemists (www.willner.com), in business since 1911, carries the city's largest selection of major brand vitamins, nutritional supplements, protein bars and powders, minerals, sports nutrition, herbs and homeopathic remedies. It also has some of New York's lowest prices: most of Willner's inventory is discounted from between 30 and 50 percent off list price, and it holds frequent half price sales on a multitude of items. Lately, I have found that when comparison-shopping large quantities of vitamins and supplements, Willner's even occasionally bests the prices at Westerly Natural Market (see above). Other Willner Chemists plusses include a large section of nutrition and health related books; a crew of pharmacists and nutritionists who are experts in vitamins and supplements; a quarterly catalog with product, health and sale information; and, getting into the carbohydrate-cutting craze, Willner's maintains a hefty assortment of low-carb foods.

100 Park Avenue at 41st Street—212-682-2817/800-633-1106

253 Broadway at Murray Street—212-682-2817/800-633-1106

Clothing

For years, the men's retailer Moe Ginsburg was *the* source for outstanding brand-name suits, shirts, shoes and ties at dirt-cheap prices. As its popularity grew, Moe Ginsburg became a little too big for its britches: its stock went upscale, prices were no longer competitive and service became lugubrious. Ultimately, Moe's loyal clientele fled, causing it to shutter its doors for good. Recently, Moe Ginsburg's grandson, Alan David Horowitz, opened a new discount men's emporium based on his grandfather's original model, and the masses are returning. The new store, **Alan David**, carries up-to-the-minute styles on suits, sportcoats, raincoats, tuxedos, trousers, shirts, ties, sportswear and more, as well as exclusive designers like Hugo Boss, Joseph Abboud, Perry Ellis, Bill Blass, Ralph Lauren, DKNY, Kenneth Cole and Hart, Schaffner & Marx, at prices that are lower than you'd pay at a department store. Suits here start at $175, tuxedos at $195, sportcoats at $95, and cashmere-blend overcoats at $149. Alan David always provides free, expert on-site alterations and has frequent sales in which every item in the store is discounted.

170 Broadway at Maiden Lane, 1st Floor—212-577-2747, www.alandavidmenswear.com

The bargain women's clothing shop **Backwoods** is a favorite of several of my actress friends. Most everything in this small store is priced from $10 to $30. Those who love Backwoods characterize the merchandise as "funky," "chic" and "cheap," and they rave about the quality, selection and helpful sales staff. Backwoods stock changes frequently, so there's always something new to see and buy.

315 West 57th Street between Eighth and Ninth Avenues—
212-459-2975

For timeless and tasteful men's and women's clothing, **Banana Republic** (www.bananarepublic.com) offers some of the best bargains to be had in the city. No, I haven't lost my marbles. Despite the perception that Banana Republic is an upscale clothier, you can find cheap **BEST MARK-DOWNS** prices. I'll explain. Every five to six weeks they introduce new inventory, which means they have to clear the shelves of the old. That "old" merchandise is marked down by 20 percent to 30 percent. The longer these unsold goods stay in the store, the more they are reduced. Make frequent trips into the stores, scope out what you want, calculate roughly when it will go on sale, and then return to the store at that time. This system has never failed me and has led to incredible buys, like two all-wool Italian suits for less than $200 each; lots of long sleeve stretch shirts for $9.99; tons of all-wool and cotton sweaters for under $20; countless crisp and colorful cotton dress shirts for $19.99; and several Italian-made silk ties for $7.99. Everything you need can be found under one roof—cashmere, cotton and merino wool sweaters, rubber rain jackets, overcoats, suits, dresses, coordinates, khakis, dress shirts, blouses, skirts, leather pants and jackets, trousers, t-shirts, underwear, accessories, bags and jewelry. The merchandise designs for men and women are mostly simple and classic, with the slight edge and influence of European designers like Helmut Lang and Prada.

Every summer and winter, no fashion-conscious, bargain-hunting New Yorker would dare miss the ritual of **Barney's Warehouse**

Sale. Thousands descend on Barney's Chelsea Co-Op Store, where the sale takes place, to devour as much low-priced high fashion as they can. During the sale merchandise can be 50 to 80 percent off Barney's regular prices. One caveat however: 80 percent savings sounds great, but Barney's is an expensive store and that percentage on a $2,000 suit or a $3,000 dress means the item is still a lot of money. For the diligent, deals can be had, especially on accessories. It's not unheard of to find designer belts, ties, scarves and even some bags for as low as $20. Even if you have no intention of buying, the Barney's sale is something every New Yorker should experience once. The warehouse becomes a war zone of rapacious shoppers grabbing, pushing, shoving, bickering, tossing and sometimes coming to blows over pieces of well-sewn cloth, providing enough spectacle to rival the Roman Coliseum during Caesar's time! The sales take place in February and August; call store for details or watch the "City" section of *The New York Times* and sales section of *Time Out New York*.

BEST SHOPPING SPECTACLE

236 West 18th Street between Seventh and Eighth Avenues—212-826-8900, www.barneys.com

Bolton's, whose motto is "If you've seen it before, you've seen it for more," carries women's clothing and accessories at discount prices. You won't find many designer items here, but there are lots of brand-name goods that are attractive and affordable: a 100 percent silk blouse for $19.99; a sweater by Rafaela for $12.99; and Harvé Benard wool separates for $29.99 (skirt), $39.99 (pants) and $59.99 (jacket). For very good end-of-season clearances, Bolton's discounts merchandise by up to 50 percent.

Broadway Generation's two Manhattan stores carry a huge inventory of inexpensive and up-to-the-minute women's footwear, casual and work apparel, accessories, winter wear, lingerie, pajamas, handbags and more, most of which are by famous designers. All Broadway Generation merchandise is marked down between 30 and 50 percent off retail; on top of this, they host constant sales for even more savings. On a recent visit to Broadway Generation, the designers found on its numerous racks and shelves included Hilfiger, Kenneth Cole, Jones NY, Diesel, Ecko, Nine West, Guess, DKNY, Cardin, Girbaud, Timberland, Børn, Naturalizer, Aerosoles and Ecco. If you're in the market for children's clothing, Broadway Generation has a huge department of girls' and boys' wear, also at discounted prices.

485 Fifth Avenue (entrance on 41st Street)—212-986-4401

23 Park Place, between Broadway and Church Street—212-608-6220

No, the **Burlington Coat Factory** (www.coat.com) chain doesn't sell just coats, even though they do carry a lot of them, many by leading designers like Calvin Klein, Nautica, Kenneth Cole, Liz Claiborne and Jones of New York. The rest of this designer discount chain's inventory doesn't have a lot in the way of designer items—and the ones they have aren't that fetching—but if you don't mind last season's styles, you will almost always find something you like at a great price.

707 Sixth Avenue—212-229-1300

625 Atlantic Avenue, Brooklyn—718-622-4057

Canal Jean Co. (www.canaljean.com) has really low prices on a wide variety of fun, casual clothes like jeans, t-shirts, lingerie, accessories, underwear and socks, bags, jewelry, shoes, vintage clothing, leather coats and pants, and club wear. Innumerable designer and brand-name products can be found here, with Levi's having the most conspicuous presence. Canal's colorful, hip and sexy merchandise is definitely suited to the young (the Manhattan store does a booming business with the students from nearby N.Y.U.), but the young-at-heart are sure to find some good buys as well. Check out the basement bargain area for some of the lowest priced garments in the city—literally thousands of pieces of new, used, closeout and irregular items, all for $10 or less, as well as several 99¢ bins.

718 Broadway at Washington Place—212-353-2608

2236 Nostrand Avenue, between H and I Avenues, Brooklyn—718-421-7590

For hardcore shoppers, serious bargain hunters and tourists in the know, **Century 21** (www.c21stores.com) is a favorite destination. This New York institution carries top (and I mean *top*) name brand and designer men's and women's fashions at fractions—from 40 to 70 percent off—of their original prices. Imagine a large department store in which their entire inventory of cutting edge, fashionable clothing is on sale *all the time*—that's Century 21. Like any department store, Century 21 carries other merchandise like accessories, cosmetics, fragrances, sunglasses, housewares, luggage and electronics—all at discount prices.

22 Cortlandt Street at Chambers Street—212-227-9092

472 86th Street, Bay Ridge, Brooklyn—718-748-3266

The national chain, **The Children's Place** (www.childrensplace.com), is one of the city's best outlets to buy inexpensive baby and children's clothing and accessories that are both durable and adorable. The merchandise here is similar to what Baby Gap and Gap Kids is doing, but always at a few dollars less. The Children's Place has frequent sales for even greater savings.

Church Street Surplus carries a huge stock of moderately priced used, vintage and military clothing. Here you'll find women's dresses, shirts and blouses from the 50s, 60s and 70s; men's retro vests and shirts; tweedy overcoats; a large selection of leather jackets (most between $50 and $90); fur coats (don't shoot me PETA members—I'm just the messenger); and bulky sweaters, suits, old Levis, military uniforms and hats. For those who need formal wear but can't afford to splurge on new duds, Church Street Surplus is an ideal place to find a decent, pre-worn tuxedo starting at around $30.

327 Church Street at Canal Street—212-226-5280

The cheap general merchandise store, **Conway**, has a handful of locations throughout Manhattan and the other four boroughs (with several stores located in the area around Macy's) where you can find low-end items at very low prices. For many of my friends, Conway is a favorite haunt for truly cheap cotton shirts, accessories, socks and underwear, knockoff purses and summer clothing.

Discount retailer, **Daffy's** (www.daffys.com), has great bargains on both designer and non-designer clothing and accessories for men, women and children. Most of what you will find are current season fashions with prices up to 60 percent less than you'd pay at a regular retail store. On top of their everyday low prices, Daffy's has frequent holiday and clearance markdowns. Several of my friends love this place for its selection and bargains, and do the bulk of their apparel shopping in it. Personally, the jumbled piles of strewn clothing and picked-over racks quickly make me nervous, and I usually end up fleeing after a couple of minutes. But if the aesthetics of shopping aren't your concern, you'll do just fine here.

Domsey's (www.domsey.com), the Goliath of discount vintage clothing stores, carries piles and piles of every imaginable item of used and funky clothing, including jeans, jackets, shoes, hats, shirts, leather goods and military garb. With a little persistence and a lot of time, you can find some real treasures in this vast warehouse store. Domsey's even has huge "Buck-a-Pound" bins where, although you're not likely to find runway-worthy fashions in them, you will find plenty of stuff to wear for painting your apartment.

431 Broadway at Hughes Street, Williamsburg, Brooklyn— 718-384-6000

1609 Palmetto Street at Myrtle Avenue, Ridgewood, Queens— 718-386-7661

Like T.J. Maxx, Burlington Coat Factory and Daffy's, **Filene's Basement** (www.filenesbasement.com) is a designer discount retailer where you'll have to do a lot of sniffing and snooping to suss out the good stuff. But fear not: there is good stuff to be had if you are willing to work. Besides reasonable prices, Filene's also has periodic clearance sales where unsold merchandise is further reduced.

620 Sixth Avenue at 18th Street—212-620-3100

2220 Broadway at 79th Street—212-873-8000

187-04 Horace Harding Expressway, Flushing, Queens— 718-479-7711

Find Outlet (www.findoutlet.com) specializes in women's very modish designer labels and high-end previous-season stock at 50 to 80 percent off the original prices. Think of this store as a remarkably inexpensive outlet for pleasingly hip clothes, shoes and accessories. New stock arrives almost every day, so call or stop in whenever you are in the neighborhood.

229 Mott Street between Prince & Springs Streets—212-226-5167

361 West 17th Street at Ninth Avenue—212-243-3177

Given that I regard myself as a know-it-all of cheap anything in the city, I am amazed that until very recently I had never heard of **Gabay's**. This popular East Village establishment has been attracting crowds for years with its unbelievable prices on an eclectic collection of exclusive designer handbags, shoes and men's and women's clothing. When I say designer, I mean designer. Most of the stuff here is the crème de la crème of the fashion world—Fendi, Kate Spade, Loro Piana, Giorgio Armani, Chanel, Calvin Klein, Ralph Lauren, Ermengildo Zegna and Donna Karan—and Gabay's charges anywhere from 40 to 75 percent below the retail price for these items. Gabay's inventory consists of irregulars and seconds from tony department stores (almost everything I saw on my most recent visit still had Bergdorf Goodman sales tags) and is in impeccable condition. Go often, as the merchandise changes nearly every day.

225 First Avenue between 13th and 14th Streets—212-254-3180, www.gabaysoutlet.com

Although **The Gap** (www.gap.com) is probably the country's most prominent retail clothing chain (God knows they are in New York) it does have attractive, comfortable, well-made and reasonably priced merchandise for men, women, children and infants. When it comes to quality, style and cost, The Gap bridges "the gap" between the more upscale goods at Banana Republic and the downscale ones at Old Navy (no surprise there since all three are operated by the same parent corporation). In addition to its affordable prices, The Gap, like its siblings, constantly introduces merchandise to its line, which means frequent sales and clearances to make way for the new stuff. For the Gap nearest you, consult your phone book, or spit in any direction—you're bound to hit one!

With several enormous stores in Manhattan, Harlem, Queens and Brooklyn that seem to have materialized out of nowhere, the

Swedish clothing super-retailer **H&M** (www.hm.com) has planted firm roots in the city and made living here that much sweeter. Why? On everything from cool men's and women's business attire to hip club clothes, fun party frocks, relaxed casual duds and trendy designer knockoffs, H&M's prices are absurdly low. This arbiter of "fashion and quality at the best price" also has amazing prices on a great selection of undergarments, accessories, bags, makeup, jewelry and women's plus sizes. H&M's inventory is the kind of stuff you see being worn by the city's beautiful people—you know, the folks who are immediately whisked past the velvet ropes at happening clubs, or who have runway-side seats at the hottest new designers' shows. These stores are always mobbed (the wait to get into dressing rooms can sometimes take an hour), but for H&M's savings, style and selection, it is worth enduring the throngs.

If you have a penchant for glitter, sequins, feathers or fake fur, you will feel right at home at **Joyce Leslie** (www.joyceleslie.com). At these emporiums of inexpensive, hot and trendy junior fashions, you can assemble a funky outfit for a night on the town or a "trailer trash" costume for the annual Greenwich Village Halloween parade. This isn't the place you'd go to outfit yourself for temp jobs or to meet the in-laws. There are racks and racks of cheap denim and polyester, as well as spangly tops for $9.99, low-cut and tight-fitting cable weave sweaters for $12.99, and jeans with revealing lace seams for $24.99.

Although **Loehmann's** (www.loehmanns.com) is categorized as a designer discount store, for quality, selection, service and goods, it is a step above the others. Here you will find the best of both household names and less mainstream designers of men's and women's fresh, hip and happening clothing. Prices on their high-end items are cheaper than department and specialty stores and boutiques—

but they are not cheap. Your Loehmann's purchase will be a splurge, but worth it if you are in the market for quality, style and value. For extra savings, get the Loehmann's no-fee member's card. With it, you get an extra 15 percent off of every purchase made four days before through four days after your birthday.

101 Seventh Avenue at 16th Street—212-352-0856

2807 East 21st Street, Brooklyn—718-368-1256

If discount designer duds are your desire, then dash down to **Loftworks**. There, you'll find three enormous floors of brand-name men's and women's formal business attire, casual clothing and sportswear, as well as children's wear and accessories, all discounted at up to 80 percent off retail prices. Loftworks, which advertises itself as "better than a sample sale," carries the world's finest designers, including Armani, Versace, Ferragamo, Dior, Prada, Hugo Boss, Dolce & Gabbano, Burberry, Ralph Lauren, Calvin Klein, Tommy Hilfiger, DKNY, Kenneth Cole, Liz Claiborne, Abercrombie & Fitch, Diesel, Nike, Puma, Guess, Reebok, Fendi, Jones NY and many more. For increased savings, Loftworks holds weekly specials and sales and has a basement clearance section. If you sign up to receive Loftworks' online newsletter, you will receive a 10 percent birthday discount and other exclusive offers.

100 Lafayette Street, one block south of Canal Street—
212-343-8088, www.loftworkslafayette.com

For basic athletic clothing, shoes and equipment, there is no better place than **Modell's**. If you are in the market for the most recent aerodynamic running shoe, or the most sought after warm-up suit, you won't find it here. What you will find is last season's hot shoes, as well as team jerseys and functional (if perhaps style-less) sports clothing at savings of 50 percent and more. Recently, men's and women's Fila warm-up suits were $25 (regularly $39.99); Adidas long-sleeve tees were $9.99 (regularly $19.99); men's Champion fleece turtlenecks were $10 (regularly $35); Nike Air Integrity walking shoes were $32.50 (regularly $64.99); Adidas women's tennis shoes were $32.50 (regularly $64.99); and Timberland men's waterproof Chukka Field Boots were $59.99 (regularly $119.99). Modell's also carries discount sports equipment. A Wilson All-Pro basketball was $5 (regularly $19.99); an Ab Slide was $19.99 (regularly $39.99); and those popular but impractical urban scooters were only $10 each. To keep customers coming back, Modell's offers free membership in their MVP (Modell's Value Plan) Club. For each purchase you make, you collect points that are turned into reward gift certificates: earn one point for every dollar you spend; spend $400 and receive a $20 gift certificate. Modell's has a low price guarantee: If you find the same item at another store for less, they will beat the price and refund 25 percent of the difference. Locations in all five boroughs; consult your phone book or the Modell's website, www.modells.com.

For great looking, dependable and affordable clothing to knock around in, there is no better place than **Old Navy** (www.oldnavy.com). Brought to you by the same people who operate The Gap and Banana Republic, Old Navy specializes in cheap cool-casual. They not only have exceptionally low regular prices, but also weekly specials, coupon sales and end-of-season blowouts, where all unsold items go for next to nothing.

The **Historic Orchard Street Shopping District** (Orchard Street and the surrounding area between East Houston and Canal Streets—www.lowereastsideny.com) on the Lower East Side has been designated New York's "Historic Bargain District," and the title is fitting. This area, which has been the bargain center of the city for the last hundred years, is a mecca for inexpensive designer apparel and much more. For maps and more information about the district, contact the Lower East Side Business Improvement District (261 Broome Street, New York, NY 10002—212-226-9010). (Note: Some of the stores in the district only take cash.)

For men's casual cotton and cotton-blend summer clothing that costs next to nothing, you can't beat **R.A.G. Transfer Clothing Co.** You'll find a varied assortment of ultra-cheap items like solid colored short sleeve button-up shirts for $13; colored t-shirts for $5 each; polo shorts for $12.50; black or blue jeans for $20 per pair; long-sleeved dress shirts starting at $12.50; cotton/linen blend tops and bottoms for $15 each; and all-cotton brightly designed Hawaiian shirts for $9.99.

Inside the A, C and E subway stop at Eighth Avenue and 42nd Street in Times Square—212-279-1829

Grand Central 4, 5, 6, 7 subway stops

34th Street between Seventh and Eighth Avenues

Broadway between 43rd and 44th Street

Rags-a-Go-Go's vintage apparel store is teeming with second-hand clothing, shoes and accessories, all at thrift shop prices. A lot of the stuff it carries is pretty basic (t-shirts, jeans, sweaters), but there is a good share of hip to outré styles that will definitely make a fashion statement (what that statement will be is up to you). Although the goods here are secondhand, most if not all are in excellent condition.

218 West 14th Street near Seventh Avenue—646-486-4011

Strawberry, a New York institution since 1932, carries a huge selection of inexpensive junior, young misses and children's clothing, shoes and accessories. You won't find much in the way of designer duds or brand-names, but the stuff here is stylish and appealing to young folk. Check your phone book for the nearest location.

With departments for men, women and children in its two Manhattan locations, **Syms** (www.syms.com) carries a large selection of quality, in-season clothing and shoes by brand-name designers and labels. For over three decades Syms has been appealing to the hearts and wallets of the city's "educated consumers" with what they call "off prices"—prices always below those found on the same or like items in department or specialty stores. Besides affordability, Syms makes shopping easier than most large discount retailers by placing color-coded price tags on all items so that sizes are located effortlessly. By signing up at the Syms website, you are automatically eligible to receive online discount coupons and announcements detailing exclusive sales. In recent forays into Syms, I've found the price and selection to be a tad better than competitors like Filene's Basement and TJ Maxx.

42 Trinity Place—212-797-1199

400 Park Avenue at 54th Street—212-317-8200

If separating the wheat from the chaff is your idea of a good time, you'll love **T.J. Maxx** (www.tjmaxx.com). This discounter of name brands from previous seasons has a lot of merchandise to sift through—aisles and racks and shelves of it. For the assiduous, however, there are huge rewards: lots of designer and retail names like Donna Karan, Calvin Klein, Express, Givenchy, Chaps and Polo Ralph Lauren, Gap, Old Navy, Nautica and more, for very little money. This is a particularly good place to buy underwear and socks: a 3-pack of Calvin Klein tighty-whities is $14.99; a 3-pack of Gold-Toe athletic socks is $4.99; and dress socks by either Dockers or Geoffrey Beene are three pairs for $7.50. The discounts on women's undergarments are just as good.

620 Avenue of the Americas—212-229-0875

136-03 20th Avenue, College Point, Queens—718-353-2727

1509 Forest Avenue, Staten Island—718-876-1995

The inexpensive, armed-services-inspired goods at **Uncle Sam's Army Navy** appeal less to military buffs and war re-enactors than they do to club kids. Sure, they have camouflage, but in shades of shimmering blue, which is guaranteed to garner attention on the dance floor. The many bargains at Uncle Sam's include Dickie work pants for $4; vintage leather jackets for around $100; flight jackets for $49.95; and Ralph Lauren vintage military pants, $8, and shirts from $4 to $8. Also for $8, Uncle Sam's will make you a set of personalized dog tags . . . you need never forget your name again.

37 West 8th Street between Fifth and Sixth Avenues—
212-674-2222, www.iamunclesam.com

In recent fashions seasons, camouflage pants and t-shirts were all the rage on the runways. Little did the fashionistas know that **Weiss & Mahoney** has been doing camouflage for years, and for a lot less ($9.99 for tees, $25 for pants) than that with a designer imprimatur. Besides the camouflage, this emporium, which bills itself as "the peaceful army navy store," carries a lot of what you'd expect at great prices. Dickie work pants were $20; jungle boots were $20; field jackets were $65; down jackets were $99.49; leather combat boots were $40; Carhartt work dungarees were $22; and all union suits, Timex watches and Columbia winter garments were 25 percent off regular prices.

142 Fifth Avenue at 19th Street—212-675-1915

Zara (www.zara.com), a Spanish owned retailer with stores throughout the world, has very low prices on modish men's and women's clothing, shoes and accessories. Most of what you will find here are well-made knockoffs of leading European designers, without the designer price tag. If you are lucky enough to catch one of their end-of-season sales, you won't pay less anywhere else for some very nice clothes.

580 Broadway near Prince Street—212-343-1725

750 Lexington Avenue at 59th Street—212-754-1120

39 West 34th Street near Fifth Avenue—212-868-6551

101 Fifth Avenue near 17th Street—212-741-0555

Shoes

By polling friends, scoping out several retailers and scrutinizing my own shoe buying habits, the following is a compilation of the places where you can find shoes at discount prices:

As I already mentioned, I love **Banana Republic** (see my valentine to B.R. in the "Clothing" chapter). The Banana carries all kinds of well-made, very fashionable shoes that are knockoffs of up-to-the-minute styles, and most are manufactured in Italy. Yeah, they aren't cheap, but all eventually go on sale after they've been on the shelves for a few weeks. And the sales are pretty spectacular. I have three pairs of Banana Republic shoes, none that I paid more than $49.99 for, and all are handsome, sturdy and comfortable. My favorite pair is complimented on all the time, and I am constantly asked, "Are those Prada?" The women I've talked to who purchase B.R. shoes on sale feel just as passionately as I do. Search the phone book for the seventeen Banana Republic locations.

Many of the **discount clothing stores**, including Burlington Coat Factory, Century 21, Daffy's, Filene's Basement, Loehmann's, Syms and T.J. Maxx, carry shoes for men and women. The roster of designer and brand-names these stores carry is impressive. You'll find (deep breath) Bass, Johnston & Murphy, Florsheim, Bostonian, Cole Haan, Bruno Magli, Giorgio Brutini, Sebago, Clarks, Hush Puppies, Sperry, Timberland, Reaction by Kenneth Cole, Steve Madden, Skechers, Enzo Angiolini, Nine West, Aerosoles, Adidas, Naturalizer, New Balance, Reebok, Avia, Liz Claiborne, Keds, Dexter, Rockport and Doc Martens, among many others. Most styles are from previous seasons and are marked down by 30 percent or more from their original prices. Unfortunately, when I explored these stores, I found that there was a better range of styles in smaller sizes for men, larger sizes for women. Men, take note: Loehmann's only sells women's shoes. (See "Clothing" chapter for store locations.)

Most of the **discount stores on Canal Street** around Broadway and Lafayette (see chapter on "General Merchandise Stores") carry one kind of shoe or another. Some have "brand-name" athletic shoes (emphasis on the quotations); some carry the real thing, albeit from two or three seasons ago. You can also find dress and casual shoes made from all kinds of materials—leather, "pleather" and canvas—in designs that are mostly utilitarian, circa 1977, Soviet-issue. You trade style for drastically low prices, but it can be worth it.

Eitan's Bootery carries women's all-leather shoes and boots made exclusively in Italy or Brazil that are obscenely inexpensive. The day I was there, most pairs were on sale for $9.99 and up to $19.99, and the highest-priced model was a whopping $29.99. Styles range from dressy to casual pumps, business heels to sandals. I did not see many brand-names (the only two I recognized were Caressa and Nine West), but most were very attractive and appeared to be extremely well made. If I were a woman, this is where I would buy all my shoes.

BEST BARGAIN FOR WOMEN'S SHOES

23 East 33rd Street near Madison Avenue—212-725-6240

The discount shoe superstore chain **Famous Footwear** (www.famousfootwear.com) has recently opened branches in New York City, and all I can say is, "Wow!" These stores carry up-to-the-minute name brand and designer dress, casual and athletic shoes for men, women and children, and all at very low prices (about half what you'd pay at a shoe or department store). Better yet, Famous Footwear always hosts promotional sales, such as their "Buy One Pair, Get the Second for Half Price." (I took advantage of the sale while on my fact-finding mission and bought a pair of Skechers dress shoes and a pair of New Balance running shoes, for which I paid less than $90 total.) Some of the many famous name manufacturers you'll encounter in Famous Footwear's aisles include Bandolino, Aerosoles, Lugz, Candies, Life Stride, Prima, Kenneth Cole, Tommy Hilfiger, Easy Spirit, Adidas, Polo Sport, Nike, Teva, Timberland, Nunn Bush, Florsheim, Bostonian, Asics, Steve Madden, Bass, Unlisted, Converse, Saucony, and K-Swiss.

BEST BET

250 West 34th Street—212-244-4810

Gateway Center, 381 Parkway Drive, Brooklyn—718-235-5683

The **Historic Orchard Street Shopping District** has thirty quality leather goods shops, most with extraordinary prices on a variety of shoe styles. Give yourself a few hours to check out all the leather vendors in the neighborhood before making your final decision, and don't be afraid to haggle. For maps and more information about the district, contact the Lower East Side Business Improvement District (261 Broome Street, New York, NY 10002—212-226-9010).

At **Make 10 Ladies and Gents Shoewear Warehouse Store** you can find lots of great looking designer men's and women's shoes for as little as $12, with a large selection priced at $20. Unlike most warehouse stores that sell low to unload undesirable merchandise, many of the shoes here are classic in style and very fashionable.

44 West 39th Street between Fifth and Sixth Avenues—212-391-2926

Parade of Shoes (www.paradeofshoes.com), with seven stores throughout the city, is a haven for bargain shoppers of women's shoes. Sorry guys, this chain only sells women's styles ... however, for those of you who are looking for a pair of pumps—and you know who you are—I'm sure they would be only too happy to help. Of the women I queried about the quality and style of Parade of Shoes' inventory, the response was overwhelmingly positive for these well made, inexpensive knockoffs of the most recent designs. One friend said, "They're surprisingly cute for so cheap." Your local listings will tell you where to find the nearest store.

The inventory of men's and women's shoes at **Payless Shoe Source** (www.payless.com) is not at all *au courant* among the fashionistas (or anyone with any sense of style for that matter). What this store does do well is sell shoes at low prices. Their shoes are cheap, cheap, cheap! At Payless, the adage holds true: you really do "get what you pay for." Check your phone book for the nearest location.

At **Pearl River Mart** (www.pearlriver.com) there are several aisles of shoes (mostly of the slipper, flip-flop and thong variety) that look well constructed and are cheaply priced. Some are decorated with brocade, beads or needlepoint; some are silk. In a section of 100 percent leather-upper and athletic shoes for men and women, none are what you'd call fashionable, but they look solid and are cheap.

477 Broadway, between Grand and Broome Streets—212-431-4770

200 Grand Street between Mott and Mulberry Streets—212-966-1010

For unbelievably low prices on fashionable men's and women's shoes, bypass the main sales area of **Shoe Mania** and go straight upstairs. There you'll find a staggering selection, most by famous designers like Kenneth Cole, Mephisto, Ecco, Rockport, Dansko, Timberland, Merrell, Diesel, Puma, Clarks, Skechers, Camper, Bacco Bucci, Durango and BCBG Max Azria, at a fraction of the price of the shoes downstairs. I have no idea why these shoes are so deeply discounted, but go often, as the selection constantly changes.

853 Broadway at 14th Street—212-253-8744, www.shoemania.com

Zara (www.zara.com), the Spanish retailer with stores worldwide has a petite selection of shoes, all fashion-forward and all made in Europe. They are mostly modestly priced, and at the end of each season are clearance-reduced, some for as low as $19.99.

580 Broadway near Prince Street—212-343-1725

750 Lexington Avenue at 59th Street—212-754-1120

39 West 34th Street near Fifth Avenue—212-868-6551

101 Fifth Avenue near 17th Street—212-741-0555

Handbags and Accessories

The bargain women's clothing shop, **Backwoods**, a favorite of several friends, carries belts, scarves, purses and other accessories for its usual $10 to $30 prices, and sometimes less. The accessories are "funky," "chic" and "cheap," too. Backwoods stock changes frequently, so there's always something new to see and buy.

315 West 57th Street between, Eighth and Ninth Avenues— 212-459-2975

For shoppers with a lot of good karma, perseverance and a willingness to dig through mounds of merchandise, excellent bargains, especially on accessories, are to be had at **Barney's Warehouse Sale**. During this semi-annual New York fashion ritual, it's possible to find high-end designer belts, bags, scarves and ties for as little as $20. The Barney's Warehouse Sale takes place every February and August. (For more information about the Barney's sale, see the "Clothing" chapter.)

236 West 18th Street between Seventh and Eighth Avenues— 212-826-8900, www.barneys.com

A good deal of the commerce on **Canal Street** (known affectionately as "Avenue of the Counterfeits"), between Lafayette and West Broadway, is the selling of designer knockoffs (or what the police would less subtly classify as "contraband merchandise"). Here, for about $15 to $35, you can buy ersatz designer bags with labels like "Kate Spade," "Gucci," "Louis Vuitton," "Hermès" and "Prada." The bags look like the real thing but cost

BEST
BARGAIN

about a tenth of what you'd pay for the real thing. Unfortunately, you do get what you pay for—don't expect these to last you more than a few months.

The **big chains** Gap, Banana Republic, Zara, and Old Navy all carry a huge, ever-changing assortment of well-made, attractive and functional accessories and bags. Old Navy has, by far, the best everyday prices on such items, but the others have frequent sales where you can pick up anything from wallets and key chains to belts, hats, scarves, briefcases, backpacks, small luggage and jewelry, for a song. (For more information on these retailers, refer to the "Clothing" chapter.)

Many of the **discount clothing stores**, including Burlington Coat Factory, Century 21, Daffy's, Filene's Basement, Loehmann's, Syms and T.J. Maxx (see "Clothing" chapter for store locations) carry lots of designer and generic handbags, as well as belts, wallets and other accessories, at low to moderate prices. Most are styles from a season or so ago, but are marked down by at least 30 percent from their original prices. On a recent expedition to each of these stores, I found handsome handbags for as little as $15, leather wallets starting at $8 and belts at $10.

In the heart of the **Sixth Avenue wholesale district** (Sixth Avenue between 24th and 32nd Streets) are two stores, **Earrings Plaza** and **Jewelry Plaza**, owned by the same parent company, both offering eye-popping prices on a leviathan assortment of costume jewelry and accessories. You'll find two heavily stocked floors of rings, earrings, bracelets, necklaces, brooches, cuff links, tie clips, evening purses, tiaras, cigarette cases, scarves, pins, jewelry and pill boxes, key chains, incense and incense holders, and belts. Most items range in price between $2 and $7. In fact, you'll find very few items that are over $10. The only glitch (and it's a minor one) is that you must spend a minimum of $10. Both shops also offer discounts on bulk shopping: you'll receive a 10 percent discount on a $100 purchase; 15 percent off $250; 20 percent off $500; and a 25 percent discount on items totaling $1000 or more. There's not much here that's really glamorous (you wouldn't wear any of this stuff to an awards ceremony—well, maybe one of the tiaras) and a lot of it is downright gaudy, but for everyday wear, you're sure to find some desirable pieces.

Earrings Plaza, 1263 Broadway, 212-685-5666

Jewelry Plaza, 1204 Broadway—212-532-3666

The goods at **Gift Show** are a step above those carried at the numerous Canal Street vendors of designer-impostor labeled handbags. For a few dollars more than its neighbors, Gift Show sells unique, well made fakes that are fashionable, functional and will last almost as long as the originals.

231 Canal Street between Centre and Baxter Streets— 212-334-8760

Rhinestones are a girl's best friend at **Girlprops.com** (www.girlprops.com). This very fun and very cheap accessory shop in Soho is packed with glittery and gleaming items for girls of all ages. Where else can you find fake fur hats, day-glo purses, faux leopard print gloves, rainbow-hued boas, colored hair spray, wigs in wild shades like chartreuse and lavender, body glitter, fishnet leggings, and tons of bejeweled belts, bobby pins, headbands, necklaces, bracelets and earrings, for prices that start as low as $1? There is a lot of kitsch here, but there's also a lot of stuff your mom would be happy to wear.

153 Prince Street near West Broadway

33 East 8th Street between University Place and Broadway

Great Value carries a huge assortment of belts, handbags, backpacks, canvas messenger bags, belts, wallets, leather watchbands, ties (which I don't recommend—UGLY!), sunglasses, costume jewelry and luggage, all at deep discounted prices. "Designer handbags from New York, Italy, Spain and Paris," their sign outside advertises, start at about $30. Most everything here (besides the aforementioned ties) is of exceptional quality, style and price.

23 East 33rd Street—212-889-5792

The Swedish chain **H&M** (www.hm.com) made an instant splash in New York with its ultra-hip, cool, trendy clothes at ultra-cheap prices. This arbiter of "fashion and quality at the best price" has a huge line of inexpensive, stylish accessories for men and women that includes wallets, backpacks, fanny packs, handbags, sunglasses, jewelry, belts, gloves, hats, scarves and watches. Prices for many of these items are in the $3–$6 range. (See my chapter on "Clothing.")

Beyond clothing and shoes, the **Historic Orchard Street Shopping District** has thirty quality leather goods shops, most with extraordinary prices on a range of accessory items from hats and bags, to purses, belts, and wallets. Allow time to check out all the leather vendors in the neighborhood before you make your final decision. On a recent foray into the area, I found well-made bags as low as $40. For maps and more information about the district, contact the Lower East Side Business Improvement District (261 Broome Street, New York, NY 10002—212-226-9010).

In **tourist-heavy areas** around the city, you will see groups of people who sell handbags right on the sidewalk. You may have seen them the last time you were on your way to Bloomingdale's, Carnegie Hall, a Broadway show, or in Soho. While hawking their goods, they always seem to be a little distracted; don't mind them, they're just watching for approaching police. You see, these bags are all faux versions of very expensive designer brands like Calvin Klein, Liz Claiborne, Gucci, Kate Spade, Louis Vuitton, and Prada. As most are counterfeits, their quality is not great, but they look like the real thing, and isn't that all that matters? Prices range from $15 to $45 for these bags, whose real counterpart would go for ten times these prices. (Note: Vendors accept only cash.) The four areas where I've encountered sidewalk vendors most frequently are:

The Upper East Side on Lexington Avenue around 60th Street, in front of, or across the street from, Bloomingdale's

On lower Broadway, between Canal and Houston

On Seventh Avenue and Broadway in the theater district, especially an hour or so before a performance

Around or in front of Carnegie Hall and the neighboring hotels

The **Sock Man** carries exactly what you'd expect—socks. His brands and styles range from athletic to business/casual, in prints of every color, thickness and design you could possibly want, at prices that are easily half what you'd find at department stores. Besides your basic socks, he also carries anklets, tights, hosiery, garters, thigh-highs, leg warmers and toe socks in all sizes, for all ages.

27 St. Mark's Place near Second Avenue—212-529-0300

Most of my socks come from the sock vendor at the Sunday **Greenflea Market at I.S. 44**. He sells every style, color and brand imaginable, at very reasonable prices. The Sunday Greenflea Market hours are from 10 A.M. to 5:30 P.M. (See the chapter on "Flea Markets.")

Columbus and 76th Street—212-721-0900

Leather Goods

When buying leather, remember one rule: there is no shame in haggling (see "Haggling" chapter). Leather dealers expect it. What a boon for consumers who hope to score some skin for very little scratch!

Domsey's the vast warehouse of discount used clothing, carries lots of dirt cheap vintage leather jackets. Because everything here is used, the selection and condition of a lot of the merchandise can be "iffy," but diligence is rewarded; the more you dig, the more likely you are to find a great, low-priced jacket. If you are at all allergic, take Sudafed before going. This place is dusty!

431 Broadway at Hughes Street, Williamsburg, Brooklyn— 718-384-6000

1609 Palmetto Street at Myrtle Avenue, Ridgewood, Queens— 718-386-7661

The city's **Garment District** (from 34th to 41st Streets, between Seventh and Eighth Avenues) has innumerable leather goods shops whose windows are filled with "too-good-to-be-true" deals on all kinds of items. Sure, there's a lot of tacky stuff in those windows, but there are also some good-looking coats and jackets (with prices starting as low as $59.99), as well as handbags and shoes. The harder you look in this neighborhood, the more apt you are to find what you want; and the more open you are to haggling, the more likely you are to arrive at a very low price.

The **Historic Orchard Street Shopping District** comes into its own with thirty quality leather goods shops, most with extraordinary prices on a number of items from coats and jackets, to skirts, pants, shoes, hats, bags, purses, belts, wallets and other accessories. Take your time to check out all the leather vendors in the neighborhood. Choose your two or three favorite items and then haggle mercilessly with the proprietors until you arrive at a price that you are willing to pay. For maps and more information about the district, contact the Lower East Side Business Improvement District (261 Broome Street, New York, NY 10002—212-226-9010).

BEST BET

Leather Friends Jackets sells its entire stock of men's and women's leather jackets for just $99.99. The jackets here are attractive, appear to be well-crafted and made of good leather. Leather Friends also carries a wide range of bags (all sell for $50 each), belts and other fine leather accessories.

142 Orchard Street—212-420-8038

Several **shops on Broadway between 11th and Canal Streets** carry very fashionable leather goods at discount prices. These shops are not above haggling with you and will often further reduce the price of an item if you pay cash. Wander up and down Broadway and comparison shop before making your final purchase; this way you can pit one store against another ("So-and-so is selling the same jacket for $30 cheaper. Can you do any better?"). It always works.

Makeup

Because it caters to the theatrical industry and professional makeup artists, everything at **Alcone** (www.alconeco.com) is always discounted. (No proof of professional status is needed.) Alcone's great appeal is that it carries brands not found in any other stores, such as Visiora, RCMA and Kryolan, and popular theatrical brands like Ben Nye and Mehron. Anything from its stock may be ordered on its website. Removers, sponges, powder puffs, and palettes are all sold here. If it is special effects makeup you want, this is the place to go; Alcone has the definitive selection of latex, blood products, bruise kits and scar-making materials in the city.

235 West 19th Street—212-633-0551

5-49 49th Avenue, Long Island City—718-361-8373

The socially conscious **Body Shop** (www.the-body-shop.com) chain is world famous for giving a portion of their proceeds to help disadvantaged peoples and endangered areas like the South American rainforest. Their environment-friendly bath and beauty aids and makeup are already moderately priced, and are often greatly reduced during sales and promotions. With eleven stores throughout Manhattan, check your phone book for the nearest location.

Just a hop and a skip from the theater district is **Cosmetic Market**, which has to be the city's cheapest place for both name brand and drugstore variety makeup, fragrances and men's colognes. Although the goods at Cosmetic Market cannot be categorized as the most up-to-the-minute, must-have products, the selection is

BEST BARGAIN

vast and eclectic and includes every kind of beauty item from makeup and perfume, to creams, lotions and grooming aids. Not everything here is perfect: some of the packaging is battered, many of the items are sloppily displayed, and there seems to be a lot of discontinued merchandise. But with prices this low (lipsticks, nail polish and the like for as little as $1), who cares about displays or packaging? (Cosmetic Market carries a big assortment of gift items too, such as picture frames, books, candles, imported olive oil, dolls, Christmas ornaments, purses and name brand candies like Droste, Guylian, Saronno, Perugina and Rocher.)

9 East 39th Street—212-725-3625

H&M (www.hm.com), the cheap yet trendy Swedish clothing store (see chapter on "Clothing"), carries its own line of makeup. H&M's quality is very good and its prices are very inexpensive.

On payment of an annual fee of $35, **MAC Cosmetics** (www.maccomestics.com) stores offer performers a generous 30 percent discount on all products through their "Preferred Professionals" program. To be eligible, you must present photo identification and any two of the following: composite card, valid union card, head shot, program/press materials with name credit, contract on production company letterhead, or crew/cast call list on production company letterhead.

113 Spring Street between Greene and Mercer Streets—212-334-4641

202 West 125th Street at Seventh Avenue—212-665-0676

139 Fifth Avenue, between 20th and 21st Streets—212-505-3563

767 Fifth Avenue at 22nd Street—212-677-6611

The **Makeup Center** stocks a large assortment of theatrical makeup by Ben Nye, Stein's and Mehron, as well as a full line of special effects products such as bald caps, stage blood, blood capsules, crepe hair, latex and glitter. The Makeup Center features its own line of theatrical and regular makeup. By presenting a membership card from any of the acting unions, actors receive a 15 percent discount on all sales.

150 West 55th Street—212-977-9494

The French beauty chain **Sephora** (www.sephora.com), new in town, is already considered the best in Manhattan. Their signature black and white design and ambient lighting makes their stores very inviting, and they stock an extensive array of name brand cosmetics and skin and hair care products. Sephora is not necessarily cheap, but their own line of cosmetics is fairly inexpensive and, I am told, very good. Seven locations citywide; check your listings for stores nearest you.

Sunglasses

If you want high-quality, stylish designer sunglasses with excellent UV protection that are the real thing and not what Canal Street and the guys in front of Bloomingdale's are hawking, but you don't want to pay Saks Fifth Avenue prices, you cannot beat the selection at **Century 21**. You won't find $5 sunglasses here (unless there is a clearance sale); but for anywhere from $20 to $100, you will find great, sturdily constructed styles for less than half of what you'd pay at the leading department stores.

22 Cortlandt Street at Chambers Street—212-227-9092

472 86th Street, Bay Ridge, Brooklyn—718-748-3266

BEST BET

At **H&M** (www.hm.com) you can find yourself some *way cool* sunglasses for prices that even the street vendors can't compete with, starting as low as $3.49 a pair. Check your local listings for the nearest H&M store locations.

Look for groups of **merchants in tourist-heavy areas** who sell sunglasses right on the sidewalk. They carry their goods in large squares of fabric. Why the fabric, you wonder? Well, not only is it used as a simple and tasteful background to display the sunglasses, but more importantly, it can be folded up in the blink of an eye if the vendor spots a cop in the vicinity. These sunglasses are all counterfeits of expensive designer brands like Armani, Calvin Klein, Claiborne, Gucci, Ray Ban and Bollé. In the nature of counterfeits, their quality is not great; but they look like the real thing, they come in cases that look like the real thing, and they are real cheap, with prices anywhere from $10 to $25. You can usually find these guys selling their wares right next to the "designer" wristwatch and handbag sellers (see my chapter on "Handbags and Accessories") concentrated in tourist areas.

The **stalls on St. Mark's Place** between Second and Third Avenues are year-round sunglasses emporiums. For as little as $5, and depending on your taste, you can buy yourself hip, conservative or utilitarian sunglasses. Don't expect a lot of UV protection, and don't expect that they will last very long. But hey, they are only $5. You're sure to find a pair that makes you look great, and let's face it, isn't that really more important than a few ultraviolet rays?

The **stalls and stores on Canal Street** are another good bet for finding cheap sunglasses. Here you will see a lot of the same goods as on St. Mark's Place and at the street fairs, the bulk of which is laughably counterfeit. It always amazes me that some of the Canal Street merchants have the *cojones* to represent such patently false junk as the true-blue, honest-to-goodness thing, when the plastic on the frames is flimsy, the logos appear to be haphazardly glued on to the temple pieces, and the lenses are so fragile that they look like *they* need protection from the sun. If you can get past the cheapness and the fact that they probably provide less UV protection than if you were not wearing sunglasses at all, there are some fun styles to be found here for very little cash.

Furniture

Setting up a home is costly but necessary. To exist with any semblance of comfort, we need a few basics like a bed, a chair, a bookcase, a table, and something to throw some clothes into. Before laying out a lot of cash, I recommend two ways to acquire furniture that won't cost anything at all.

First, go hunt the streets for discarded pieces. A favorite pastime of many New Yorkers is to **comb through trash bins and curbside garbage piles** for cast-off furniture. Believe it or not, there are a lot of treasures to be found on the street. Wander around the city on trash pickup day, or the night before, and take a good look at the garbage. Newcomers to the Big Apple will be surprised at the incredible things New Yorkers throw away. Often these pieces are in impeccable condition—just no longer wanted by their original owners—and once they hit the street, they are fair game to stake a claim. Most young urbanites, myself included, have, or have had, a piece or two of refuse furniture. For a complete rundown of collection days and times, call the Department of Sanitation 24-hour information line—212-219-8090. (Note: For high quality refuse, street-shop in the city's tonier neighborhoods, such as the Upper East Side, Murray Hill and Greenwich Village.)

Second, **network with friends and colleagues**. In our cramped city quarters, people can't afford to hold on to furniture they don't need—they don't have space for it. So, mention to everyone you know that you're looking for a couch, a table, whatever. You may find, from among those you have alerted, some who will be only too happy to part with what they no longer want or have room for. Over half of the contents of my first city apartment were hand-me-down pieces, and all served me well until I could afford the things I really wanted.

If neither of these alternatives is appealing, or you've grown tired of living with other people's tastes, it's time to go shopping. Hopefully the following will help keep you from breaking the bank:

EQ3 on the Upper West Side has a great selection of attractive, contemporary Ikea-esque furniture at affordable prices. Here you'll find stylish, quality-built pieces for every room, including bed frames, desks, chairs, entertainment centers, sofas, dining tables, lamps and storage units. Some of EQ3's great deals include a maple 41″ x 41″ coffee/cocktail table for $135; a solid wood queen size bed frame for $285; and their very hip "2morrow" computer desk for a reasonable $270. For greater savings, you may purchase your EQ3 items with their very own no-interest credit card (for details and an application, contact the store).

750 Columbus Avenue at 96th Street—212-865-4754,
www.eq3.com

Green Village Used Clothing and Furniture Warehouse, named the "Best Junk Shop" by *New York Magazine*, is an enormous place stuffed to the rafters with, yes, you guessed it, used clothing and furniture. All kinds of gems are to be found here, most in very good shape and for very little money (haggle, haggle, haggle!). If your thing is priceless antiques at bargain prices, go somewhere else (and if there is such a place, please tell me.) But if you're in the market either for newish stuff or vintage pieces, you'll have lots to choose from. The inventory here changes constantly, so check in periodically.

276 Starr Street, Brooklyn—718-599-4017

IKEA, the Sweden-based furniture company, with superstores throughout the world, is a godsend for dorm room dwellers, new homeowners and fresh-off-the-bus émigrés to the big city. IKEA's corporate philosophy is to offer a wide range of well designed, comfortable, functional and durable home furnishing products at prices so low that as many people as possible will be able to afford them. On this promise, IKEA delivers the goods. The IKEA store is a marvel of home furnishing products—a whopping 12,000 products in all—with something for every room and every taste at prices that are unbelievably low. Hands down, this is the city's least expensive outlet for attractive, quality furniture. (Okay, there isn't actually a store in New York City, but a free IKEA shuttle bus leaves from and returns to the Port Authority bus station several times each Saturday and Sunday). How do they thrive selling stuff so cheap? They buy in bulk and require you to schlep it home and assemble it yourself. (Lugging some of that stuff on the bus isn't pretty. I once bought two 4-foot-tall bookcases that I had to drag home from the bus by myself...living two blocks from Port Authority does have its rewards!) But for the money you save, it's definitely worth it. The only negative thing I can say about Ikea is that most of the furniture requires assembly, which can be time consuming and frustrating if you're not skilled in this area. That free IKEA shuttle departs every thirty minutes from 10 A.M. to 2:30 P.M., Saturdays and Sundays—Port Authority Bus Terminal, Gate 5— and returns every thirty minutes from 12 noon to 6 P.M. Call 800-Bus-IKEA for more information. (Note: An Ikea is expected to open in the Red Hook section of Brooklyn in early 2005.)

Elizabeth Center, New Jersey—908-289-4488, www.ikea.com

About twice a year, the **Props for Today** warehouse opens its doors to the public and sells most of its contents at unbelievable prices. Props for Today's primary business is renting furnishings and props for photography, film and parties; most of what you will find has been used in commercials, magazine ads, films shot in the area and New York -based TV shows and soaps. Once these items are no longer needed (the film has wrapped, the ad is shot, the TV show's designer gives the set a facelift) and Props for Today determines they cannot be recycled, they are unloaded at the warehouse sale. Although a lot of the stuff here is technically "used," it is in excellent condition. Better yet, it is priced to move. Who knows? You could walk away with Erica Kane's sofa, "Mango's" nightstand, or Starr Jones's chair from *The View*. Call for dates or ask to be put on the warehouse sale mailing list.

330 West 34th Street between Eighth and Ninth Avenues—212-244-9600

Straight From the Crate's (www.straightfromthecrate.com) merchandise is ideal for people who are outfitting a new home on a budget. Although the stuff is glorified dorm room furniture, it is attractive, functional, sturdily built and inexpensive. You can furnish every room from this store's inventory of office furniture, dining tables, and all kinds of chairs, armoires, bookcases, entertainment centers, CD/DVD racks, coffee tables, futon frames and lamps. Recent bargains included a computer workstation on coasters for $149; a halogen torch lamp with bulb for $39; a 5-drawer dresser for $159; a 24-inch solid wood stool for $30; a 2-tier tech trolley for $69; and a 60-inch heavy steel CD rack for $99.

1114 First Avenue at 61st Street—212-838-8486

261 Madison Avenue at 38th Street—212-867-4050

1251 Lexington Avenue between 84th and 85th Streets—212-717-4227

161 West 72nd Street between Columbus and Amsterdam Avenues—212-579-6494

464 Park Avenue South at 37th Street—212-725-5383

50 West 23rd Street between Fifth and Sixth Avenues—
212-243-1844

An ideal way to save money on furniture (and exercise some creativity at the same time) is to buy unfinished pieces and paint or varnish them yourself. Several stores in the city offer excellent savings on **unfinished furniture** for every room in your home and have a variety of styles and woods to choose from. If you're useless with a paintbrush, for an extra charge, the furniture can be finished for you.

The mother of all unfinished furniture stores is **Gothic Cabinet Craft** (www.gothiccabinetcraft.com) with its twenty-five retail outlets throughout the five boroughs. Here you will find a huge selection of inexpensive tables, chairs, dressers, desks, bookcases, beds, entertainment centers, and even mattresses by Sealy and Serta. If you don't see what you want, Gothic can custom-build a piece to your specifications at an affordable price. Gothic's solid wood dressers start as low as $99; pine bookcases at $38; 3-drawer pine Captain's beds at $125 (birch are $229); pine platform beds at $89; and nightstands at $69. Gothic Cabinet Craft has periodic sales and frequent coupon specials (look for their ads in the *Village Voice*). Consult your phone book for the nearest Gothic Cabinet Craft location.

Innovative Woodwork claims that they stock the largest variety of unpainted solid wood furniture available for same day or next day delivery in New York. It is hard to imagine that they have a larger selection than Gothic Cabinet Craft, but as their prices are comparable, I will forgive them the hyperbole. Among the many bargains I saw on a recent trip was a solid butcher-block, drop-leaf dining table for $199; a 7-drawer

Aspen wood dresser for $349; a solid pine storage chest for $119.99; and a 4-drawer desk for $229. Innovative carries a large assortment of bookcases in a variety of sizes and woods (pine, maple and oak), and fills custom orders at discounted prices.

> 355 Third Avenue at 26th Street—212-683-2127

Mike's Furniture Store on the Upper West Side sells excellently crafted and reasonably priced finished and unfinished furniture, such as tables, chairs, bookcases, computer and entertainment centers, beds and wall units. Mike's also carries a large group of furnishings for kids and babies and does special orders.

> 520 Amsterdam Avenue at 85th Street—212-873-1336, www.mikesfurniturestore.com

Although you probably won't be furnishing your new home from New York's premier (and expensive) furniture stores like ABC Carpet and Home, Domain, Maurice Villency, Roche Bobois, E.J. Audi, and Palazzetti, these emporiums periodically hold **warehouse sales**, where a lot of unsold and "as is" items go for a fraction of their list prices. To reach the warehouses, you usually have to schlep out to some obscure corner of Brooklyn, Queens or Long Island, but the savings are worth the trip and the quality is always very high. These sales are usually advertised in the "House & Home" or front-page sections of *The New York Times*.

- **ABC Carpet & Home**, 888 Broadway at 19th Street— 212-473-3000, www.abchome.com
- **E.J. Audi**, 160 Fifth Avenue at 21st Street, 4th Floor— 212-337-0700, www.stickley.com
- **The Terence Conran Shop**, 407 East 59th Street at First Avenue—212-755-9079, www.conran.co.uk

- **Roche Bobois**, 200 Madison Avenue at 35th Street—212-725-5513, www.roche-bobois.com

- **Domain**, 938 Broadway at 22nd Street—212-228-7450, www.domain-home.com

- **Knoll**, 105 Wooster Street—212-343-4000, www.knoll.com

- **Maurice Villency**, 200 East 57th Street at Third Avenue—212-725-4840, www.mauricevillency.com

The catalog furniture retailer **West Elm** has recently expanded its profile (and market share) by opening stores in Brooklyn and Manhattan. Brought to you by the folks at Pottery Barn, West Elm has moderate prices on attractive, comfortable, functional furniture and housewares for every room in your home. If your design proclivities tend toward traditional, "shabby chic," Colonial stoicism, Victorian kitsch, Empire stateliness, medieval rustic or anything else antique, this is definitely not the store for you. However, if ultra-mod, Asian-inspired furnishings are your thing, you'll find plenty here to feather your nest. Be sure to explore West Elm's sales area, where discontinued and slightly damaged pieces as well as floor samples are discounted.

115 West 17th Street between Sixth and Seventh Avenues—718-797-6340

75 Front Street at Main Street, DUMBO, Brooklyn—718-875-7757

Mattresses

Buying a mattress is not easy. There are countless brands and models to choose from, as well as stores that sell them. Furthermore, everyone claims to have the lowest prices, but it is nearly impossible to comparison shop. The same Serta model at Sleepy's is given a completely different name at Macys's and a different name again at 1-800-Mattress, and so on. Prices vary wildly from store to store. And then there are those constant nagging TV news-magazine exposés about mattress retailers who are covering old mattresses with new fabric and selling them to unsuspecting consumers. What's a shopper to do?

First, steer clear of the 1-800-Mattress merchants. I don't infer that they sell a shoddy product, or that they have exorbitant prices. Generally, the opposite is true. The problem with these phone retailers is that you don't know what you're getting.

Next, visit a few showrooms. Since it's impossible to comparison shop by make and model, you will have to do it by feel and comfort. You must try out several mattresses to determine which is the most comfortable, which gives the best support, and which will help you get a good night's sleep. Once you have narrowed down the two or three mattresses that suit you, don't be afraid to haggle. Play one retailer against another. Tell the salesman at store B, "I like this bed, but a similar one at store A was $100 dollars cheaper. What can you do for me?" This may make you uncomfortable, but mattress salespeople expect it.

Finally, make sure you shop in stores that have some longevity in the business, a good selection of mattresses to choose from, and positive customer feedback. The following merchants fall in this

category and all offer bedding at affordable prices as well as free
or cheap delivery and set-up:

Sleepy's (www.sleepys.com), which has been in business for
eighty years, claims to carry the world's largest selection of name
brand mattresses at the lowest prices. They back up this statement
with their "Incredible Price Guarantee" offer: if you find the same
mattress for less, anywhere, Sleepy's guarantees to beat the price or
you get your purchase free plus $500. As I note above, though, it is
often difficult to prove this, because similar mattresses are given different names at the various retailers. Sleepy's reassured me that
they use "comparison charts" to determine which of their mattresses are comparable to those carried in other stores. In fact,
Sleepy's doesn't beat Town Bedding (see below) when it comes to
price (Sleepy's explains that Town Bedding models are mostly from
last season, which is true enough, even though Town's merchandise
is brand new and top-of-the-line), but they come close. Sleepy's
does outdo Town Bedding when it comes to selection and brands;
they carry Aireloom, Serta, Sealy, Back Care, Kingsdown, Stearns &
Foster, Spring Air, Simmons Beauty Rest, Masterpiece and Chatham
& Wells. Besides their low prices and selection, Sleepy's offers customers "when you want it" delivery, removal of old bedding and a
sixty-day home trial exchange policy. Look in your phone book for
the nearest of Sleepy's sixteen city-wide store locations.

Located in the center of Chelsea's self-consciously glamorous emporiums, restaurants, cafes and male boutiques, **Town
Bedding** is an eyesore. What a dump! If you can get
past this store's defiant lack of décor, organization
**BEST
BARGAIN** and cleanliness, you can find yourself a great bed,
futon or sofa bed for very little money. Town Bedding
does not carry a lot of stock, but what they do carry
(Serta, Simmons, Continental, Therapedic and Spring Air) is very

good and much less expensive than their competitors. You can save literally $100 to $200 on a mattress comparable to what you would find anywhere else. Town Bedding offers an unconditional money back guarantee on all its merchandise, provides free delivery in the five boroughs, and will remove your old bed at no charge. Better still, the salesmen could not be more laid back.

205 Eighth Avenue, between 20th and 21st Streets— 212-243-0426, www.townbedding.com

If sleeping on a **futon** is your preference, there are many stores in the metropolitan area that carry this inexpensive option to conventional mattresses. Several advertise in the *Village Voice* and often have sales or offer discount coupons:

Futon Furniture Center (www.futonfurniturecenter.com) carries futons, frames, loft beds, tatami beds and thousands of covers.

265 West 72nd Street near Broadway—212-712-2133

51 West 14th Street between Fifth and Sixth Avenues— 212-727-1252

Not only does **Futonland** (www.futonland.com) have a large selection of frames, futons, covers, pillows and throws, they offer same-day delivery and free assembly.

730 Amsterdam Avenue, between 95th and 96th Streets— 212-663-8454

89-12 Queens Boulevard, Queens—718-779-5766

55-18 Myrtle Avenue, Queens—718-497-5181

255 Calyer Street, Brooklyn—718-349-8008

Futon Plus (www.futonplus.com) offers low-priced futons, frames and living room sets, as well as same-day delivery and free assembly.

375 Broadway at White Street—212-941-1384

313 Sixth Avenue—212-741-1335

Futon Warehouse, the store where there is "always a sale," advertises itself as having the largest selection of futons in New York. You'd be hard-pressed to argue with them—the stock here is immense. In addition to futons, they sell frames, covers, pillows, shelving, tables, chairs and bookcases; a clearance center is on their second level.

113 University Place at 13th Street—212-473-4400, www.futon-warehouse.com

Housewares

Located in the newly spruced up meatpacking district, **Bodum Café and Home Store** has to be the city's most whimsical housewares retailer. The shop's credo is, "Good design should not be expensive"; it could also be, "Good design should not be dull." There's nothing here that isn't brightly colored or artfully designed, and completely practical, to boot. Best of all, this stuff is cheap: Bodum's famous Caffettiera coffee maker is $14.95; multihued tissue boxes are $4.95 to $5.95; wastebaskets start at $5.95; shopping trolleys are $9.95; beech paper towel holders are $9.95; nail brushes are $1.95; a set of four punch glasses are $4.95; and bast place mats are $1.95 each. If you need office supplies, look no further: you can pick up a lemon-colored paper-clip holder for $2.95, a cherry-hued stapler for $2.95, a blueberry pencil sharpener for $1.95 and a pomegranate tape dispenser for $1.95. They also carry a huge line of bathroom gadgets and linens, as well as closet organizing systems. Breeze through the back clearance area, which is swarming with extra cheap home necessities; and once you've finished shopping, grab a cup of coffee and a nibble at the Bodum Café.

413-415 West 14th Street between Ninth and Tenth Avenues—
212-367-9125, www.bodum.com

Catering to master chefs and civilian gourmands, **Broadway Panhandler** carries the best tools of the cooking and baking trades. Appealing to such a discerning demographic, the inventory, unfortunately, is composed of mostly high-end items at high-end prices. But city foodies are in luck because they have constant sales, clearances and promotions, discounting a large portion of the merchandise from 10 percent to 50 percent below regular prices.

477 Broome Street at Wooster Street—212-966-3434,
www.broadwaypanhandler.com

Fishs Eddy's (www.fishseddy.com) two New York locations feature inexpensive new and never-used vintage china and glassware. Appealing to diners with a sense of humor, most of the stock here has been gathered from stores, restaurants, golf and country clubs, universities, ocean liners, government institutions and manufacturers. I saw logos decorating a wide array of china recently that included "Petroleum Club of Maitland," "Migis Lodge on Sebago Lake," "Isla Del Sol Yacht and Country Club," and "Four Diamond Award Dinner—Black Point Inn Resort." Fishs Eddy also features sets of reasonably priced dishware with zany border patterns like a ticker tape, baseball lingo, the Manhattan skyline (including the World Trade Center), a checkerboard and the San Francisco skyline. This store's best bargains are on its basic white china: mugs are $1.50 each, bowls and dinner plates are $3.50, bread plates are $1.25, and cups are $1.95.

889 Broadway at 19th Street—212-420-9020

2176 Broadway at 77th Street—212-873-8819

1338 Third Avenue at 79th Street—212-737-2844

For myriad household items that you don't want to spend a lot on, check out the various cheap general merchandise and **99¢ stores** such as Conway or Odd-Job. (See "General Merchandise Stores" for a complete listing.)

Home to Go carries towels, sheets, pillows, curtains, tablecloths and place mats, items for the bathroom, and some kitchen and cooking supplies—all at very cheap prices. Cotton bath towels start at 99¢; twin-size poly-cotton sheet sets start at $7.99.

89 Chambers Street

The giant home furnishings superstore **IKEA** has an enormous housewares section, which carries just about everything (except appliances) that a home will ever need. These home necessities, gadgets and decorative items are attractively designed, functional and incredibly inexpensive—probably the least expensive in New York. Okay, as I already mentioned, IKEA isn't actually in New York; but you can get there easily on their free shuttle bus out of Port Authority. For details on the IKEA bus, call 800-Bus-IKEA. (For more information on IKEA, see the "Furniture" chapter.)

Elizabeth Center, New Jersey—908-289-4488, www.ikea.com

Kaufman Electrical Appliances, an obscure, dumpy little shop on the Lower East Side, has amazing prices on all kinds of small appliances. Some examples: a half-gallon PUR water filter, $15; a Toastmaster toaster, also $15; a Remington men's automatic precision personal groomer, $20; a mini Dirt Devil vacuum cleaner, $35; a Braun 10-cup coffee maker, $30; a small Cuisinart food processor, $28; and a Braun Oral-B plaque remover/automatic toothbrush was $25. Kaufman also has a large selection of stainless steel flatware starting at $10 for a 20-piece set, and fine china place settings that sell at close to wholesale.

365 Grand Street between Essex and Norfolk Streets— 212-475-8313

Kmart (www.kmart.com) devotes thousands of square feet to inexpensive housewares, from kitchen gadgets and small appliances, to bedding, linens, towels, cookware, glassware, dishes and curtains. What Kmart does really well, and sells at great prices, is their complete line of Martha Stewart products for the home. Martha's 100 percent cotton sheets and towels are the least expensive I've found, of excellent quality, and frequently put on sale for even greater savings. My entire apartment is painted with Martha Stewart brand paints purchased at Kmart. She offers hundreds of colors (256 to be exact), provides swatches that recommend which colors go well together and even a how-to book that demonstrates the proper way to paint a room. From my experience, the quality of the paint is very good; it has not faded, cracked or peeled, and it is washable. Best of all, it's really cheap and goes on sale all the time. Martha's latest Kmart venture is a line of inexpensive home organizers. Everything to get your office, kitchen, bathroom, closet and desk into Type A order can be found here, and all reasonably priced (see "General Merchandise Stores").

> One Pennsylvania Plaza on 34th Street between Seventh and Eighth Avenues—212-760-1188

> 770 Broadway at Astor Place—212-673-1540

The Bowery, between Grand and Delancey Streets, is the lighting center of the city. Here you will find dozens of retailers selling their wares at discount, contractor and even wholesale prices. My favorite is **Lighting by Gregory**, a huge four-store complex staffed by helpful experts that carries (or can get for you very quickly) just about any brand or type of lighting fixture you desire. Their prices are always several dollars below retail.

> 158 Bowery—212-226-1276, www.lightingbygregory.com

Contrary to what you might think, **Macy's**, the "biggest store in the world," has great prices on its huge assortment of kitchen tools and small appliances, pots and pans, baking utensils, vacuum cleaners, bathroom electronics, dinnerware, bed linens, curtains, towels and much more. Their seasonal and semi-annual sales, where prices are slashed below anything you'd find at even the cheapest discount stores, are especially good. My Proctor-Silex toaster, Mr. Coffee coffee maker and Sunbeam iron, all purchased on sale in the **Cellar** at Macy's, were only $9.99 each and have lasted for years. Recent Macy's bargains have been a 10-piece set of Teflon cookware, including tea kettle and steamer, for $59.99; tablecloths for $11.99; fan or ceramic heaters for $39.99; a Salton rice cooker for $14.99; king or queen sheet sets for $24.99; a 45-piece stainless steel dinner set for $34.99; a Hoover upright vacuum for $99.99; and bath towels for $3.99 each. Watch out for their frequent coupon sales that offer an additional savings of between 10 and 25 percent. Where Macy's really excels is in its customer service: the sales staff (admittedly, when you can find them) is very knowledgeable and helpful, and the store has a liberal return policy. If you're going to buy a big-ticket item, open a Macy's charge account. On the first day you use the card, Macy's gives you an additional 10 percent off. As a Macy's cardholder, you will have privileges such as access to Customer Appreciation sales and advance notification of future promotions.

151 West 34th Street between Sixth and Seventh Avenues—212-695-4400, www.macys.com

National Wholesale Liquidators

(www.nationalwholesaleliquidators.com) sells brand-name manufacturer's overstocks and seconds in its vast inventory of household basics, all at discount prices. You can find everything from flatware and appliances, to pots, pans, bedding, bath accessories, china, glasses and stemware, and home-furnishing items, marked down 20 to 40 percent off retail. I found a 4-pack box of GE soft white light bulbs for 99¢; a Goldstar microwave oven for $39.97; a Proctor-Silex toaster for $10.97; a 7-piece set of nonstick cookware for $19.97; and a Black & Decker cordless Dustbuster for $14.97.

632 Broadway, between Bleecker and Houston Streets—212-979-2400

71-01 Kissena Boulevard, Flushing, Queens—718-591-3900,

Whether it's a vacuum cleaner, microwave, toaster, refrigerator, dish washer, oven or stove, washer, dryer, freezer, air conditioner, heater, fan, humidifier, iron, water purifier, coffee maker, food processor, hair dryer, blender, food mixer, or just about anything else you might need in the way of housewares, **P.C. Richard & Son** (www.pcrichard.com) has it, and for less than you'd find at most other housewares/electronics retailers. P.C. Richard & Son offers "next day" delivery, low-cost installation and repairs, customer service that is a notch above the city's other large chain retailers, and a guarantee that it will meet or beat its competitors' price for the same item if you bring in an advertisement within forty days of your initial purchase. P.C. Richard & Son's two Manhattan stores are located at 120 East 14th Street between Third and Fourth Avenues—212-979-2600, and 205 East 86th Street between Second and Third Avenues—212-289-1700. Consult your phone book for P.C. Richard & Son locations in the Bronx, Brooklyn and Queens.

For price and selection, the housewares section at **Target** (www.target.com) is unparalleled by any of the city's other general merchandise stores (except perhaps National Wholesale Liquidators). I especially love their Michael Graves designed blenders, coffee pots, flatware, cooking utensils, toasters, alarm clocks, teakettles, picture frames, and knife sets. These ultra-hip domestic items are practical, stylish and designed with a sense of humor. For the bedroom and bathroom, Target features a large collection of inexpensive and moderately priced items. Unfortunately, there are only four Target stores in New York City (New Jersey has two, but you need a car to get to them). If you are willing to make the trek outside of Manhattan, a wondrous world awaits you. Look for Target's periodic sales and specials circular inside the Sunday edition of *The New York Times*. (See chapter on "General Merchandise Stores.")

13505 20th Avenue, Flushing, Queens—718-661-4346

Queens Place, Queens Boulevard and 55th Avenue, Elmhurst, Queens—718-760-5656

139 Flatbush Avenue, Brooklyn and 55th Avenue, Elmhurst, Queens—718-290-1109

40 West 255th Street, Bronx—718-733-7199

The high-style furniture purveyor **West Elm** (see "Furniture" chapter) carries an array of moderately priced housewares and decorative items. Everything you'll find is functional and attractive, and, though ultra-mod and Asian inspired in design, will coordinate with any décor. Some of the many household things you'll find include rugs, curtains, towels, bed linens, storage boxes, photo albums, tableware, picture frames, accent pieces, lighting and lamps, vases, and candles and candle holders. Be sure to explore West Elm's sales area, where discontinued and slightly damaged pieces, as well as floor samples, are discounted.

115 West 17th Street between Sixth and Seventh Avenue—718-797-6340

75 Front Street at Main Street, DUMBO, Brooklyn—718-875-7757

For anyone who likes to cook, **Zabar's** is culinary heaven. The second floor housewares section of this revered Upper West Side institution has the city's largest and best selection of products, from adequate to top-of-the-line—everything needed to outfit a kitchen. There is virtually every type, brand and price range of toaster, blender, mixer, processor, pot, pan, dish, wok, colander, utensil, vacuum, dust buster, air purifier, space heater, humidifier, microwave, scale, coffee maker, water filter, cappuccino maker, mug, glass, pitcher, linen, bowl and hotplate available on the market—they even have an entire department devoted to knives for God's sake—and most at very reasonable prices. Even their high-end inventory is several dollars cheaper than the competition. Better yet, Zabar's always puts a large portion of its stock on sale at jaw-dropping discounts.

2245 Broadway at 80th Street—212-787-2000, www.zabars.com

Electronics

For eons, J & R Music World (see below) was considered by in-the-know New Yorkers as the best source for affordable electronics. In recent years, however, J & R has lost that title to **B & H**. This superstore, located just south of the theater district, has the city's lowest prices on photo, video and audio equipment. Priding itself as the "professional's source," B & H inventories what has got to be the city's (if not the world's) largest selection of electronic equipment, and maintains a knowledgeable and courteous service staff. Not only do they deal with the newest, latest, rarest and most desired equipment at the lowest prices, but they are also one of the very few stores to trade or buy used electronics that they service and sell at bargain prices. If you're not intimidated by the sheer size of the store and the heft of the inventory (not to mention the crowds), you'll never want to shop for electronics anywhere else.

420 Ninth Avenue at 34th Street—212-444-6608, www.bhphotovideo.com

Canal Street in Chinatown is a bargain shopper's paradise where you'll find row upon row of shops, storefronts and cubicles crammed with all kinds of electronic equipment. Know, though, that like most of the other merchandise in this area, the quality and legality of this stuff is dubious—and don't even think about getting a warranty. You pay your money and you take your chances! If you need something temporary until you can afford what you really want, and dependability and durability aren't your first priorities, Canal Street is calling. (See chapter on "General Merchandise Stores.")

On three packed floors in midtown, **Datavision**, the "intelligence superstore," carries about every electronic product known to man, and at very competitive prices. On a recent visit, Datavision was having an amazing sale on Sony Vaio computers, with most models discounted up to $200 below list price. Other great deals included Vivistar 50-pack 700 mb blank CDs for $9.99 (regularly $19.99); a Compaq Presario desktop computer with Intel Pentium 4 processor and DVD for $1,249 (regularly $1,498); and an Evolution mp3 player for $99 (regularly $119). Depending on what you purchase and how much you spend, Datavision offers freebies like software, speakers, CD-R media, headsets, VCRs and gift certificates.

445 Fifth Avenue at 39th Street—212-689-1111, www.datavis.com

One of the best places in the city to buy electronics is **J & R Music World**. They've got it all: an incomparable, large selection of quality merchandise, low prices and frequent sales. Best of all, they will match or beat the price of any other store if you bring in an ad. This year I found a pair of Klipsch speakers at a competitor for $80 less than J & R; I told the J & R salesman, who immediately offered them to me for $85 below his store's original price. Taking up an entire block across from City Hall, J & R's huge inventory encompasses every electronic product and accessory you can imagine, from notebooks and desktops to scanners, fax machines, internet appliances, printers, monitors, CD burners, peripherals, software, video games, mp3 players, sound cards, palm computers and handheld organizers, telephones, cordless phones, cell phones, home office equipment, DVD players, CD players, VCRs, minidisk players, videos and DVDs, TVs, camcorders, cameras, receivers and amplifiers, mini stereo systems, speakers, radios and clock radios, keyboards, personal care products, watches, and even some housewares. If you don't mind schlepping all the way downtown, you're sure to find what you are looking for at a great price. J & R delivers large items; rates for delivery are determined by weight.

23 Park Row—212-732-8600, www.jandr.com

Recently voted "Best Discount Shopping" by the editors of *New York Magazine's* "The Best of New York" issue, **National Wholesale Liquidators** (www.nationalwholesaleliquidators.com) is by far the city's superior discount merchandise store. In addition to its other great deals, it carries a wide assortment of well-known electronics merchandise, marked 20 to 40 percent below retail. On a recent visit, I found both a Sharp 19-inch color TV and a Sharp DVD/Video/CD player for $139.97 each; a Conair Trimline phone for $5.97; an Emerson portable stereo CD player for $39.97; an AT&T digital answering machine for $24.97; and a Curtis portable AM/FM radio for $6.97. Unlike most other closeout and overstock specialists, everything on National Wholesale Liquidators' three floors is in perfect condition. (See chapter on "General Merchandise Stores.")

632 Broadway between Bleecker and Houston Streets— 212-979-2400

71-01 Kissena Boulevard, Flushing, Queens—718-591-3900

Popular among New Yorkers for its everyday low prices and weekly sales specials, the retail chain **P.C. Richard & Son** (www.pcrichard.com) carries a huge inventory of electronics and appliances. Although the stock here is uninspired—more low-end and functional than state-of-the-art—you'll find just about everything you'll need to outfit your home, including kitchen appliances and housewares, audio and video equipment, air conditioners, washers and dryers, vacuum cleaners, cameras, video games, telephones, computers, printers and computing peripherals. P.C. Richard & Son offers "next day" delivery, low-cost installation and repairs, customer service that is a notch above the city's other large chain retailers, and a guarantee that it will meet or beat its competitors' price for the same item if you bring in an advertisement within forty days of your initial purchase.

Explore, also, the superstore **Target** (www.target.com). This chain carries just about any electronics item you might need or desire, and at low prices. Although you won't find the top-of-the-line stuff here, you will encounter most of the major brand-name manufacturers. (See the "General Merchandise Stores" chapter.)

13505 20th Avenue, Flushing, Queens—718-661-4346

Queens Place, Queens Boulevard and 55th Avenue, Elmhurst, Queens—718-760-5656

139 Flatbush Avenue, Brooklyn and 55th Avenue, Elmhurst, Queens—718-290-1109

40 West 255th Street, Bronx—718-733-7199

Books

Once upon a time, Manhattan was the "Land o' Books." Almost every neighborhood in the city supported great small to medium-sized specialty, independent and mom-and-pop book peddlers, doing their best to raise the literary standard of all New Yorkers. The demise of these stores began in the real estate boom of the 1980s, when greedy landlords gouged their tenants for everything they could, which put those who couldn't afford exorbitant rents out of business. Adding insult to injury, along came the corporate mega-bookstores (they know who they are), who, by under-pricing the competition, drove a final nail into the coffins of many of the last-gasping little guys. Although several of the great Manhattan bookstores are gone, there are still a number of wonderful places to acquire books, plays and scripts. Lucky for those of us who live on a budget, several are discount vendors:

The 24-hour **Accidental Records** in the East Village sells a huge array of mostly new and used paperbacks at 30 to 40 percent off list price. A majority of the inventory here is modern fiction and, as Accidental's owner Craig Lopez says, "primarily the books you always meant to read but never did." A word of caution: this place is a disaster area. The clutter of books, CDs and junk is overwhelming, partly because the books are not placed in any order and are (a first for me) stacked from floor to ceiling instead of shelved. These are minor irritations, however, since the helpful staff can locate just about anything in stock.

131 Avenue A, between St. Mark's Place and 9th Street— 212-995-2224, www.accidentalcds.com

Located around the corner from Strand, **Alabaster Bookshop** carries a variety of cheap used and rare titles. Particularly good is their selection of books on art, photography, theater, film and New York City. On my last visit, Alabaster had a couple hundred Dramatist Playservice and Samuel French acting editions, clearly once part of the library of a theater professional. Be sure to rummage through the outdoor $2 carts where you're likely to find a must-have.

> 122 Fourth Avenue at 12th Street—212-982-3550,
> www.abebooks.com/home/alabaster

Applause Theater and Cinema Books carries a small but adequate collection of scripts, screenplays and film and theater-related books, periodicals and magazines. Unlike the city's other theatrical bookstores, Applause has an inventory of discounted used volumes, occasionally reduces on select titles, and has periodic sales. When I was there last, all hardcover books were 20 percent off.

> 211 West 71st Street, just off Broadway—212-496-7511,
> www.applausebooks.com

The behemoth **Barnes & Noble** (www.barnesandnoble.com) gives discounts of up to 40 percent off hardcover bestsellers, up to 30 percent off paperback bestsellers, and has numerous bargain racks of remaindered merchandise. Is it my imagination, or have the discounts at this store diminished? It seems to me that while in the process of obliterating most of their competition, B & N offered consumers more generous savings. Coincidence? I'm not sure what to think, but feel compelled to put it out there. Discuss amongst yourselves. Kvetch as I do about Barnes & Noble's domination in the book market, I'd be lying if I said I didn't shop there.

The subterranean **Book Ark** sells, buys and trades quality used and rare hardcovers and paperbacks in all subjects, including foreign titles. The selection here is small but good in all areas and prices are low. Although this shop is housed in a low-ceilinged basement, there is always soothing new age music playing to enhance the browsing.

173 West 81st Street at Amsterdam Avenue—212-787-3914, www.bookark.com

If there were such a thing as bookstore hierarchy, for me **Coliseum Books** would be king. A few years ago, Coliseum's original location at the corner of 57th Street and Broadway (a true New York institution and premier destination for city book lovers) became another victim of the mega-chains and real estate boom, and bit the dust. Bibliophiles freaked: we viewed its death as the symbolic end of New York's reign as the cultural and intellectual center of the world. Well, thankfully, Coliseum has come back with a vengeance at a new location, and those of us who were in mourning have doffed our widow's weeds believing all is well with the world once more. This wonderful store, which calls itself "a gym for your brain," carries over 100,000 titles at any given time, presents a weekly author series, and has the city's most knowledgeable and devoted staff. For budget-conscious readers, Coliseum Books has a huge discount book section, as well as a table with lots of new soft and hardbound editions for just one dollar. In its attempt to keep up with the big guys, Coliseum even has a café that is less sterile and less expensive than those of the others.

11 West 42nd Street between Fifth and Sixth Avenues— 212-803-5890, www.coliseumbooks.com

There are several **curbside book-peddlers** who set up tables throughout the city and have a huge presence around Union

Square and on the Upper West and Upper East Sides. Their supply seems to have mysteriously "fallen off of the back of trucks." Fortunately, we New Yorkers reap the benefits of these "accidents" by being charged about half the price of what we'd pay for the same book in a legitimate bookstore. Their supply is usually of the best-seller and coffee table art book variety and are usually in mint condition.

The Drama Book Shop, by far the best theatrical bookstore in the city, has gotten even better now that it has moved into new, more spacious quarters in the Garment District. If it is in print and has anything to do with the theater, you can find it here. Besides carrying just about any play ever published, The Drama Book Shop has a huge selection of books devoted to theater-related subjects, ranging from stage makeup and design, to dialects, history and drama therapy. You'll find a very good assortment of books on film and video, as well as lots of industry newspapers and magazines, agent and casting director mailing labels, and DVDs of acclaimed theatrical performances. The very helpful and friendly staff (I assume most are actors) are put through rigorous training. This store, which I consider "actor church," is a sanctuary for anyone who works in, or is passionate about, the theater.

BEST DRAMA BOOK STORE

250 West 40th Street between Seventh and Eighth Avenues— 212-944-0595, www.dramabookshop.com

Fifty percent of the profits from donated used books at **East Village Books** supports local causes. Most of East Village's books are general interest and extremely cheap. The people working behind the counter are helpful but not intrusive and really know their stock. A bonus: If you are looking to make some fast scratch,

East Village Books claims to pay the highest prices in the city for used books, CDs and tapes.

101 St. Mark's Place, between First Avenue and Avenue A—
212-477-8647

Gotham Book Mart, a New York landmark since 1920, carries a combination of new and used books and journals on literature, the arts, philosophy and myriad special interests. Famous for smuggling books into the U.S. by authors James Joyce, Henry Miller and D.H. Lawrence when their books were banned under inflexible obscenity laws, Gotham has been a pilgrimage destination for some of the greatest literary figures of the twentieth century, including Tennessee Williams, Noel Coward, Arthur Miller, Gertrude Stein, Nathaniel West, Thornton Wilder, Eugene O'Neill, Saul Bellow and T.S. Eliot. Although Gotham does not discount its new books, it reduces its large collection of used merchandise by 50 percent and more off original prices. In fact, Gotham has huge reductions on its entire inventory of used film and drama books. On Gotham's "Buck and Below" wagons, books are as cheap as 10¢, and many are even free. A word of warning: although the staff is very knowledgeable, they are a surly bunch. I've been coming here for years and Gotham's gruffness has been as dependable as its selection and good prices. Make sure to pop into Gotham's upstairs art gallery, which features the works of the late illustrator Edward Gorey, as well as changing exhibitions.

16 East 46th Street between Fifth and Sixth Avenues—
212-719-4448, www.finneganswake.org/GothamBookMart

At the **Housing Works Used Book Café** there is a very eclectic collection of books at rock-bottom prices. Unlike most of the city's used bookstores, a majority of the more than 55,000 volumes here are in new or nearly new condition. All proceeds from the Used

Book Café benefit Housing Works, an organization that assists homeless people with AIDS. (See chapter on "Thrift Shops.")

> 126 Crosby Street between Prince and Houston Streets—
> 212-334-3324, www.housingworks.org/usedbookcafe

Ivy's Books on the Upper West Side is the best organized and most inviting of the city's many small book emporiums. Besides its new and used titles, this quaint shop also sells rare books, including first editions, and vintage paperbacks, as well as cards, stationery and some gifts. Ivy's size doesn't allow for a large inventory, but it does a good job of stocking its shelves with the same gamut of topics and genres that are found at larger stores. Prices on used volumes are very low, and Ivy's also has a cart of sale books on the sidewalk out front with titles never more than a couple of dollars.

> 2488 Broadway, between 92nd and 93rd Streets—212-362-8905

I know most used bookstores wear their disarray as a badge of honor, but does **Mercer Street Books** really have to be so slapdash? It feels like the store hasn't shelved a book properly in years. Interspersed among the mostly used offerings are some new volumes and review copies; and if you are interested in art, theater or fiction, you're in luck—each of these areas has a great range of titles. Prices here are comparable to most of the other used book dealers around town. Now, if they'd only spruce the place up a bit...

> 206 Mercer Street at Bleecker—212-505-8615,
> www.mercerstreetbooks.com

The entire inventory of **Murder Ink Books of Mystery and Suspense** is devoted to, well, mystery and suspense. Here you will find more new, used, rare and signed whodunits than you ever imagined existed; and since most are paperbacks, they are affordably priced. Murder Ink also has tons of out-of-print titles starting at just $4.99, and a great collection of vintage collectible paperbacks with provocative titles like *The Gallows in My Garden, Cry Hard, Cry Fast, The Only Girl in the Game,* and *Marihuana.*

2486 Broadway between 92nd and 93rd Streets—212-362-8905, www.murderink.com

Of course, the absolute cheapest way to get your hands on the books you want is to utilize the New York, Queens and Brooklyn **Public Library Systems**. With great services, branches throughout the five boroughs and free membership, there is no reason not to join. And most branches hold ongoing and occasional sales, where hardcover books go for about $1; paperbacks for 50¢. For more information, including locations, hours and services, call or visit their website:

- **New York Public Library**—212-930-0800, www.nypl.org
- **Brooklyn Public Library**—718-230-2100, www.brooklynpubliclibrary.org
- **Queens Borough Public Library**—718-990-0700, www.queens.lib.ny.us

Ruby's Book Sale, which has deep discounts on new and used hardcovers and paperbacks, has an impressive section of low-priced reference and computer books, and an assortment of art volumes comparable to the city's leading book retailers. Used paperbacks and backdate magazines are 50 percent off the cover price.

119 Chambers Street between West Broadway and Church Street—212-732-8676, www.rubysbooksale.com

Samuel French, the world's foremost publisher of plays for over 170 years, has a modest-sized drama bookshop in the foyer of its offices in Chelsea. The books concentrate in film and theater, with lots of acting editions, even those published by Samuel French's competitors. Pick up a free copy of their catalog, which lists all the plays and musicals the company publishes.

45 West 25th Street—212-206-8990, www.samuelfrench.com

Skyline Books and Records has a vast assortment of inexpensive used books, covering every genre imaginable, from art and architecture, to cooking, philosophy, history, religion, literature, children's, poetry, sociology, erotica and even steamy vintage pocketbooks from the 50s and 60s.

13 West 18th Street between Fifth and Sixth Avenues—
212-759-5463, www.skylinebooksnyc.com

The Strand Bookstore (www.strandbooks.com) is the city's biggest, best and perhaps cheapest purveyor of used and rare books. They boast "sixteen miles" of merchandise, and after visiting their three floors, you won't dispute the claim. For me, this store is nirvana; if I haven't made it at least once every couple of weeks, I suffer from withdrawal. Under one roof you will find hardcovers and paperbacks on every subject, a rare book department, review copies and recent releases (that are always 50 percent off the retail price), an astonishing assortment of art books, overstocks, and publishers' closeouts. On the sidewalk outside, Strand packs several carts with cheaper than cheap volumes of fiction and nonfiction. Have I mentioned service? The staff here, mostly scruffy middle-aged men and young women in glasses and uncombed hair, is passionate about books and extremely helpful. The only negative thing I can say about this store is that its organization is helter-skelter. As a friend says, "I can never find what I am looking for, but I always find what I didn't know I

BEST USED
BOOKSTORE

wanted." If you don't mind spending a lot of time browsing for that bargain Kafka, Woolf, Williams or Wharton, you will love this store. Strand has a second location at South Street Seaport that, although it doesn't compare in size and scope with the mother-store, is a great vendor in its own right.

828 Broadway—212-473-1452

95 Fulton Street—212-732-6070

Their location in a basement notwithstanding, **Twelfth Street Books** is a brightly lit, well-organized and cheerful shop specializing in used and rare books. There is an enormous variety here, most in very good condition, at affordable prices.

11 East 12th Street between Fifth Avenue and University Place—212-645-4340

My favorite place to buy brand new books is the ironically named store **Unoppressive Non-Imperialist Bargain Books**. No vendor of new merchandise in the entire city comes close to the low prices this wonderful shop charges. Unoppressive's inventory is all publisher closeouts and overstocks, so there isn't a broad selection, but there is always something of interest and the prices are irresistible. They sell gift books, biographies, fiction, art volumes, poetry collections, tomes on religion and eastern philosophy, children's titles, calendars, cookbooks, and much more.

BEST PLACE
TO BUY
NEW BOOKS

34 Carmine Street near Sixth Avenue—212-229-0079

The diminutive, two-story emporium **Westsider Rare and Used Books** is packed solid with cheap, mostly used and rare paperbacks and hardcovers. Books are everywhere, covering every surface, creating obstacles in the aisles and making it hard to negotiate the stairs. One man's clutter is a book lover's paradise. The helpful staff, who are undoubtedly responsible for the mess, knows their inventory inside and out—if they have what you are looking for, they will point you in the right direction. Westsider's outdoor bargain shelves have deals on all kinds of books you never wanted to read and probably never will, but are worth a look just the same.

2246 Broadway between 80th and 81st Streets—212-362-0706, www.westsiderbooks.com

CDs

According to many of those I polled, **Academy Records** is the best used CD store in New York, and as one friend said, "Anywhere, for that matter." I agree wholeheartedly. Academy's prices and selection are unsurpassed anywhere else in the city. Most CDs average $8.99, with walls and walls of classical CDs for $3.99, many of them still in shrink-wrap. There are great jazz, rock, opera, soul, Broadway and country sections too, as well as VHS movies and vinyl albums galore (mostly classical). While you are there, be sure to check out Academy's budget area, where all merchandise goes for around 99¢. In the ten years I have been shopping there, I have found innumerable treasures and never paid full price.

BEST BET ON USED CDS

12 West 18th Street between Fifth and Sixth Avenues—
212-242-3000, www.academy-records.com

Academy has two satellite shops that sell jazz, pop and genre LPs:

77 East 10th Street—212-780-9166

96 North 6th Street Williamsburg, Brooklyn—718-218-8200

Craig Lopez, the owner of **Accidental Records** in the East Village, claims that his is the only music shop "on the planet that is open 24 hours." I haven't verified this, but for this neighborhood that never sleeps, it's a real plus. The overwhelming clutter and junk store ambience of the place can be off-putting, but don't let it keep you from going inside. Accidental stocks over 10,000 new, shrink-wraped CDs representing every genre, with an especially large selection of Pop/Alternative—all for between $10 and $12 for single albums; $15 to $20 for doubles. A large bargain bin holds CDs priced from $1 to $5. Of the many music styles to be found here, a section, unknown to me before now, of "Antifolk" CDs, is explained by Lopez as a collection of works composed and burned by local artists.

131 Avenue A between St. Mark's Place and 9th Street—
212-995-2224, www.accidentalcds.com

Contrary to what you might think, you can occasionally save money on CDs when shopping at many of the major music **chain stores**. Here's how:

Although the international mega-chain **HMV Records** sells their huge inventory at top prices, they hold several sales throughout the year and frequently offer their "Best of the Best" CDs at greatly reduced prices.

565 Fifth Avenue at 46th Street—212-681-6700

308 West 125th Street—212-932-9619

At **Record Explosion's** two Manhattan locations, $5.99 is the going rate on a glut of new closeout CDs, including many boxed sets. There is a reason why these are closeouts: there isn't much here (to me, at least) that is desirable. In the many years that I've ducked into Record Explosion looking for the titles I want at discount prices, my search has been futile. You may have better luck. This chain also sells new releases of pop, rock and Latin at list price, and has discounts as low as $1.99.

142 West 34th Street—212-714-0450

176 Broadway near Maiden Place—212-693-1510

Tower Records (www.towerrecords.com), which charges top retail prices on their outstanding selection of CDs, does have periodic sales and discounts in which select labels or genres are greatly reduced. On my last visit to Tower, hundreds of titles were on sale, with some like Simon and Garfunkel's "Bridge Over Troubled Water," "The Freewheelin' Bob Dylan" and "The Best of Eric Clapton" for only $5.99. Check for sales circulars in *The New York Times* Sunday edition and ads in the *Village Voice*.

692 Broadway at 4th Street—212-505-1500

1961 Broadway at 66th Street—212-799-2500

725 Fifth Avenue near 56th Street—212-838-8110

The gargantuan **Virgin Megastore** (www.virgin.com) has frequent sales and clearance blowouts on a host of music from all genres. Their weekly sales ads can be found in the *Village Voice*; or stop in whenever you are in Times Square or Union Square.

52 East 14th Street at Broadway—212-598-4666

1540 Broadway between 45th and 46th Streets—212-921-1020

Maurice Chevalier once sang, "Thank heaven for little girls..." I continually sing, "Thank heaven for **Disc-O-Rama**." This bargain institution has the city's best prices on brand new CDs. The entire inventory of mostly pop, rock, hip-hop and dance (with some classical and other genres) is just $9.99 per CD. That's right, $9.99! And it's not clearance or closeout crap. Disc-O-Rama's stock is comprised of mainstream, top 40, new releases and popular fare—the stuff that's going for $14.99 and higher at most other stores. Disc-O-Rama (www.discorama.com) carries tons of cheap used CDs. At its Classical and Clearance outlet store, prices start as low as $2.99. Even better, they have occasional sales. On my last

BEST BARGAIN

visit, they were offering $2-off coupons on all used and clearance items marked at $5.99 or higher.

186 West 4th Street between Sixth and Seventh Avenues—
212-206-8417

40 Union Square East—212-260-8616

146 West 4th Street (Classical and Clearance store)—212-477-9410

Bypass the ground floor sales area (no bargains here) at **Generation Records** and head straight downstairs to their used CD section. Here you will find lots of music, actually organized (wonder of wonders) alphabetically and by genres, with low prices ranging from $2.99 to $11.99. A small bargain rack contains CDs for just 50¢. Most of Generation Records' inventory is rock, hardcore, industrial, punk, metal and electronica, so don't even think about asking the sales staff for the latest Patti Lupone or a box set of show tunes; you're liable to evoke leers, guffaws or worse.

210 Thompson Street between Bleecker and 3rd Streets—
212-254-1100

Gryphon Records has a smattering of classical, soundtrack, jazz and Broadway CDs for between $5 and $9. What they do really well here is old, rare and out-of-print vinyl, and there is a heap of it at reasonable prices. I especially love this store for their "spoken word" albums. I've found many of Ruth Draper's monologues, as well as original cast recordings of plays like *The Cocktail Party* and *Who's Afraid of Virginia Woolf,* and versions of classic plays like *A Doll's House* with Claire Bloom and *Saint Joan* with Siobhan McKenna.

233 West 72nd Street—212-874-1588

Couple the ambience of a St. Mark's Place music store with an Upper West Side address and you have **N.Y.C.D.**, where you get deep discounts on a slew of used rock, pop, jazz and soundtrack CDs. Most sell for between $6.99 and $11.99. Search in the several $1 crates and the table outside, where all CDs are $2 or ten for $15. For every four used or sale CDs you purchase, N.Y.C.D. will give you a fifth gratis.

173 West 81st Street between Amsterdam and Columbus Avenues—212-724-4466, www.nycd-online.com

Other Music isn't really a discount outlet, but this great store warrants a mention for its excellent and eclectic collection of alternative and indie CDs. Much of the inventory here you can't find anywhere else (this is the only store in New York to carry Kiki and Herb's anarchic Christmas album) and prices are competitive. To keep bargain hunters happy, Other Music has frequent sales on selected items, and there is a big section of discounted used merchandise.

15 East 4th Street off Broadway—212-477-8150, www.othermusic.com

If you're looking for brand new CDs at bargain prices, **Rebel Rebel Records** is not your place. All new merchandise sells at list or even slightly higher than seen at the megastores. What is cheap here are used CDs. Prices on their stock of mostly rock and dance music, range between $4.98 and $9.98, with several clearance CDs dropping to $1.98 or six for $10. You'll have to do a lot of digging to find what you are looking for, as most everything is placed haphazardly in several cardboard boxes scattered throughout the tiny store.

319 Bleecker Street near Seventh Avenue—212-989-0770

Rocks In Your Head sells, you guessed it, mostly rock. It has a very small section of used CDs with prices ranging from $2.99 to $7.99. If you're looking for something other than rock, check this store out anyway, as they have a handful of discs from other genres, such as blues, country, world, soundtracks, trip hop, Arab, jazz, and 60s and 70s.

> 157 Prince Street between Thompson Street and West
> Broadway—212-475-6729, www.rocksinyourhead.com

Interspersed between all of the vintage clothing stores, t-shirt shops, junk jewelry stands, sunglass booths and tattoo parlors on **St. Mark's Place** between Third and Fourth Avenues, are several joints selling new and used CDs. Given the neighborhood, most deal in the rock/punk/rap realm. Comb carefully through the collections of each of the shops on the block and you are sure to find what you want (and perhaps what you didn't know you wanted) at prices that are a few to several dollars below retail:

Joe's Compact Discs, which specializes in the music that makes one dance (trance, metal, rap, rock, hip-hop and techno), has a good selection of both new and used CDs at prices that are only about a dollar more than Sounds (see below) across the street. Upstairs at Joe's you'll find sections of most non-dance musical genres that are, like the other shops on St. Mark's, barely or badly organized. Although Joe's has the block's largest selection of 99¢ CDs, you'll have to do a lot of trawling through the bad stuff to get to the good. But then, who am I to call anything "bad"? Once, in my callow youth, I actually paid hard-earned money for an album by Wham! Sheesh.

> 13 St. Mark's Place—212-477-4376

Mondo Kim's Video and Music, beloved by the city's cinephiles for its extraordinary selection of both mainstream and non-mainstream films (see chapter on "Videos and DVDs"), also carries a great assortment of music at reasonable prices.

Kim's appeals to a broad range of tastes—everything from establishment to independent, metal to techno, psychedelia to show tunes. Prices here on new releases are about what you'd pay at the larger music outlets, but used CDs start around $5.99 and don't go much higher. Kim's also has a "Bargain Cove," where all CDs are 99¢.

6 St. Mark's Place—212-598-9985, www.kimsvideo.com

Wowsville Records has a great selection of punk rock, soul and country CDs, LPs, videos, DVDs and rock 'n roll memorabilia, including stickers, buttons, t-shirts, framed photographs by Roberta Bayley, and full catalogs by the venerable Crypt Records and Norton Records. A narrow purple strip of cement and mortar, frequented by everyone from Benicio del Toro to Wayne Kramer, Wowsville is a veritable shrine to New York's punk rock princes, the Ramones, and is a regular hangout for local bands. The customer service is second to none.

125 Second Avenue near St. Mark's Place—646-654-0935, www.wowsville.net

For the area's best prices and selection on new and used mainstream music, look no further than the two **Sounds** stores in the middle of the block. Here you'll find a huge assortment of new releases and catalog titles at very low prices. Used CDs run from $3.99 to $10.99, and new average from $9.99 to $13.99 (double CDs are $15.99). Sounds also has a few large bargain bins where all CDs are just 88¢.

16 St. Mark's Place—212-677-2727

20 St. Mark's Place—212-677-3444

Videos and DVDs

Why rent (or pay late fees!) when you can buy, especially if the video is only a dollar? If you are in the market to by DVDs or videos of "camp" crap (as opposed to "camp" classics)—old episodes of "The Lucy Show" or "Alfred Hitchcock Presents," bad Kung Fu movies, pornography from the 70s, or just about anything that Kevin Costner ever appeared in—you need look no further than **NYC Liquidators**. This place carries movies no one wanted to see and CDs no one wanted to hear. But with NYC Liquidators' low prices—DVDs starting at $9.95, previously viewed videos starting at $1, newly released vids at $3.98 and CDs starting at $2.98—who cares? The junk you'll find here can be great for gag gifts, the centerpiece of your very own "Bad Film Festival," and a source of mockery and derisive laughter for years to come. The act of shopping in this joint is a trip in itself. The merchandise is thrown haphazardly onto shelves with no attempt at categorizing or organizing it in any way. In fact, this place gets my award for the most ramshackle shop in New York, (and in the process of living in this city and writing this book, I've seen *a lot* of ramshackle shops). Who knows though, the store's crappy layout may be a premeditated (and unfortunate) attempt to thematically market the crappy stuff they sell. All kidding aside, if you're diligent and give yourself plenty of time to search, you'll find some gems here.

158 West 27th Street between Sixth and Seventh Avenues—
212-675-7400, www.nycliquidators.com

Party Supplies

For the launch of the first edition of this book, my publisher and I planned to have a party and our goal was to do it in the spirit of the book . . . inexpensively. Not an easy thing to do when expecting two to three hundred guests. Although I'd written about mastering living on a shoestring, I had no idea where to find cheap party supplies. One afternoon, as I wandered along West 14th Street doing some comparison shopping among the area's many dollar discounters, I stumbled upon **Party City**. "Could this be the solution?" I asked myself as I went in. It was. Party City is New York's "party central," with an enormous inventory of everything you'd need for an event of any size and occasion, and all at the lowest prices. Party City has huge discount birthday, bridal and baby shower sections and carries seasonal items for any gathering, be it Christmas, Easter, New Year's, Fourth of July or Arbor Day; it also has a large selection of greeting cards and invitations for every occasion. Besides its everyday low prices, Party City has a clearance department; its own brand of cut-rate supplies like paper and plastic goods; the cheapest balloon bouquets in the tri-state area; weekly sales (recently, all birthday tableware was 60 percent off and its entire stock of solid color paper plates, napkins, cups and table covers was 50 percent off); organization discounts; and a price match policy that says if a competitor has an identical item at a lower price, they will match it and take off an additional 15 percent. There are several Party City locations throughout the five boroughs.

38 West 14th Street—212-271-7310, www.partycity.com

Flowers and Plants

One of the things that most of the New Yorkers I know have at the top of their "To Do" list but never get around to doing, is take a predawn jaunt through the **Chelsea Flower District**. For a few hours each early weekday morning, this nondescript area in midtown pulsates with startling colors and exhilarating aromas as it vends its blooms to the city's flower peddlers. Once you've recovered from sensual overload, you'll want to take advantage of the district's low prices on plants and flowers. Although you won't receive wholesale rates, you will find prices at most shops are lower than other city florists and gardening centers. (Recently, phalaenopsis orchids in the Flower District were going for $35, about half the price of several city florists I checked out.) If you're not a morning person, no need to worry: most of these vendors are open until early afternoon. But be advised, most of the good stuff will have been snapped up.

28th Street between Sixth and Seventh Avenues

The **Chelsea Wholesale Flower Market**, which promises "unique variety and quality unsurpassed," isn't really a wholesale place, but the prices on most flowers and indoor and outdoor plants are competitive. You'll find every kind of seasonal blossom, freshly picked and arranged in a user-friendly way so that you may easily coordinate your arrangements. If your particular talents don't include artfully assembling roses and Queen Anne's Lace, the experts at the Chelsea Wholesale Flower Market will do the arranging for you at prices that are probably a few dollars less than you'd pay at your neighborhood florist. Balcony gardeners will have a field day here choosing from the market's abundant range of potted vegetables, plants and trees. Those who want to add a dash of the southwest to their Manhattan abodes can choose from a large selection of exotic cacti, starting at just $7. The Chelsea Wholesale Flower Market stocks plenty of inexpensive gardening and plant supplies, including pots, soil, baskets, liquid fertilizer, fungicides and insecticides.

> 75 Ninth Avenue at 15th Street—212-620-7500,
> www.chelseaflowersny.com

If you, or the person you are buying flowers for, aren't fussy about freshness or quality, the city's countless **corner grocers and ethnic delis** provide alternatives to expensive florists. Most of these merchants carry a varied selection of decent to beautiful, durable blooms at low prices. Almost all have a similar array of quality flowers for about the same price: carnations sell for around $3 a bouquet, or two for $5; hothouse tulips (when in season) are $6 a bunch or two for $10; alstroemeria are around $3 a bunch; irises sell for $3 a bunch, or two for $5; colored roses are two dozen for $8 to $10 (except on Valentine's Day or Mother's Day). Most also carry large, colorful arrangements of mixed flower bouquets that start at just $9.99.

New York Flower and Plant Shed hails itself as "New York's Houseplant Supermarket." With over 16,000 square feet of greenery, flowers and plant and gardening supplies (including a rooftop greenhouse) and a staff of thirty-five "artisans," botanists and clerks, this claim isn't just bravado. The plants here are all fresh, lush, and well cared for by the expert staff, but the prices aren't exactly budget: corn plants (some as tall as six feet) are $39.99; snake plants are $19.99; spathiphyllum are $29.99; rubber trees are $14.99. However, because of the quality, they are worth the money.

The New York Flower and Plant Shed sells a stunning assortment of flowers and offers a full range of florist services.

209 West 96th Street at Broadway—212-662-4400, www.plantshed.com

Roses and Blooms in the Citicorp Building is, at best, a moderately priced retailer of huge selections of imported flowers. They do, however, offer one generous bargain (which qualifies them for inclusion in this book): they will assemble and deliver a boxed bouquet of a dozen beautiful 24-inch stem roses, complete with ferns and baby's breath, for just $35. At this price, you can say "Thanks," "I love you," "Happy Whatever," even "Screw you, I have enough friends," without breaking the bank!

599 Lexington Avenue at 52nd Street—212-758-7673

New York's biggest, best and oldest farmer's market is the **Union Square Greenmarket**. Colorful displays of food and produce are upstaged by the many vibrant and aromatic stands heaving with newly harvested, locally grown flowers, potted plants and herbs. Most of these seasonal beauties, picked or potted earlier that same morning, are sold at moderate prices. Better yet, at the end of each market day, many vendors discount their goods as much as 50 percent so they won't have to cart them home. Market hours are Mondays, Wednesdays, Fridays, and Saturdays from 7 A.M. to 6 P.M.

Union Square at 17th Street between Broadway and Park Avenue South—212-477-3220, www.cenyc.org

Art Supplies

Whatever your medium may be, **The Art Store** has just about everything you'd need to create a masterpiece. The selection of brand name (as well as their own line) of art supplies in this two-story emporium is vast, and prices are low: most everything is below list, with students receiving an extra 10 percent discount. Moreover, the Art Store has a sizable 50 percent off clearance section and a price match policy that guarantees they will match any local competitor's advertised prices.

1-5 Bond Street between Broadway and Lafayette—
212-533-2444, www.artstore.com

With an enormous selection of goods spread over six floors, the giant retailer **Pearl Paint** is the city's best resource for art, drafting and architectural engineering supplies. Pearl carries just about anything an artist would need or want and has an outstanding picture framing department, home décor section and craft center. Best of all, everything here is sold at discount prices. Pearl also features monthly sales (look for their circular at the store entrance) and offers a 10 percent student discount on all merchandise. Not a student? No problem—just tell them you are—they never ask for ID. Pearl also promises to match any competitor's advertised price (with proof of ad). Recent Pearl deals included a 9″ x 12″ stretched canvas for $2.59; 4-ounce tubes of acrylic paint (assorted colors) for $2.59 each; 37 ml. tubes of oil colors for $2.19; Rembrandt brand oil color set (6 tubes) for $17.99; set of four bristle brushes for oil and acrylics for $9.99; Reeves set of 12 watercolors or gouache colors

BEST
BARGAIN

for $2.99; Loew Cornell pottery tool kit for $5.99; 19″ x 25″ pastel and charcoal papers for 98¢ each. The staff at Pearl Paint is comprised mostly of artists, and is knowledgeable, friendly and attentive.

308 Canal Street at Mercer Street—212-431-7932,
www.pearlpaint.com

Respected by artists working in all mediums, **Utrecht Art Supplies** (www.utrecht.com) sells the finest quality paints, brushes, canvases, art boards and papers, as well as graphic art, printmaking, drawing and sculpting materials and more at substantial savings. In fact, Utrecht's low price guarantee states that if you find an exact item for less at any of their competitors' stores, they will match the price (a valid competitor's ad, coupon or flier is required). Moreover, Utrecht has monthly sales on a wide variety of items, everyday discounts on their store-brand paints and supplies, and a clearance section where everything goes for next to nothing. Utrecht's knowledgeable and helpful sales staff contributes to this chain's reputation as one of the country's leading art supply retailers.

237 West 23rd Street between Seventh and Eighth Avenues—
212-675-8699

111 Fourth Avenue between 11th and 12th Streets—
212-777-5353

General Merchandise Stores

With New York real estate prices soaring to astronomical heights, it is getting harder and harder for warehouse-size general merchandise stores to make a go of it. Gone are the Woolworth's and the Bradlees of my early days in Gotham. However, there are still several places in the city where you can buy essentials (and nonessentials) inexpensively:

Canal Street in Chinatown, known affectionately as "Avenue of the Counterfeits," is a bargain shopper's paradise. On it you will find row upon row of shops, storefronts, cubicles and jerrybuilt booths crammed with everything you'd ever need to stock your pantry, medicine cabinet, closet, desk, cutlery drawer, breakfront, kitchen cupboard, jewelry box and CD rack. The disparate arrayed items here might be plumbing supplies, stereo equipment, kimonos, dishes, 14k gold chains, scarves, slippers, handbags and sunglasses, to name a few. A good deal of the commerce on Canal Street—and what draws the crowds on the weekends to the point where the sidewalks are barely passable—involves the sale of designer knockoffs (what the police less subtly classify as "contraband merchandise"). Here, for about $5 to $25, you can buy ersatz everything: pirated CDs and videotapes, "Kate Spade," "Louis Vuitton" and "Prada" handbags, sunglasses, athletic shoes, and "Rolex" and "Philippe Patek" watches. Most of these are shabby items that wouldn't fool even the least discerning from twenty paces. Between the born-every-minute suckers and those who want a "Cartier" watch without paying for a Cartier watch, counterfeit merch is big business. A warning: occasionally there are raids on these places because of their questionable goods. If a proprietor of a shop suspects a raid is about to take place, he will suddenly slam his metal gates shut and the rest of the stores on the block follow his lead. It's not unheard of for shoppers to be locked in while the proprietors scramble to hide the fake goods. A friend of mine actually experienced this and said it was the most fun he'd had in a long time, especially trying to comfort a woman tourist from Ohio who panicked and screamed over and over, "We're going to die. We're going to die. We're going to...."

The **Conway Store** has a handful of locations throughout Manhattan and the boroughs, with its biggest concentration of outlets around Macy's on Seventh Avenue and 34th Street. Here you can find mostly low-end items and designer knock-offs at very low prices. Conway is a favorite place for truly cheap cotton shirts and summer clothing, as well as toothpaste, toys, makeup, perfume, laundry and dish detergent, cleaning supplies, some brand-name items and a good selection of linens.

One of the best ways to save money is to buy in bulk. Unfortunately, most New York apartments can't accommodate twenty-four rolls of toilet paper, fifty boxes of rice, sixteen cans of spray starch or enough sticky buns to feed a small army (and try getting all that home on the subway). But, if you happen to have the space (and perhaps a car), or enough friends that you can divide it all up between, you should consider joining **Costco** (www.costco.com). For $45 a year (join with a friend and split the membership cost), you can find amazing bargains on industrial sized toiletries, frozen and packaged foods, herbs and spices, vitamins, paper goods and household cleaning supplies. Costco also has great prices on items like clothing, computer equipment (hardware, software and peripherals), DVDs, CDs, videos, books, electronics, furniture, hardware, video games, jewelry, office products, tires—you name it.

32-50 Vernon Boulevard, Long Island City, Queens—718-267-3680

976 Third Avenue at 37th Street Sunset Park, Brooklyn—718-965-7603

2975 Richmond Avenue, Staten Island—718-982-9525

A rung (or two) below Kmart, Costco and Target in the quality and ambience department are the many **discount and 99 cents stores** scattered throughout the city. Most are concentrated around Herald and Union Squares and City Hall, each a sanctuary to a wildly eclectic assortment of items that range from essential to nonessential, including everything from paper towels, canned goods and chocolates, to floral-print slippers, "Last Supper" wall clocks, leopard-print toilet seats, American flag beach towels and yellow smiley face nightlights. Although the quality of the items can be hit or miss, there is literally something for everyone at these stores and they are definitely worth a look. You can find your first set of dishes, glasses and silverware here, as well as cheap bed linens, clocks, phones, bath towels, party supplies and even socks and underwear. Discount stores and locations:

- **99¢ Creation**, 244 West 23rd Street between Seventh and Eighth Avenues

- **99¢ Dreams:**

  2 West 46th Street between Fifth and Sixth Avenues—212-840-1995

  1657 Metropolitan Avenue, Bronx—718-863-8005

  870-888 Hunts Point Avenue, Bronx—718-328-7297

  74-80 East Burnside Avenue, Bronx—718-466-2618

  2397 Hylan Boulevard, Staten Island—718-980-6526

1245 Broadway, Brooklyn—718-574-0124

275 Broadway, Brooklyn—718-782-7144

9415 Church Avenue, Brooklyn—718-485-8410

218-13 Jamaica Avenue, Queens—718-479-8922

92-45 Guy Brewer Boulevard, Queens—718-739-4434

- **Amazing 99¢ or Less**, 122 Chambers Street between West Broadway and Church Street

- **The Bag Man**, 261 West 34th Street at Eighth Avenue—212-502-5452

- **Broadway Job Lot**, 8 West 25th Street between Fifth and Sixth Avenues

- **Chambers Brothers Closeouts**, 100 Chambers Street at Church Street—212-766-9660

- **Dee & Dee:**

  22 West 14th Street—212-243-5621

  97 Chambers Street at Church Street—212-233-3830

- **Jack's World** has a two-level price system: items for 99¢ or less are sold on the ground floor; $1 and over items are on the second floor. Three locations:

  16 East 40th Street off Fifth Avenue—212-696-5767

  110 West 32nd Street between Sixth and Seventh Avenues—212-268-9962

  45 West 45th Street between Fifth and Sixth Avenues—212-354-6888

- **M & S Bargain Hunters**, 519 Eighth Avenue at 36th Street

- **New York 99¢:**

  85 Chambers Street between Broadway and Church Streets

- **Odd-Job and Odd Job Trading:**
  169 East 60th Street between Lexington and Third Avenues—
  212-893-8447
  36 East 14th Street at University Place—212-741-9944
  299 Broadway at Duane Street—212-964-6574
  465 Lexington Avenue between 46th and 47th Streets—212-949-7401
  149 West 32nd Street between Sixth and Seventh Avenues—
  212-564-7370
  390 Fifth Avenue at 36th Street—212-239-3336

- **R & R Everything 99¢,** 207 West 14th Street between Seventh
  and Eighth Avenues

- **Ralph's Discount City,** 72 Nassau Street between Fulton and
  John Streets—212-964-9386

- **Self-Service Stores,** 395 Broadway at Walker Street—212-966-3069

- **Weber's Closeout Center,** 116 West 32nd Street between Sixth
  and Seventh Avenues—212-564-3606

- **Westside Home Center,** 778 Ninth Avenue at 52nd Street—
  212-265-1010

- **Yes 99¢,** 92 Delancey Street between Ludlow and Orchard
  Streets—212-473-9428

When **Kmart** (www.kmart.com) announced years ago that they
would be opening stores in Manhattan, most New Yorkers, me included, collectively gasped and cried aloud "There goes the neighborhood." We feared that this was the beginning of the end, the
"suburbanization" of our cosmopolitan home. If Kmart could open
here, would Chuck E. Cheez, Costco and an outpost of Branson,
Missouri, be far behind? Well, Kmart's presence here in Gotham
has not hurt our status as retail capitol of the world. Instead, it has

provided an outlet where we can buy everything from office supplies to toiletries, baby clothes, women's lingerie, gardening tools, wristwatches, prescription drugs, perfume and air conditioners under one roof. Although most New Yorkers won't readily admit to shopping at Kmart, my very unscientific poll shows we do. Even the most vocal and jaded Blue Light Special naysayers—preening Chelsea boys, snooty Upper East Side matrons, East Village artists and sunglasses-at-midnight TV actors can all be found taking advantage of Kmart's low to moderate prices.

One Pennsylvania Plaza on 34th Street between Seventh and Eighth Avenues—212-760-1188

770 Broadway at Astor Place—212-673-1540

Recently voted "Best Discount Shopping" by the editors of *New York Magazine's* "The Best of New York" issue, **National Wholesale Liquidators** (www.nationalwholesaleliquidators.com) is by far the city's superior discount merchandise store. Here you can find great deals on food, toiletries, housewares, electronics, toys and hardware. Everything

BEST BARGAIN

from cotton balls to cookies, clocks, cleanser and Clearasil is marked down 20 to 40 percent off retail. Best yet, unlike most other discount stores, everything on National Wholesale Liquidators' three floors of manufacturers' overstocks and seconds are in pristine condition and don't have dubious expiration dates.

632 Broadway between Bleecker and Houston Streets—212-979-2400

71-01 Kissena Boulevard, Flushing, Queens—718-591-3900

The best and largest of all the discount stores in the Canal Street shopping district is **Pearl River Mart** (www.pearlriver.com).

When I sent out my initial e-mail query to friends asking for their suggestions for this book, several wrote back about Pearl River. I was intrigued because I had never heard of the store. So, down I went to Canal Street to check it out, and I'm glad I did. This multi-level emporium is a marvel of very cheap, mostly Asian import products. The aisles teem with both basic necessities and some luxury items, and include everything from imported foods to clothing, cooking supplies, silk handbags, Chinese herbs, loose tea and teapots, wallets, gongs, stationery, Japanese paper lanterns, bamboo shades, wind chimes, metal lunch boxes covered with printed silk and lots of decorative objects at unbelievable prices. Two locations:

477 Broadway between Grand and Broome Streets—212-431-4770

200 Grand Street between Mott and Mulberry Streets—212-966-1010

In my opinion, of all the general discount merchandise stores out there, **Target** (www.target.com) is Valhalla, the big Kahuna. This community-conscious store carries *everything*, and at good prices. The Target housewares section is unparalleled by any other store of its kind. I especially love their Michael Graves designed blenders, coffee pots, flatware, cooking utensils, toasters, alarm clocks, teakettles, picture frames, and knife sets. These ultra-hip domestic items are practical, stylish and designed with a sense of humor. Target features some easy-to-assemble furniture, and carries a large selection of items for the bedroom and bathroom. Penny-pinching fashionistas will have a field day poring through the racks of inexpensive and trendy gear by designers Isaac Mizrahi and Mossimo. Unfortunately, there are only four Target stores in the New York boroughs (although there are two fairly close by in New Jersey, but you need a car to reach them), and are a pain to get to. Make the trek, however, and a wondrous world awaits you. Look for Target's sales and specials circular inside Sunday editions of *The New York Times*. You may not know this but Target is a huge supporter of Broadway Cares/Equity Fights AIDS. Over the years, they have contributed millions to this worthy organization.

13505 20th Avenue, Flushing, Queens—718-661-4346

Queens Place, Queens Boulevard and 55th Avenue, Elmhurst, Queens—718-760-5656

139 Flatbush Avenue, Brooklyn and 55th Avenue, Elmhurst, Queens s—718-290-1109

40 West 225th Street, Bronx—718-733-7199

Sample Sales

One of the many benefits of living in New York is that we have the opportunity to take advantage of the sample sales that dozens of New York's leading designers and manufacturers hold almost every week. Originally, the term "sample sale" meant exactly that—a sale of designers' samples. Samples are what designers use to entice buyers to purchase their clothing line; at the end of a season when these samples are no longer needed, they are sold to the public at wholesale prices. Today the term is more all encompassing and includes the sale of any leftover inventory after orders have been filled for retail stores. As you can imagine, these clearance blowouts offer amazing discounts on top-of-the-line clothing, shoes, furniture, linens and housewares, and attract hordes of bargain seekers hoping to save megabucks on high-ticket items for their wardrobe and home.

To make your sample sale-ing an easy and rewarding experience, I recommend the following:

* **Arrive an hour or more before the sale opens**; hardcore sample salers (and there are a lot of them) get there before dawn and almost immediately snap up the best bargains.

* **If you see something you like, buy it**—chances are, if you put it down, it won't be there when you return.

* **If you are in the market for something for your home, bring a tape measure as well as pictures and dimensions of the area where you want the item to go.** Doing this will help insure that the item fits proportionally and goes with your décor. (Note:

Purchases from sample sales are usually not refundable or exchangeable.)

- Most of these sales don't have dressing rooms, so **go prepared to try things on in the aisles**. That means wearing slim, stretchy clothes that you can slip things over or under. A lady friend who frequents sample sales always wears a sports bra and Lycra tights. She gets a few strange looks, but, as she says, "Who cares? I'm not there to impress people. I'm there to save a fortune."

How can you find out about these weekly wonders? Both the **"Sales and Bargains" section of** New York Magazine and the **"Shoptalk" section of** Time Out New York provide detailed listings of the dates and locations of sample sales throughout the city. The **website www.nysale.com** constantly updates its comprehensive list of sales. Also, on any given weekday, **saunter through the Garment District** and you are sure to see signs or be handed flyers advertising present or future sales. (The Garment District is bounded roughly by Sixth and Eighth Avenues and 35th and 41st Streets.)

SSS Sample Sale in the Garment District holds weekly overstock and sample sales of goods by designers and manufacturers at wholesale and below wholesale prices. These sales feature both single and multiple designers, with names like Tahari, Theory, Diesel, and Diane von Furstenberg among many others. The savings here are tremendous—from 50 to 80 percent below retail prices. Advantages of shopping at SSS Sample Sale are that they do have dressing rooms and they do allow you to exchange any item (with the exception of underwear, bodysuits and swimwear, of course) from the same manufacturer as long as the exchange is done within the duration of that manufacturer's sale. For information about present and future sales or to be put on their snail-mail or e-mail lists for upcoming events, call SSS Sample Sale or visit their website at www.clothingline.com.

261 West 36th Street, 2nd Floor—212-947-8748

"Borrowing" Apparel from Leading Retailers

Need some nice clothes for a special occasion or work-related event but don't have the cash? An industry secret, told to me long ago, allows you to get around this. Out of the necessity for full disclosure, please don't assume that my inclusion of the following is in any way sanctioning such behavior (as I've said before: I'm just the messenger). In that function, it is my duty to pass this secret on to you. Shop at any of the major department or apparel stores that have a *liberal return policy*. Select the items you want, price being no object, and purchase them with a credit card (unless of course you are maxed out—then you're out of luck). Do not remove any of the garment care labels or price tags and wear your purchases very carefully. The next day, return the items to the store with a fully rehearsed excuse as to why you no longer want them ("My husband's dot-com tanked," "My fiancée left me for her secretary, Fritz, and I had bought these things to wear on our honeymoon," "We should have unloaded that Enron stock a long time ago") and have the store credit your charge card. You must return these things looking and smelling brand-new, so when wearing them, make sure to use a generous amount of unscented deodorant, refrain from colognes, stay out of smoky environments, use armpit guards and don't have them dry-cleaned—the lingering smell of dry cleaning fluid is a dead giveaway. Also, make sure that the items fit right off the rack. Once they are tailored, they become yours forever.

Flea Markets

The famous and popular **Annex Antique Fair and Flea Market** is not, I repeat, *not* a place for the bargain-hungry. There are all kinds of beautiful vintage and antique treasures to be found here: furniture, clothing, china, watches, clocks, decorative pieces, books, collectibles, objets d'art, purses, pens, lamps, jewelry, art work, silver and eyeglass frames—all at prices that you'd expect in this expensive and style-conscious city. Don't let the prices deter you, however. View your time at this flea market as a visit to an outdoor museum and enjoy the eye candy. And the people watching isn't bad either—you'll see all kinds of characters from celebrities and politicians, to designers, fashion models, buff Chelsea boys, East Village punks and regular Joes fingering the wares and bargaining with dealers. Perseverance here can pay off: a little diligence and a stomach for haggling can reap gems whose prices will be acceptable to you. I've also found that at the end of the day the dealers are happy to unload their goods at lower prices instead of hauling them home, so don't hesitate to negotiate. The Annex, which averages around 600 dealers and attracts close to 10,000 people per weekend is open on Saturdays and Sundays from sunrise to sunset year-round. Admission is $1.

Sixth Avenue between 25th and 26th Streets—212-243-5343

If the $1 admission price to the Annex gives you pause, check out the side streets surrounding the Sixth Avenue market and the nearby **Garage Antique Show**. This poor cousin to the Annex is a huge, two-level, (barely) heated flea market that specializes in kitsch, the unusual and a lot of junk. As the saying goes, though, "one man's junk is another man's treasure," and there are a lot of treasures to be discovered here at prices that are much more reasonable than those on Sixth Avenue. If old photos, art by unknowns, reams of nondescript fabric, glass marbles, drawings of plants and insects torn out of ancient encyclopedias, vintage undergarments, antique spectacles, 70s decorative pieces, or old magazines, prints and books hold sway over your life, you will hit the jackpot here. Open weekends 7 A.M. to 5 P.M.

112 West 25th Street between Sixth and Seventh Avenues—
212-647-0707

The indoor/outdoor **Greenflea Market at I.S. 44** has something for everyone and in regard to price and selection is New York's best flea market. This huge "flea" has an abundance of everything you could possibly desire

BEST FLEA MARKET

or need, such as antique, vintage and new furniture, clothing, jewelry, books, decorative items, handmade crafts, prints and records. But it also carries foodstuffs like fresh canned jellies, cider, produce and plants. This market also has lots of stalls that sell necessities like underwear (all new of course), socks, sunglasses and bedding. The prices here are low and the vendors will haggle. Besides these, there are all kinds of beautiful, handmade, collectible, and one-of-a-kind things to grace your home and body that can be bought for a song. The Greenflea at I.S. 44 hours are Sundays from 10 A.M. to 6 P.M., year-round.

Columbus Avenue at 76th Street—212-721-0900

The small **Greenflea Market at P.S. 183** is ideal for those who want to combine a little antiquing with some grocery shopping. Here you will find produce, prepared foods, fish, eggs and plants, as well as items that would not be out of place in Miss Havisham's bedroom. There is more lace, jewelry (costume and real) and silver crammed in here than you'd ever hope to see, unless of course those things are your passion. Open Saturdays, year-round, from 6 A.M. to 6 P.M.

419 East 66th Street at First Avenue—212-721-0900

The **Hell's Kitchen Flea Market**, the city's newest, is still experiencing growing pains: most weekends there is a paucity of vendors and visitors. But, as the saying goes, "Rome wasn't built in a day," and the Hell's Kitchen Flea Market is slowly gathering steam. Although the crowds are underwhelming, you can find all kinds of high quality goods here, including new and vintage furniture, handcrafted items, fresh produce, home canned and jarred foods, jewelry, clothes and artwork. Open Saturday and Sunday from 9 A.M. to 5 P.M.; the Hell's Kitchen Flea "hibernates" in the winter from December to April.

West 39th Street between Ninth and Tenth Avenues— 212-242-1217

The no-delusions-of-grandeur **M.H.C. Flea Market** has exactly what you'd expect to find in an Alphabet City bazaar: lots of funky junk and edgy treasures at truly cheap prices. The stuff here is a real hodge-podge of old, used, vintage and retro items. You'll find records and CDs, furniture, toys and games, clothing, books, "art," bicycles, costume jewelry, bric-a-brac and more, most of which has seen better days. Open Saturday and Sunday from 8 A.M. to 6 P.M.

Corner of Avenue A and 11th Street

The **Noho Flea Market**, located in a lot next to the downtown Tower Records store, vends lots of clothing, jewelry, tapes and

CDs, sunglasses, bongs, pipes and more. The Noho flea is open year round, seven days a week.

Broadway and West 4th Street

The **Soho Antiques Fair and Collectibles Market** isn't huge but has a pretty eclectic selection of goods similar to those found at the Annex and the Greenflea at I.S. 44, and for less money. Don't be fooled by this market's "Antiques" name; only about half of the dealers sell antique or vintage items. The other 50 percent deal in clothing, accessories and handmade jewelry, as well as not-old-enough-to-be-antique furniture, decorative pieces and books, most at prices that won't break the bank. Open every Saturday and Sunday from 9 A.M. to 5 P.M.

Grand Street and Broadway

Thrift Shops

In New York, there are dozens of outlets for low-priced, mostly used, donated goods, whose proceeds benefit numerous charitable organizations throughout the city. Ostensibly you could furnish your apartment and fill out your wardrobe buying from any one of these, especially if your fashion sense is shabby-not-so-chic. Still, many of these stores have rendered treasures (I've found several myself) and are definitely worth a look.

Besides price, the other great thing about thrift shops is that anything you donate to them is tax deductible, which will save you a little money at tax time. (Note: To insure against disputes with the I.R.S. over a tax deduction, make sure to get a receipt from the charitable organization where you have made your donation; the government requires a photocopy of receipts for any donations whose value exceeds $500.) Most places will pick up furniture as well as donations of exceptional quality and value. Call the thrift shop of your choice for drop-off locations, pick-up appointments or further information.

If the city's thrift shops had a flagship store, the **City Opera Thrift Store** would be the place. The design and layout of this two-story emporium makes you feel (if you don't look too closely at the merch) as if you are in a trendy boutique. The condition of most everything here is very good and includes lots of never-used items. The women's section is full of designer dresses, suits, skirts, blouses, sweaters and shoes from a season or two ago with labels like Manolo Blahnik, Dior, St. Laurent, Calvin Klein, Nina Ricci, Adolpho and Jacqueline de Ribes. Upstairs you can locate a good selection of mostly antique and vintage furniture although there are a few modern pieces (a chaise longue upholstered in a sand-colored wool fabric in impeccable shape was selling for $400). There are pictures and frames galore, housewares, dishes, cups, glasses, books (50¢ for paperbacks, $1 to $3 for hardcovers), records ($1 each) and CDs ($4). On a recent visit, the store's window displayed dozens of gold and cream-colored Mary McFadden "mother-of-the-bride" (or so they seemed to me) shoes for $35. Women's designer suits were marked around $65; evening gowns from $10 to $80. In the men's section, there were an inordinate number of pairs of tuxedo pants and black patent leather shoes (did these appear in a recent City Opera production?) for $10 each; designer sport coats and suits between $15 and $25; and men's shirts were $5.

222 East 23rd Street between Second and Third Avenues—
212-684-5344

Goodwill Industries of Greater New York is a not-for-profit organization serving people with mental and physical disabilities, the unemployed, people who are economically disadvantaged, mature workers and disadvantaged youth. Goodwill stores provide a service to the community by offering new and gently used clothing, toys, household items and furniture at low costs. The stores also provide a training ground in retail for persons with disabilities and other barriers to employment, and your purchases help finance Goodwill's rehabilitative programs. The quality and type of goods at these stores is what you'd expect (as are the prices—very low with daily half-price sales on designated items), but unlike many of the city's other thrift shops, there is a surprising paucity of furniture. Goodwill has several locations in the New York area; check your phone book or www.goodwill.org for the store nearest you.

Housing Works (www.housingworks.org) has five stores that help fund its programs to provide housing, support services, job training and advocacy for homeless men, women and children living with HIV and AIDS. You can find some great items at these hip and stylish thrifts at very low prices. Good-quality furniture, eclectic decorative items, books, CDs, housewares and clothes are, for the most part, fashionable and in good condition. Some of the best stuff is held for display in each of the store's provocative windows and sold by silent auction. Housing Works has a high turnover on its goods so that you can shop at any one of the stores several times a week and never see the same items twice. Locations:

BEST THRIFT SHOP

202 East 77th Street between Second and Third Avenues— 212-772-8461

157 East 23rd Street between Third and Lexington Avenues— 212-529-5955

306 Columbus Avenue between 74th & 75th Streets—212-579-7566

143 West 17th Street between Sixth and Seventh Avenues— 212-366-0820

126 Crosby Street south of Houston (Used Book Café)— 212-334-3324

The proceeds of the **Parish of Calvary/St. George's Vintage Furniture Shop** support the church's outreach programs for shelters, AIDS patients and alcohol and drug programs. These stores carry exquisite pre-50s vintage furniture, as well as paintings, Oriental rugs, lighting fixtures, mirrors, chandeliers and decorative bric-a-brac. Most of the items are in antique store condition at moderate prices. This shop has an especially good selection of both dining room sets (some art deco) and bedroom sets.

The church also runs a clothing thrift shop in the basement offering contemporary (okay, last year's model) items at very affordable prices.

277 Park Avenue South between 21st and 22nd Streets—
212-475-6645

61 Gramercy Park North—212-475-2674

The very cramped **Out of the Closet Thrift Shop** feels like it is really two stores—a thrift shop and an antique emporium. The antiques here are mostly the kind of stuff you'd see in your grandmother's home, with an abundance of porcelain figurines and dainty lamps, at prices that are on par with local antique dealers. The shop's real bargains are on books and records (starting as low as $1) and men's and women's clothing. Dresses and blouses can be as little as $10; men's suits can be had for $45 and lots of trousers and shirts at $10. One hundred percent of Out of the Closet's proceeds from sales of items that also include silver, crystal, china, framed artwork, collectibles, furniture, crafts, linens, rugs and appliances, supports over fifty-five organizations and institutions fighting AIDS.

220 East 81st Street between Second and Third Avenues—
212-472-3573

After the Salvation Army's 2002 mischief during which they secretly lobbied the Bush White House to gain exemption from the nondiscrimination order that all organizations receiving federal funds are bound to, I can't enthusiastically recommend patronizing their thrift shops. The Salvation Army wanted to create a loophole in the law that would allow it to continue receiving taxpayer dollars, but *legally* exempt it from hiring gays and lesbians. Fortunately, the gay press uncovered the imbroglio, and the White House, in an attempt to save face, withdrew its support for the effort. Worse yet, the Salvation Army rescinded its earlier decision to allow its West Coast division to offer health care benefits to the domestic partners of its employees, after Salvation Army officials received a barrage of criticism from fundamentalist Christian and anti-gay groups, who complained that the popular charitable organization was bowing to pressure by "militant homosexuals." Under this reversal of policy, the Salvation Army will withdraw from or decline to enter into contracts with any city or municipality that requires a domestic partner benefits program as a condition for providing social services programs. It's too bad that this organization, which does so much good, has done so much bad. Having said that, I will now hop off my soapbox...

The **Salvation Army** (www.salvationarmyusa.org) uses the proceeds from its many thrift stores to fund its residential facility for substance abusers. The goods at these stores, which include furniture, housewares, clothing, knickknacks, toys and more (all used, of course), are real hit or miss; hits, however, can be homeruns. Women should note that the Salvation Army has no dressing rooms.

I have had two great Salvation Army successes: I paid $700 for a huge, vintage (it was built in the 30s) Empire-style breakfront that I use as a bookcase/storage cabinet/room divider and that always elicits oohs and ahhs from first-time visitors to my home. It is my favorite piece of furniture and the one thing I'm sure I will hang onto until I have shuffled off this mortal coil. For $17.85, I picked up a pair of blond wood Alvar Aalto stools that I've been told are worth $1,000 a piece. There's gold in them thar stores! There are eight Salvation Army locations in the greater New York area; consult your local listings for the nearest store.

The boutique-like **Spence-Chapin Thrift Shops** (www.spence-chapin.org), which fund this nonprofit organization's commitment to finding homes for infants and children, carry a variety of items at very low prices. At both Upper East Side stores, there is new and gently used "better" clothing, accessories, shoes, jewelry and handbags, with separate sections selling designer fashions and furs. Other items for sale include books, records, tapes, CDs, furniture (some antique and vintage), art, china, silverware, glassware, linens, housewares, computers, software and video games. The prices in the stores' clearance areas are so low, they're practically giving the stuff away. Recently, I found racks of women's overcoats and dresses for $20, a case of $5 jewelry, a basket of slightly used purses for $10, new purses for just $15, and a box containing china and glassware for $1 each item. Furs and furniture were all 50 percent off marked prices. Hardcover books are always $1 each; paperbacks are 50¢ each or three for $1. These shops are definitely a step above the Salvation Army and Goodwill stores, with most merchandise in good condition.

1473 Third Avenue between 83rd and 84th Streets—212-737-8448

1850 Second Avenue between 95th and 96th Streets—212-426-7643

Other New York City Thrift Shops include:

- **17 @ 17 Thrift Shop**, 17 West 17th Street between Fifth and Sixth Avenues—212-727-7516

- **Angel Street Thrift Shop**, 118 West 17th Street between Sixth and Seventh Avenues—212-229-0546

- **Cabrini Thrift Store**, 532 Main Street, Roosevelt Island—212-486-8958

- **Cancer Care Thrift Shop**, 1480 Third Avenue at 84th Street—212-879-9868

- **Care Partners Thrift Shop**, 475 Atlantic Avenue, Brooklyn—718-852-2437

- **Council Thrift Shop**, 246 East 84th Street between Second and Third Avenues—212-439-8373

- **Good Old Lower East Side Thrift Shop**, 17 Avenue B at 2nd Street—212-358-1041

- **Marble Thrift Shop**, 382 Third Avenue between 27th and 28th Streets—212-532-5136

- **Memorial Sloan-Kettering Center Thrift Shop**, 1440 Third Avenue near 82nd Street—212-535-1250

- **Monk Thrift Shop**, 165 Avenue A at 9th Street—917-534-0511

- **St. Luke's Thrift Shop**, 487 Hudson Street between Christopher and Barrow Streets—212-924-9364

- **St. Margaret's House Thrift Shop**, 49 Fulton Street near Gold Street—212-766-8122

- **Sirovich Thrift Shop**, 331 East 12th Street between First and Second Avenues—212-228-7836

- **Stuyvesant Square Thrift Shop**, 1704 Second Avenue between 88th and 89th Streets—212-831-1830

- **Vintage Thrift Shop**, 286 Third Avenue between 22nd and 23rd Streets—212-871-0777

Street Fairs

Hardly a weekend goes by from late spring through the summer to early fall that a street fair is not going on in some part of the city. Although they take place in the city's many diverse neighborhoods, every one of them is mostly composed of the same kinds of stuff—lots of funnel cake vendors, Italian sausage sandwich makers and "Pina Colada" stands. So much for diversity! However, the street fairs also attract several entrepreneurs who are selling all kinds of things you might want for prices that are less than you'd pay at a retail store. Visit the street fairs for deals on everything from plants and 100 percent cotton sheet sets to jewelry, art, men's/women's/children's clothing, sunglasses, pottery, Japanese crockery and tea sets, toys, internet service providers and long distance phone companies, CDs, videos, towels, candles, home furnishings, hats, makeup, temporary tattoos, leather handbags and wallets, and even cheap ten-minute massages. For a complete listing of street fairs, consult either the "Weekend Fine Arts/Leisure" section of the Friday edition of *The New York Times*, the "Around Town" section of *Time Out New York*, *The New York Press* or the *Village Voice*.

Outlet Stores

Although there are no outlet stores in New York City, a few are reasonably accessible to us by bus, car or train. These discount upscale malls feature the best and brightest designers, manufacturers and retailers of clothing, housewares, handbags, accessories, perfumes, linens, china, stemware, and luggage. They are oases for designer-addicted bargain shoppers who can find most merchandise discounted between 25 and 70 percent off their original prices.

Although these malls host stores that outfit the trendsetters of taste and fashion, their décor and settings have a distinctly "camp" quality. The urban-edged New Yorker in me can only take so much of the squeaky-clean kitsch of faux Colonial and fake cobblestone before I start breaking out in hives. Fortunately, the savings these outlet malls provide is the perfect salve:

Considered the oldest Outlet Mall in the nation, **Liberty Village** is the area's most intimate outlet center. Liberty Village has only sixty stores, including Calvin Klein, Donna Karan, Tommy Hilfiger, Perry Ellis, Nautica, Jones New York, Izod, Bass, Nine West, Etienne Aigner, Fossil, Sunglass World, and Villeroy & Boch. Because of its size, Liberty Village draws smaller crowds than the other area malls, which is a blessing for mob-phobic, long-line-loathing shoppers. From Manhattan, take the Trans-Bridge bus from the Port Authority Bus Terminal (800-962-9135).

One Church Street, Flemington, New Jersey—908-782-8550, www.premiumoutlets.com

Tanger Outlet Center, located on Long Island, is a short, pleasant journey from the city. This discount shopping center, really two separate malls linked by a trolley, has over 160 stores featuring a "Who's Who" roster of designers, manufacturers and retailers. Brands include Aldo, Anne Klein, Barney's New York, Bath and Body Works, Benetton, Bombay, Books Warehouse, Children's Place, Christmas Market, Club Monaco, Dana Buchman, Danskin, Disney, Eddie Bauer, Harry and David, Hugo Boss, Hoover, Joe Boxer, Lillian Vernon, Lindt Chocolate, Mikasa, Noritake, Pepperidge Farm, Pottery Barn, Skechers, Samsonite, The Wiz, Zales. There are two ways to get to the Tanger Center: By bus, take Sunrise Coach Lines, which departs several times a day from Port Authority (800-527-7709); by train, take the Long Island Rail Road from Penn Station (718-330-1234, www.lirr.org) to Riverhead. Call Sunrise Coach and LIRR for fares and a schedule of departures.

1770 West Main Street, Riverhead, New York—800-407-4894, www.tangeroutlet.com

Woodbury Commons, the mother of all area outlet stores, offers everyday savings of 25 to 65 percent on the world's greatest designers. Here you'll find Armani, BCBG Max Azria, Dolce & Gabbana, Christian Dior, Frette, Gucci, Kenneth Cole, Malo, Max Mara, Judith Leiber, Neiman Marcus, Saks Fifth Avenue, Polo Ralph Lauren, Salvatore Ferragamo, TSE, Versace, Waterford, Wedgwood, Le Creuset, and more. In addition, outlet mall regulars like Banana Republic, Nike, Patagonia, Gap, Guess, Brooks Brothers and Cole Haan are here. To get to Woodbury Commons, take the Short Line (800-631-8405—www.shortlinebus.com) or Gray Line Bus (www.grayline.com—800-669-0051) from Port Authority. Round-trip is $36, $17.50 for children; several buses leave throughout the day, the first at 8:30 A.M., the last at 2:45 P.M.

498 Red Apple Court, Central Valley, New York—845-928-4000, www.chelseagca.com

BEST
OUTLET
MALL

Haggling

"Haggle," in *Merriam-Webster's Collegiate Dictionary*, is defined as "to annoy or exhaust with wrangling," and according to the Random House *Dictionary*, as "to bargain in a petty, quibbling manner." Until recently, haggling was regarded by many (shopkeepers, the shy, cowards) with the same negative connotations and considered the bailiwick of people termed ballsy, aggressive and terminally cheap. In New York, haggling was solely the province of specific neighborhoods (the Lower East Side and Canal Street) and restricted to particular products such as antiques, leather goods, jewelry, mattresses and electronics. These negative connotations notwithstanding, the practice of haggling has become *de rigueur* throughout the five boroughs and at a number of retailers. Even department stores are getting into the act: a *New York Times* article about haggling cited a Bloomingdale's customer who negotiated down the cost of two sofas and got them at half their marked price.

Chalk this change up to the sagging economy and the aftermath of September 11, as more and more consumers are using haggling as a way to get the best for less and hold on to a little more of their hard-earned cash. Retailers are encouraging negotiation as a way to finalize a sale they might not make otherwise.

How does one haggle? Easy. If there is a product or service you desire but don't want to pay the list price for, ask for a discount. There are a lot of ways to do this: "How much will you come down?" "Can you do any better on the price?" "I saw this at such-and-such a place for less. Can you match it or do better?" The worst that can happen is that you will be told no.

Fancying myself an expert at haggling (I've gotten everything from furniture to books, clothing, paint and appliances, as well as services like gym memberships, yoga classes and medical care by doing this), the following are my sure-fire suggestions to become a savvy negotiator:

Bargain with confidence. If you act at all timid or embarrassed, the merchant will see it and will barely deal with you.

Don't reserve negotiating only to stores that honor or better a competitor's advertised price. Many more retailers than you'd imagine will haggle. You won't know which ones until you try.

Start with a number lower than you're willing to pay, as the retailer may accept this figure. If not, wrangle up to the amount you deem satisfactory while acting as if you're being forced to go higher than you wanted.

Cash speaks louder than credit; retailers are more likely to haggle for the paper stuff than the plastic.

Be prepared to walk away from a sale if the negotiation breaks down. More often than not, if you start to leave, the retailer will agree to your proposal or, at the very least, make a counteroffer. For a lot of merchants, a lesser sale is better than none at all.

Craigslist

The wonderful community-based website **Craigslist** (www.newyork.craigslist.org) is an ideal place to find almost anything you're looking for at rock-bottom prices. This free site, which is part classifieds, part forums, and part civic outreach, was established to "provide a trustworthy, efficient means for folks to get the word out regarding everyday stuff, and connect with others locally to find jobs, housing, companionship, community." Craigslist makes good on this by offering copious "help wanted" listings, as well as those for community needs and events (everything from childcare to classes, ridesharing, activity partners, pets, artists, musicians and more), personals and housing. Its "Forums" section offers discussion groups on hot topics like politics, restaurants, housing, the job market, nightlife and romance.

Craigslist's huge "Stuff for Sale" section gives New Yorkers the opportunity to list whatever it is they want to unload. Here you'll find a multitude of offerings from bicycles, motorcycles, cars, trucks, computers, technical equipment and electronics, to tickets to arts and sporting events, furniture, general merchandise and much more. Also listed are moving and apartment sales, "items wanted," and people looking to swap or barter goods and services. Craigslist is totally free to browse, provides an easy and accessible way to search for the items you're looking for, and allows no ads. Prices are set by individual buyers and seller, which means . . . anything goes.

Freecycling

Freecycling, an environmentally and community conscious movement, provides New Yorkers a free electronic forum to recycle functional but unwanted items. This practice, which is sweeping the nation, connects the "haves" (those with most anything including clothing, furniture, housewares and electronics that they no longer want, need or have room for) with the "have-nots" (those in need of what the "haves" want to unload) via the internet. Freecycling's purpose is to minimize the size of dumps and landfills while at the same time help those without the cash to obtain the items they need. As www.freecycle.org states, "One person's trash can truly be another's treasure!"

Freecycling works this way: simply sign up with one of these volunteer moderated websites—www.freecycling.com or www.freecycle.org—and scroll through the listings. If you see something you want or need, respond to the posting. If you're the first to express interest, the item is yours. There are only two rules to freecycling. First, everything posted by the "haves" must be free. Second, if you agree to pick up something, you must indeed pick it up.

Items up for grabs on a recent visit included, among many other things, a coffee table, a pine desk, various shades of house paint, a double frame bed and headboard, a hamster cage, a baby car seat, a 19-inch color television, an ironing board, a futon, a minidisk player, a toaster oven, skis, exercise equipment and file cabinets. (Note: Craigslist.org also has a large posting of items that are offered gratis.)

Weekly Sales Listings and Discount Coupons

Each week read **New York Magazine** and **Time Out New York** to locate all kinds of sales that are happening throughout the city. The categories vary widely—from clothing and accessories stores, to food purveyors, health clubs, beauty spas, home emporiums, hair salons, opticians, and even service businesses like dog-walkers, dry cleaners and personal shoppers. **New York Magazine Shops**, published twice a year by *New York Magazine*, not only lists the best stores in Manhattan, but also includes articles on sample sales, bargains and discounts.

The **Village Voice** a free, left-leaning newspaper, hits the newsstands every Tuesday evening. Besides its comprehensive articles on everything from New York City politics, to music, art, theater and concerts, it is a veritable guide to everything cheap in New York, packed with ads for inexpensive stores and services. Be sure to check out the column, "Elements of Style," which covers the retailers that have hip stuff at humble prices. The *Voice's* Classifieds section is considered one of the best resources for finding an apartment (see chapter on "Apartment Hunting") in the city—not to mention a job, a "massage" or even a potential life partner!

The website **www.nysale.com** is a great tool for the sales savvy New York shopper. This one website lets you search for current and future sales by specific products, date, category or store. Each day, nysale.com lists sample sales, going-out-of-business sales and clearances from department stores like Bloomingdale's and Barney's, to small boutiques and designer showrooms. Store categories on the site include women's, men's and children's apparel, accessories, jewelry, furnishings, eyewear, maternity and much more. Membership at nysale.com is free, but you must register if you want to surf the site or receive their daily e-mail messages about current sales.

Bargain Retail Areas

Why not combine shopping with a walk? Even in this very expensive city there are whole corridors of bargain retail areas where you'll find incredible deals while becoming acquainted with several distinctive neighborhoods:

Atlantic Avenue between Nevins and Bond Streets in Brooklyn has several shops that carry antique, vintage and retro furniture and accessories at prices that are about half what you'd pay for the same items in Manhattan.

The **Bowery below Houston** has many discount lighting and restaurant supply stores.

The side streets near **City Hall** from Broadway to Church Street swarm with discount retailers. Particularly noteworthy are Chambers, Duane and Reade Streets, where you can find a glut of cutrate linens, toiletries, books, paper goods, party supplies and clothing.

Canal Street, of course, which I have already discussed in my chapter on "General Merchandise Stores," has innumerable electronics and surplus stores, as well as other shops carrying a surfeit of cheap counterfeit everything.

14th Street between Union Square South and Eighth Avenue has several stores that carry a multitude of cheap items. Here you'll find lots of toys, sheet sets, umbrellas, towels, paper goods, party supplies and CDs.

Many of the streets between Sixth and Eighth Avenues in the **Garment District** (41st Street to 34th Street) have discount fabric, notions, trim, button, ribbon and lace shops, as well as "Wholesale to the Public" clothing stores.

The entire **Lower East Side** has been designated New York's "Historic Bargain District" (for more information call 212-226-9010) and the title is apt. This area, which has been the bargain center of the city for the last hundred years, is a mecca for inexpensive goods like CDs, sunglasses, designer apparel, fabric, luggage, retro furniture, lighting fixtures and much more. Also, some of the city's best cheap restaurants, bars and cafes are in this neighborhood.

The **Madison Square Garden/Penn Station area**, especially the **north side of 34th Street between Seventh and Eighth Avenues** (the anchor on this block is the Conway Department Store; see chapter on "General Merchandise Stores") houses several low-price clothing, shoe and gift stores.

St. Mark's Place, home to New York's punkers, club kids and other colorful characters, has tons of inexpensive CD stores lining both sides of the streets. You'll also find tattoo parlors, jewelry stores, booksellers and street vendors hawking everything imaginable.

Sixth Avenue between 24th and 32nd Streets is lined with all kinds of discount specialty stores selling shoes, hats, clothing, plants, fabric and notions, gifts, watches, Army/Navy surplus items. costume jewelry and more.

All Work and
No Play

Icons of New York

There's a world of wonders to explore in this great big city of ours. Many of these marvels are free or incredibly cheap. Now that you've taken care of the nuts and bolts of living in New York— gotten settled, found a home and furnished it, opened a bank account, discovered the cheap places to buy groceries, scoped out the stores that carry the affordable clothes you like, learned how to get around town, gotten a haircut and massage, found a doctor, and shared all your frustrations with a shrink—it's time to enjoy your life. Hopefully the following will help you do that:

With more than 6,000 animals cavorting over 265 acres, the **Bronx Zoo/Wildlife Conservation Society** is the nation's largest urban zoo and one of the first in the world to showcase its animals in habitats recreated to match their native environment and terrain. Of special note is the zoo's newest attraction, Congo Gorilla Forest, a habitat for several primates, including two troops of gorillas, indigenous to the African rainforest. Although this is primarily a walking zoo, there is a train, an aerial tramway and a monorail to whisk you from one area to another. FREE ON WEDNESDAY (SUGGESTED DONATION).

Bronx River Parkway at Fordham Road, Bronx—718-367-1010, www.bronxzoo.org

Whether by foot, bicycle or skate, the trek across the **Brooklyn Bridge** provides the most awesome view of New York. Looking south you can see the Statue of Liberty, New York Harbor and the Verrazano Narrows Bridge; looking north you can see some of the network of bridges (all of which were built after the Brooklyn

Bridge) that connect Manhattan to Brooklyn and Queens. To the west are the shimmering buildings of the Financial District, and to the east, the rooftops and trees of Brooklyn spread to the horizon. The bridge itself is a thing of beauty. Sixteen years in the making and completed in 1883, its graceful gothic towers have been immortalized in paintings, film and poetry. As you stroll along the pedestrian walkway, be sure to read the plaques detailing the bridge's history and commemorating its architects and the twenty workers who died during its construction.

The **Brooklyn Heights Promenade**, which runs along the East River between Cranberry and Remsen Streets in Brooklyn Heights, provides romantic views of the sceptered isle of Manhattan, the Statue of Liberty and Ellis Island. Ever since the events of September 11, 2001, the view, sans the World Trade Center, is heartbreaking; what was once a favorite spot to ogle the Manhattan skyline has become a quiet place for reflection. To get to the Promenade, take the N, R, 2, 3, 4, or 5 subway to Court Street/ Borough Hall.

The **Cathedral of St. John the Divine**, home to the Episcopal Diocese of New York and already the world's largest cathedral, is (and will be for the foreseeable future) under construction. This very progressive church is not only a place of worship, but also a monument and memorial to famous writers, immigrants, firefighters who have lost their lives in the line of duty, victims of genocide, and those who have died from AIDS. Throughout the year, St. John offers concerts, art exhibitions, poetry readings, lectures and dance performances. ADMISSION TO THE CATHEDRAL IS ALWAYS FREE, (although donations are encouraged) and guided tours are $3.

Amsterdam Avenue and 110th Street—212-316-7540, www.stjohndivine.org

When you're in the mood to splurge, and it's well worth the money, take a **Circle Line** boat ride around Manhattan. It's a fun, relaxing way to see our famous skyline in all its glory and to get a feel for the size of the island. On a 90-degree day, this aquatic tour provides relief for apartment dwellers with a breath of fresh air. Circle Line's two- and three-hour cruises depart from Pier 83. The two-hour trip travels around lower Manhattan, while the three-hour cruise circles the island; both excursions include a close up view of the Statue of Liberty. Prices for the two-hour cruise: adults (13 and over) $21, seniors (65 and over) $17, children (3-12 years old) $10; for the three-hour cruise: adults $26, seniors $20, children $13. Operating hours vary throughout the year; call for a schedule or visit www.circleline.com. (Note: If you purchase your tickets over the web at either www.ticketweb.com or www.destination-coupons.com, adult tickets for the three-hour tour are just $21, and children's tickets are $10.)

West 42nd Street at Hudson River—212-563-3200

The Cloisters. EVERY DAY EXCEPT MONDAY IS "PAY-AS-YOU-WISH." This museum, a branch of the Metropolitan Museum of Art, is pieced together from parts of 12th and 13th century European monasteries and houses the Met's vast medieval art and architecture collection. The Cloisters' grounds and gardens is a tranquil oasis and presents spectacular views of the Hudson River, making it one of New York's favorite retreats.

Fort Tryon Park, Washington Heights—212-923-3700, www.metmuseum.org

The **Columbia University Observatory** is FREE AND OPEN TO THE PUBLIC TWO FRIDAYS PER MONTH FROM SEPTEMBER THROUGH MAY. Show up an hour after sunset and follow the signs to the roof, where you can spend two hours stargazing under the guidance of an astronomy grad or professor.

Pupin Hall, 2960 Broadway at 116th Street

Coney Island, one of the first and most flamboyant amusement parks in the country, is now a shell of its former self. Most of the rides have been abandoned or ravaged by time and fire, and the feeling of lost opulence is palpable. Still though, there is a lot to do and see here. There are several moderately priced rides, attractions and sideshows you can catch, including the 75-year-old Cyclone wooden roller coaster that continues to induce near heart attacks. For me, Coney Island's major draw is people watching along the three mile boardwalk. Nothing tops some of the colorful folks you'll see here. Make sure to check out, at least once, Coney Island's Mermaid Parade, held on the last Saturday in June. This very campy parade marches from Surf Avenue and 10th Street to Steeplechase Park, and features some of the zaniest mermaid-inspired floats and costumes ever assembled.

Coney Island is also home to the new (as of 2001) and beloved minor league baseball team, the Brooklyn Cyclones. Playing at the brand new KeySpan Park ballpark, the championship-winning Cyclones have brought baseball back to Brooklyn after a 44-year hiatus and a lot of pride back to the borough. For a complete game schedule or to purchase tickets (which are a fraction of the cost of a Mets or Yankees game), visit the Cyclones website at www.brooklyncyclones.com.

1000 Surf Avenue at West 10th Street, Brooklyn—718-372-0275, www.coneyislandusa.com

Ever since the devastating events of September 11, the **Empire State Building** has once again become the tallest skyscraper in

New York. This Art Deco masterpiece, completed in 1931, is one of the most famous structures in the world. Not only is it a landmark, an office building, and a one-time perch for King Kong, it also offers visitors spectacular vistas of our tenacious metropolis: from the observatories on the 86th and 102nd floors, you can see as far as eighty miles away in all directions. Bring out-of-towners for some oohing and ahhing or someone special for a romantic interlude. Admission to the observation decks is an affordable $12 for adults, $11 for seniors, and youths (ages 12 to 17), $7 for children (6 to 11), and free for children under 6. Due to tightened security, prepare to wait on line an hour or more, especially during peak summer months.

350 Fifth Avenue at 34th Street—212-736-3100, www.esbnyc.com

The enormous and intimidating **Federal Reserve Bank of New York**, modeled after a Florentine Renaissance palace (and just as impenetrable), processes approximately $400 million dollars a day and holds about a quarter of the world's gold bullion in vaults five stories below street level. Free one-hour tours of the gold vault, cash area and money-related exhibits are held weekdays on the half-hour between 9:30 a.m. and 2:30 p.m. To book one of these popular tours, phone at least two weeks in advance.

33 Liberty Street between Nassau and William Streets—
212-720-6130, www.ny.frb.org

Grand Central Terminal has completed a years-long cleaning/
restoration/renovation, which has returned this transportation hub to its former sparkling beaux arts glory. Be sure to take in the constellations of the zodiac that grace the ceiling on the Main Concourse, as well as the famous clock atop the information kiosk in the center of the hall. Grand Central is a fully operational train station and a des-

tination in its own right with frequent art exhibits, upscale restaurants and bars, international food purveyors, an extensive food court, trendy retail shops and occasional classical music performances. Two groups offer FREE organized tours of the terminal—Grand Central Partnership leads tours every Friday at 12:30 P.M. (meet across the street at the Philip Morris Building, 120 Park Avenue at 42nd Street—212-883-2468); and the Municipal Art Society conducts tours every Wednesday at 12:30 P.M. (meet at the central information booth on the Main Concourse—212-439-1049).

East 42nd Street between Madison and Lexington Avenues, www.grandcentralterminal.com

Reputed to have been built on the spot where the film *West Side Story* was shot, **Lincoln Center** is one of the world's largest and most famous arts complexes (see chapters on "Viewing Theater," "Viewing Dance," "Viewing Opera" and "Listening to Music"). Lincoln Center's main performing halls include Alice Tully, Avery Fisher, Metropolitan Opera House, New York State Theater, Vivian Beaumont Theater and the Mitzi E. Newhouse Theater, and can accommodate over 13,000 audience members on any given night. Lincoln Center is also home to the newly renovated New York Library of the Performing Arts (see chapter on "Books"), the Juilliard School of Music, the Fiorello La Guardia High School of the Performing Arts and the Walter Reade Movie Theater. The Center's Italianate plaza, large water fountain, reflecting pool and Damrosch Park (home to the Big Apple Circus in winter and various performances during the Lincoln Center Out-of-Doors Festival in the summer) are peaceful havens for spectators as well as anyone seeking a respite from the city.

For a "behind-the-scenes" look at the Center, you may take a tour of the Met, Avery Fisher Hall and New York State Theater: $12 for adults, $9 for seniors and students with ID, and $6 for children. Tours last about an hour and depart from the desk at the downstairs concourse level at 10:30 A.M., 12:30 P.M., 2:30 P.M. and 4:30 P.M. For more information regarding tours or to make reservations, call 212-875-5350. For a glimpse backstage of the Metropolitan Opera House, call 212-769-7020; cost is $10, $5 for students.

65th Street at Columbus Avenue—212-546-2656, www.lincolncenter.org

The **Metropolitan Museum of Art**, which is always "PAY-AS-YOU-WISH," welcomes more than five million visitors annually, and its unrivalled collections span 5,000 years of art, culture and history from every part of the world. (See chapter on "Museums" for a more in-depth description.)

1000 Fifth Avenue at 82nd Street—212-535-7710, www.metmuseum.org

Famous the world over for the stone lions posted in front of its gorgeous beaux arts façade, the **Humanities and Social Sciences Library—New York Public Library** is the main branch of the library system and one of the city's architectural gems. Be sure to check out the Rose Reading Room—about as ostentatious and awe-inspiring a main reading room as anything I've ever seen. If you find yourself at the library on a warm sunny day, sit on the steps out front for some of the best people watching in New York. FREE GUIDED TOURS ARE CONDUCTED AT 11 A.M. AND 2 P.M. MONDAY TO SATURDAY.

455 Fifth Avenue at 42nd Street—212-869-8089/212-661-7220/212-930-0855, www.nypl.org

Located in Flushing Meadows Park, the **Queens Wildlife Center** features mostly animals found in North America, a walk-through aviary and a children's petting zoo. ADULT ADMISSION IS $5, $1.25 FOR SENIORS, AND $1 FOR CHILDREN 3 TO 12.

> 53-51 111th Street, Queens—718-271-1500,
> www.wcs.org/home/zoos/queenswildlifecenter

Riverside Church, built by the Rockefeller family, is home to the world's largest carillon. The 400-foot tower, which holds 74 huge bells, also offers dramatic views of the city and across the Hudson. ADMISSION IS ALWAYS FREE.

> 490 Riverside Drive at 120th Street—212-870-6700,
> www.theriversidechurchny.org

Give yourself a free, self-guided tour of the Art Deco masterpiece **Rockefeller Center**. In nineteen buildings occupying twenty-two acres of some of the most expensive real estate in the world, Rockefeller Center has a vast array of public art on view: murals, mosaics, sculpture, metalwork and enamels, the famed Prometheus statue that soars above the ice rink, and the majestic Atlas who balances the world on his shoulders in front of the International Building. Rockefeller Center is also home to Radio City Music Hall and NBC studios. During the Christmas holidays, be sure to take in the colossal Christmas tree, which is decorated with thousands of colorful lights.

> Fifth Avenue between 48th and 51st Streets—212-632-3975,
> www.rockefellercenter.com

The four-minute ride on the **Roosevelt Island Tramway** (www.ny.com/transportation), for $1.50, gives you expansive views of Manhattan and Queens from 250 feet above the East River. Once you've arrived on Roosevelt Island, stroll along the promenade that faces the city or take the minibus tour of the island for only a quarter. For a bit of romance, board the tramway at night with your companion and (if you're discreet) a bottle of wine.

St. Patrick's Cathedral, the seat of the Catholic Diocese in New York and a supporting player in the film *Easter Parade*, is a Gothic Revival masterpiece inside and out. ADMISSION FOR WORSHIPPERS AND VISITORS ALIKE IS ALWAYS FREE; religious services daily.

> Fifth Avenue and 50th Street—212-753-2261,
> www.stpatrickscathedral.ie

The round-trip ride on the **Staten Island Ferry**, half an hour each way, is ALWAYS FREE and has breathtaking views of the city, the harbor, the Brooklyn Heights Promenade, Governor's Island, Ellis Island and the Statue of Liberty. Taking the ferry on a balmy summer night is without a doubt the most romantic (not to mention cheapest) way to woo a potential life partner. You can catch the ferry at Manhattan's southernmost tip at Battery Park.

BEST
CHEAP
DATE

> 311, www.siferry.com

The **Staten Island Zoo**, which is tiny in size but enormous in ambition, is home to a large and varied menagerie of creatures, including those found in the tropical rainforest and the African savannah. The zoo houses aquarium displays, a definitive collection of reptiles, and a farmlike setting where children may feed and pet animals and ride ponies. ENTRANCE IS A VERY AFFORDABLE $5 FOR AGES 15 AND UP, $3 FOR CHILDREN BETWEEN 3 AND 14, $4 FOR SENIORS, AND FREE FOR CHILDREN UNDER 3; WEDNESDAYS AFTER 2 P.M. IS ALWAYS "PAY-AS-YOU-WISH."

> 614 Broadway, Staten Island—718-442-3100,
> www.statenislandzoo.org

Standing one hundred fifty-one feet above a ten-story pedestal and built of three hundred sheets of copper, the **Statue of Liberty** is one of the nation's greatest landmarks and most enduring symbol of freedom. Designed by French sculptor Frederic-Auguste Bartholdi and built soon after the Civil War, the Statue of Liberty was originally a gift to commemorate the Franco-American alliance. By the end of the 19th century, however, its significance changed: seen by sea-borne immigrants making their way into the harbor toward Ellis Island, the statue came to be synonymous with immigration and the freedom these people would experience in their new homeland. To get to the Statue of Liberty, you'll need to take a ferry, which leaves from Castle Clinton in Battery Park. Although access to the statue has been restricted to visitors since September 11, you can still get a close-up view of Lady Liberty by disembarking the ferry at Liberty Island. ADMISSION TO THE ISLAND IS FREE, BUT THERE IS A $10 CHARGE FOR THE FERRY ($8 FOR SENIORS, $4 FOR AGES 4 TO 12, FREE TO TOTS UNDER 4). The ferry ride is an experience in itself. You get a real sense of the awe immigrants must have felt making their historic passage through New York Harbor en route to their new homeland. Purchase tickets for the Statue of Liberty ferry at Castle Clinton or across Battery Park from the South Ferry terminal. Ferries run every 30 minutes between 9:00 A.M. and 5 P.M. on weekdays and every 20 minutes between 8:30 A.M. and 4:10 P.M. on weekends; there are extended hours in the summer.

212-363-3200, www.nps.gov/stli

Take a Hike

The best and least expensive way to see New York's many diverse and interesting neighborhoods is to walk. From Inwood to Battery Park, Harlem, the Lower East Side, Upper West Side, Times Square and the Theater District, the West Village, Soho, Tribeca, Little Italy, Chinatown, Washington Heights, Financial District, Murray Hill, Turtle Bay, Upper East Side and Morningside Heights on Manhattan to the Bronx, Brooklyn, Staten Island, and Queens, there is an abundance of places to discover. Whether you wander haphazardly, meander with a guidebook in hand or take a walking tour, there is no better way for you to become familiar with this place you now call home.

Of the infinite number of New York City guidebooks out there, my favorite is **Frommer's Memorable Walks in New York** (4th Edition), by Reid Bramblett. This inexpensive guide lists at $12.99 (and $10.39 on Amazon) and offers ten great walking tours that are educational and entertaining through the city's most colorful neighborhoods.

If you'd like some expert guidance while navigating through Gotham, there are several outfits that offer a variety of low-priced **walking tours** covering almost every inch of the city. Although many of these excursions attract tourists, the majority are devised for New Yorkers, natives and transplants who wish to have a more penetrating sense of the city's history and culture. Enthusiastic professionals who have an encyclopedic knowledge and obsessive love of the neighborhoods they cover usually conduct these enlightening tours, and they take joy in imparting that love and knowledge to their listeners. For a complete listing of the current week's walking tours, be sure to check out either the "Weekend Fine Arts/Leisure" section of the Friday edition of *The New York Times* or the "Around Town" section of *Time Out New York*.

Adventure on a Shoe String, at just $5 per person, is the least expensive walking tour in the city. This company has a large and always changing selection of tours led by fun, informative Manhattanphiles.

300 West 53rd Street—212-265-2663

Big Onion Walking Tours, founded and guided by Columbia grad students, offers informative visits into many of New York's historic areas and ethnic neighborhoods. Most tours are $12, $10 for students and seniors.

212-439-1090, www.bigonion.com

Brooklyn Center for the Urban Environment offers several inexpensive tours throughout the year, concentrating on the architecture and neighborhoods of Brooklyn.

Tennis House, Prospect Park, Brooklyn—718-788-8500, www.bcue.org

Joyce Gold History Tours of New York features two- to three-hour weekend walking excursions covering the history, culture, architecture and evolution of New York's liveliest neighborhoods. Joyce Gold, a history professor at NYU, conducts these jaunts with themes ranging from Diplomatic New York to Rockefeller New York, Religious Manhattan, Colonial New

York, Broadway Theatrical, Ethnic New York, A Day in Brooklyn and Noshing Manhattan. Tours are $12 each.

141 West 17th Street—212-242-5762, www.nyctours.com

I'll Take Manhattan Tours conducts weekend trips through many of the city's interesting and historic neighborhoods, including Tribeca, Greenwich Village, Soho, Millionaire's Mile, Chinatown, Gramercy Park, Lower East Side and the Metropolitan Museum of Art Historic District. All tours are $12 and depart at 1 P.M.

732-270-5277, www.lowereastsideny.com

The Lower East Side Business Improvement District will send you a free guide to the Historic Orchard Street Shopping District, which not only contains an extensive listing of the area's merchants, but also has a map and walking tour detailing the Lower East Side's historic immigrant past. Every Sunday at 11 A.M. from April through December, an escort from the Lower East Side Business Improvement District conducts a free walking tour of the area (meet at Katz's Deli, corner of East Houston and Ludlow Streets).

261 Broome Street—212-226-9010, www.lowereastsideny.com

New York City Cultural Walking Tours highlights the architecture, culture and history of Manhattan's varied neighborhoods. They also offer theme walks covering such topics as gargoyles, Italian, Irish and Jewish history and public art. Tours are $10.

212-979-2388, www.nycwalk.com

Radical Walking Tours of New York offers fifteen different excursions, all led by political activist Bruce Kayton, to many of the sites of the city's revolutionary and political movements. Tours last about three hours and cost $10.

539 53rd Street, Brooklyn—718-492-0069,
www.he.net/~radtours

Street Smarts N.Y. leads entertaining themed weekend hikes to some of New York's most tony neighborhoods, as well as areas of "ill repute." All tours are $10.

212-969-8262, www.streetsmartsny.com

Somewhere That's Green

Contrary to the cliché that New York is nothing but a series of glass and concrete canyons, there are several extraordinarily beautiful parks, gardens and serene swaths of green scattered throughout the five boroughs. Each is a refuge from the hassle of city life. With beauty aplenty and myriad athletic and cultural activities, the city's parks and gardens contribute much to the mental and physical health of all New Yorkers.

The following is only a sampling of the city's many wonderful green spaces. For more information and a complete directory of city parks, call the New York Parks Department or visit their website at www.nyc.gov/parks.

Located at the southern tip of Manhattan on the Hudson River and built on landfill from the construction of the World Trade Center, **Battery Park** (www.batteryparkcity.org) offers exquisite views of the Statue of Liberty, Ellis and Governors Islands and New York Harbor. City folk come to picnic, roller blade, bicycle, jog, play sports, attend the many music and dance performances, gawk at the yachts, visit the Museum of Jewish Heritage, and watch the sunset. Although set among office and apartment buildings, Battery Park is one of the most tranquil places in Manhattan.

Open March to October, the **Brooklyn Botanic Garden** features over fifty acres of plants and flowers in specialized gardens. The Cranford Rose Garden is home to over a hundred varieties of roses and the Japanese Garden has several cherry trees (a "must see" in May when they are in bloom), weeping willows and one of the world's largest collections of bonsai trees. Of special interest is

the Shakespeare Garden, which grows eighty plus plants that the
Bard names in his works. FREE ALL DAY ON TUESDAY AND ON SAT-
URDAY FROM 10 A.M. TO NOON.

900 Washington Avenue between Eastern Parkway and
Empire Boulevard, Prospect Heights, Brooklyn—718-623-7200,
www.bbg.org

Bryant Park, located behind the main branch of the New York
Public Library and built right above some of the library's stacks, is
a sanctuary. On warm days, the park is an ideal place to kick off
your shoes, sit on the grass and watch the world go by. In the summer, you can catch a free concert or cinema classic on the Great
Lawn (see chapters on "Viewing Film" and "Listening To Music").

Sixth Avenue at 42nd Street—www.bryantpark.org

Created in 1858 by Frederick Law Olmstead and Calvert Vaux,
Central Park encompasses over 840 graceful acres in the very
center of Manhattan. It was built over a desolate area of marshy
swamps, garbage dumps and shantytowns inhabited by the city's
poorest residents, and today provides a "green" escape from the
hustle and bustle of this hectic city. The park's carnival-like atmosphere on weekends in the spring, summer and fall makes it the favorite retreat of thousands of New Yorkers. There are innumerable
free and inexpensive things to do here: jog, skate or cycle around
the park's 6.5 mile loop; hear free concerts at the Central Park
Summerstage Bandshell or on the Great Lawn; play softball, foot-
ball, tennis, soccer or basketball at fields or courts located throughout the park; see free Shakespeare performances at the outdoor
Delacorte Theatre; Zen out at the tranquil Strawberry Fields; run,
power-walk or saunter around the reservoir; commandeer mini-
sailboats at the Conservatory Water; fish in the Harlem Meer; take
a carousel ride; play with the kids in any one of several play-

grounds; ice skate at the Wollman or Lasker rinks in winter; rent a rowboat at the Loeb Boathouse; dine at Tavern on the Green; soak up some rays in the Sheep Meadow; walk the dog or commune with nature just about anywhere. If you'd like to know more about the park's history, flora, fauna or the stories behind its many statues, there are several free walking tours year-round that are overseen by the Central Park Conservancy.

From 59th Street to 110th Street between Fifth Avenue and Central Park West—212-360-2726, www.centralparknyc.org

Want to escape the heat but can't face the schlep to the beach? Then get yourself over to the two **Christopher Street Piers**. These narrow strips of grass that jut deep into the Hudson River (they are the result of the ongoing Hudson River Park redevelopment and a perfect example of the good that public works projects do) provide an oasis from the heat and madness of a New York City summer day. If you like to people watch, especially the hunky and buff male variety (a majority of those who come to the piers are gay boys from the Village and neighboring Chelsea), you'll have a field day. You'll encounter men, women and children of all stripes and persuasions who have come to the piers for the respite they provide and for their festive atmosphere. In fact, once on the piers you'll feel as if you've been invited to a large outdoor party. It can seem as if everyone has left their attitudes and prejudices across West Street and have come here to relax, visit with friends, meet new people and have a good time. The piers have bathrooms, food vendors, a playground for the kids, picnic tables and chairs, and lots of bike racks.

Christopher Street and West Street

Flushing Meadows-Corona Park in Queens, home to the 1939 and 1964 World's Fairs, has sculpted gardens, lots of rambling lawn, an 18-hole pitch 'n' putt golf course, and a lake where you may rent paddle and row boats. The park houses a few remnants of the '64 World's Fair, like the Unisphere, the New York Hall of Science and the New York State Pavilion. After Shea Stadium, the park's second most popular attraction is the Queens Museum of Art; here you may view a scale model of the city that is constantly added to and altered to reflect New York's ever-changing cityscape (see chapter on "Museums"). Flushing Meadows-Corona Park is also home to the Queens Science Museum, Queens Zoo and the U.S. Tennis Association National Tennis Center.

Located on the highest natural point in Manhattan, **Fort Tryon Park** (212-408-0100/212-795-1388) in Washington Heights has resplendent views of the Hudson River and the Palisades of New Jersey. Created by Frederick Law Olmsted (who also designed Central and Prospect Parks), Fort Tryon Park is home to the Cloisters (see the "Museums" and "Icons of New York" chapters) with miles of footpaths that wind through natural stone terraces and spectacular floral gardens.

Presently under construction, **Hudson River Park** (www.hudsonriverpark.org) will eventually stretch almost the entire length of the West Side, connecting the existing Battery and Riverside Parks. When completed, a lawn, together with flower and plant beds will parallel the expanse of the West Side Highway, incorporating most of the abandoned piers into its design. Also planned, believe it or not, are sand beaches. Pedestrian and bike/skate paths are already finished, allowing you to go from the Staten Island Ferry to the George Washington Bridge without ever leaving these paths.

Several ghosts of "Old New York" seem to haunt **Madison Square Park**, which is more famous for what it was than what it is. Originally a public cemetery, it was in Madison Square Park that a game called "New York Ball," the precursor to baseball, was played. The torch held aloft by the Statue of Liberty was displayed here while funds were being raised to construct her pedestal. P.T. Barnum's Hippodrome stood here, as did the original Madison Square Garden. And it was here on the night of June 25, 1906, that Harry Thaw, the enraged husband of Evelyn ("the girl on the velvet swing") Nesbitt, murdered Stanford White, the father of New York's beaux arts architecture, for ravishing his bride. Today, the atmosphere of the park is more low-key and serene than in its historic past. The lush green lawn and towering trees provide a perfect setting for reading, relaxing or meditating. After a long reconstruction and the addition of some fanciful new public art, Madison Square Park is now more appealing than ever.

23rd Street to 26th Street between Madison and Fifth Avenues—
www.madisonsquarepark.org

The **New York Botanical Garden**, across the street from the Bronx Zoo, is considered one of the world's best horticultural preserves. Set in two hundred fifty vibrantly colorful acres, the New York Botanical Gardens features twenty-eight specialty gardens and plant collections, including the Peggy Rockefeller Rose Garden, a forty-acre uncut hemlock forest, the T.H. Everett rock garden and waterfall, the Enid A. Haupt Conservatory (a glass greenhouse reminiscent of London's Crystal Palace), and the "Please Touch" Everett Children's Adventure Garden. The Garden offers several money saving passes with FREE GROUNDS ADMISSIONS ALL DAY WEDNESDAY, AND SATURDAYS FROM 10 A.M. TO 12 P.M. Metro-North trains depart from Grand Central Terminal and stop at the Botanical Gardens throughout the day. By subway, take the B or D train to Bedford Park and then walk east eight blocks.

200th Street at Kazimiroff Boulevard, Bronx—718-817-8700,
www.nybg.org

Designed by Frederick Law Olmsted and Calvert Vaux (the architects who created Central Park), **Prospect Park** is a green retreat amassing five hundred twenty-six acres in the middle of Brooklyn. Although covering less real estate than Central Park, Prospect Park is no less ambitious in its offerings. Here you may rent paddle boats, stroll through a vast network of footpaths, ride the Carousel (built in 1912 and accompanied by a Wurlitzer calliope) for just 50¢, picnic, bird watch, jog, cycle, ride horses that may be rented at the Kensington Stables, and in-line skate. Season-specific park activities include ice-skating at Wollman rink in winter, musical concerts, and children's theater and storytelling at the Prospect Park Bandshell in the summer (see chapters "Listening to Music" and "Viewing Dance"). You may also take a free tour of the Park's two historic homes, Litchfield Villa (built in the 1800s) and Lefferts Homestead, a preserved Dutch farmhouse built in the 1700s, which serves as the Park's headquarters and is home to the Children's Historic House Museum.

718-965-8951, www.prospectpark.org

Smaller but no less dramatic than its cousin in the Bronx, the **Queens Botanical Garden** is a feast for the visual and olfactory senses. The Botanical Garden features a rose garden with 5,000 beautiful bushes, an arboretum, several specialty gardens, and for those New Yorkers who have a backyard (or a balcony), a home compost demonstration. The Queens Garden is open April to October and is ALWAYS FREE.

Flushing Meadows-Corona Park—718-886-3800, www.queensbotanical.org

Riverside Park is a huge playground for young and old alike. Everywhere you look there are sunbathers, cyclists, rollerbladers, joggers, strollers, chess players, children romping on swing sets, al fresco diners, park bench jockeys and frazzled mothers (or are they nannies?) pushing prams. If you'd like to play an organized sport, there are tennis/basketball/handball/volleyball courts and baseball and soccer fields aplenty. For those with a yen for some aesthetic stimulus, there are lots of sculptures to gaze on, flowers to adore and views across the Hudson to glory in.

From 72nd to 125th Streets along the Hudson River—
212-408-0264

Once considered unsavory and unsafe, **Union Square Park** had a facelift a decade or so ago and has become a favorite gathering spot for local residents and workers. The park now pulses with activity—hot-dogging rollerbladers and skateboarders dominate the south end of the park and the north end features a wonderful year-round farmer's market (see chapter on "Provisions"). In between, stallvendors sell books, CDs and art prints at reasonable prices; street musicians strum guitars and croon to no one in particular; and bench-perchers watch the parade of life pass by. In summer, a large outdoor bar that resembles a German beer garden caters to a crowd of mostly models, trendoids and model/trendoid wannabes.

Between Broadway and Park Avenue South, and 14th and 17th Streets—www.unionsquarenyc.org

Before becoming a park, **Washington Square** had many incarnations. Originally home to Native Americans, by the mid-1600s it had become an enclave for freed slaves. By the late 1700s, it became an anonymous burial ground for the area's poor (it is believed there are 15,000 bodies buried here), and during the Revolutionary War, a place for public executions. It was not until the early 19th century that it became a park and the center of life in Greenwich Village. Today, Washington Square Park still hums with activity: musicians and street performers vie for loose change, NYU students catch a few rays between classes, not-so-discreet marijuana entrepreneurs ply their wares, hard-core chess hustlers focus intently on their games, locals trade gossip as they walk their dogs, and children scamper everywhere.

Between 4th Street and Waverly Place and Fifth Avenue and MacDougal Street

The Bronx estate **Wave Hill**, once home to such luminaries as Teddy Roosevelt, Mark Twain, Arturo Toscanini and William Thackeray, has one of the city's most beautiful European gardens. Overlooking the Hudson River and Bronx Palisades, Wave Hill's internationally acclaimed gardens and horticultural collection (over 3,200 seasonal plants and flowers in formal settings and greenhouses) provide a serene and idyllic landscape in which to commune with nature. Besides the bountiful flora, Wave Hill has educational programs such as garden basics, and tours, talks, workshops, cooking demonstrations and lectures. Other programs include poetry readings, art exhibitions and music concerts (see "Listening to Music" chapter). OPEN YEAR-ROUND, WAVE HILL IS FREE NOVEMBER 25 TO MARCH 14, AS WELL AS EVERY TUESDAY AND SATURDAY MORNING UNTIL NOON.

675 West 252nd Street, Riverdale—718-549-3200, www.wavehill.org

Museums

New York is undoubtedly the greatest museum city in the world. The diversity and magnitude of the collections here is unrivalled anywhere and enriches the cultural and social lives of all New Yorkers. The best part about our museums is that we have free or inexpensive access to almost all of them. Although most of the major museums charge an admission fee, many suspend their usual fees at some point during the week. The following is a list of New York museums that have free, "Suggested" or "Pay-As-You-Wish" admissions. (Note: There are several museums I'm omitting because they don't meet my free or almost free criteria.)

American Museum of Natural History/Hayden Planetarium
ADMISSION IS "SUGGESTED"; FREE SUNDAY TO THURSDAY FROM 4:45 P.M. TO 5:45 P.M., AND FRIDAY AND SATURDAY FROM 7:45 P.M. TO 8:45 P.M. Every time I visit this museum I think of Holden Caulfield's field trip to the Museum of Natural History in J.D. Salinger's *The Catcher in the Rye*. So much of the museum is still exactly as Salinger described it in his 1951 novel. The old-fashioned dioramas of the Akeley Hall of African Mammals make me feel as though I've suddenly been transported back to the museum of the 50s. However, other parts of the museum (the newly renovated Hall of Ocean Life and Hayden Planetarium, the Rose Center for Earth and Space and the dinosaur halls on the top floor) are so new and modern that they seem to have opened only yesterday. Be sure not to miss the Hall of Human Biology and Evolution, which displays the mysteries of human development and includes bones and fragments of "Lucy," who is believed to be the oldest early human. Other must-sees are the Morgan Hall of Gems,

which glitters with diamonds, emeralds and rubies and contains the Star of India Sapphire, the world's largest; and the Wallace Wing, which contains the world's largest assembly of fossilized mammals. The museum also houses an Imax movie theater and a stunning light and sound show (both for an additional charge).

79th Street and Central Park West—212-769-5000, www.amnh.org

The **American Numismatic Society** houses a vast collection of coins and paper money from the last 26 centuries. FREE.

140 William Street—212-234-3130, www.amnumsoc.org

The Asia Society FREE FRIDAYS 2 P.M. TO 6 P.M. The Asia Society presents exhibitions of Asian art including Asian-American works. Free or inexpensive symposia, musical performances, film screenings and a "Meet the Author" series are also scheduled here throughout the year.

725 Park Avenue at 70th Street—212-288-6400, www.asiasociety.org

Audubon Terrace Museum Group ALWAYS FREE. Once part of the Audubon estate and game preserve, it now houses two museums and societies:

613 West 155th Street between Broadway and Riverside Drive

The **Hispanic Society of America** is dedicated to the arts and culture of Spain and Portugal and includes works by El Greco, Velazquez and Goya. The Society also contains ceramics, mosaics, an ornate Spanish Renaissance court, religious artifacts and a 100,000-volume research library.

212-926-2234, www.hispanicsociety.org

The **American Academy of Arts and Letters** honors American writers, composers, painters, sculptors and architects. Although it is not actually a museum, the Academy occasionally sponsors free public exhibitions of works drawn from its permanent collection.

212-368-5900, www.nyc-arts.org/nyc-arts/name/
name_by_borough/manhattan/upper/artsltrs.html)

Bronx Museum of the Arts ALWAYS "PAY-AS-YOU-WISH" AND FREE ALL DAY WEDNESDAY. This small museum of contemporary art, located in the Bronx Courthouse, showcases its permanent collection of established artists as well as exhibitions by emerging Bronx artists.

1040 Grand Concourse at 165th Street, Bronx—718-681-6000, www.bxma.org

The **Brooklyn Museum of Art** ALWAYS "PAY-AS-YOU-WISH" AND FREE ON THE FIRST SATURDAY OF EVERY MONTH FROM 5 P.M. TO 11 P.M. (THE MUSEUM'S FREE SATURDAYS OFFERS "FABULOUS" FREE ENTERTAINMENT AS WELL.) The Brooklyn Museum's million plus permanent collection contains significant Asian, African, Oceanic and New World works, as well as American painting, sculpture and decorative art. Notable are the museum's extensive ancient Egyptian collection and contemporary art galleries, with works by Louise Nevelson, Larry Rivers and Leon Polk Smith, among many others. The museum itself, originally designed by the beaux arts masters McKim, Mead and White in 1897, has had a recent facelift, making it, as a *New York Times* review said, "one of the most attractive public spaces to be found anywhere in town." Especially striking is the new entrance pavilion with its cantilevered glass roof that resembles a cascade, and amphitheater-like seating out front that faces a magnificent fountain of dancing waters.

200 Eastern Parkway, Brooklyn—718-638-5000, www.brooklynart.org

Castle Clinton National Monument FREE. Though Castle Clinton has been many things since its incarnation in 1808, it has never been a real castle. Built originally as a sandstone fort to defend New York Harbor against the British, by 1824 it had become a setting for concerts and other performances. Since then, it has been an immigration center (the precursor to Ellis Island), and home to the New York City Aquarium until 1941. Today, this national monument is a launching point for the ferries to Ellis Island and the Statue of Liberty and once again a performance space for live music and dance. Housed in the Castle is a small museum depicting the changing history of the fort. Open daily from 8:30 A.M. to 5 P.M.

Battery Park—212-344-7220, www.nps.gov/cacl

The Cloisters EVERY DAY EXCEPT MONDAY IS "PAY-AS-YOU-WISH." This museum, a branch of the Metropolitan Museum of Art, is a tranquil oasis in Washington Heights. Pieced together from parts of 12th and 13th century European monasteries, it houses the Met's vast medieval art and architecture collection. Not to be missed are the world-famous Unicorn Tapestries and the Treasury, which contains incredibly delicate illuminated manuscripts and miniature carvings. The Cloisters offers spectacular views of the Hudson River, making it one of New York's favorite retreats on hot summer days and an ideal place to bring a date or loved one on a cool, clear spring evening.

Fort Tryon Park, Washington Heights—212-923-3700, www.metmuseum.org

Coney Island Museum 99¢. This museum exhibits remnants of old rides along with pictures, antiques and memorabilia chronicling Coney Island's happier, more carefree days. The view out of the Museum's windows is also a lot of fun, as they look directly onto Coney Island's landmark rides like the Cyclone roller coaster, the WonderWheel and the Parachute Jump.

Astroland Amusement Park, 1208 Surf Avenue at West 12th Street, Brooklyn—718-372-5159, www.coneyisland.com/museum

Dahesh Museum of Art FREE FROM 6 P.M. TO 9 P.M. THE FIRST THURSDAY OF EACH MONTH. This is the only museum in the U.S. dedicated to the collection, preservation, exhibition and interpretation of European academic art of the 19th and 20th centuries. The collection includes Orientalism, landscapes, and pastoral scenes by artists whose work you rarely, if ever, see in any other collections.

580 Madison Avenue at 57th Street—212-759-0606, www.daheshmuseum.org

Ellis Island Immigration Museum FREE. This museum pays tribute to the 12 million immigrants who passed through the island on their way to resettling in America. The personal artifacts, photos, oral histories and memorabilia on exhibit here are a moving reminder of the struggles our forebears endured to create a new, more prosperous life for themselves on these shores. At the end of your tour of the island, be sure to check the database of the American Family Immigration History Center to search for names of your ancestors. (Note: Although admission is free, for adults there is a $10 fee for the ferry that transports you to the island; $8 for seniors; $4 for ages 4 to 12; free to tots under 4.

Ellis Island—212-363-3200, www.ellisisland.org

El Museo del Barrio FREE THURSDAYS FROM 4 P.M. TO 8 P.M. El

Museo del Barrio features the art and culture of Puerto Rico, the Caribbean and Latin America through its extensive collections and varied exhibitions of video, painting, sculpture, photography, theater and film.

1230 Fifth Avenue at 104th Street—212-831-7272, www.elmuseo.org

Federal Hall National Memorial FREE. Housed in a Greek Revival style building that was originally a Customs House, Federal Hall is home to exhibits on both customs collections (revenues collected from imports) and a history of the site on which the Customs House was built. It was here that George Washington gave his inaugural address in 1789. (Upon your arrival to Federal Hall, you'll be met out front by a statue of Washington, which faces the New York Stock Exchange across the street.) It was also here that Congress first met and drafted the Bill of Rights and passed the Northwest Ordinance, allowing for the admission of new states.

26 Wall Street—212-825-6888, www.nps.gov/feha

Forbes Magazine Galleries ALWAYS FREE TUESDAY TO SATURDAY, 10 A.M. TO 4 P.M. The Forbes Galleries collection contains jewelry, fine art, fully decorated miniature rooms, an array of antique toy boats and toy soldiers, Presidential and important American historical papers, antique trophies and several original versions of the game Monopoly.

62 Fifth Avenue at 12th Street—212-206-5548

Freakatorium "PAY-AS-YOU-WISH." Set in a storefront on the Lower East Side, this museum is filled with sideshow memorabilia. Collected and curated by sword swallower and magician, Johnny Fox, the 1,000 plus artifacts and curiosities here are, well. . .freaky! (Where else can you see Sammy Davis, Jr.'s glass eye, the bones of St. Matthew, and Frik and Frak the two-headed turtle?)

This place is a definite change of pace from the Metropolitan and Natural History Museums.

57 Clinton Street between Rivington and Stanton Streets— 212-375-0475, www.freakatorium.com

Garibaldi-Meucci Museum "PAY-AS-YOU-WISH." This 1840s Gothic Revival home is a memorial to the lives and works of inventor Antonio Meucci and Italian patriot Giuseppe Garibaldi, both of whom lived here. The Museum also collects, preserves and interprets artifacts and ephemera detailing the history of the Italian community in New York.

420 Tompkins Avenue, Staten Island—718-442-1608

Grant's Tomb National Monument FREE. At this landmark in Riverside Park on the Upper West Side, you can actually find out who is buried in the tomb! There is an exhibit focusing on Ulysses S. Grant's very interesting life and a history of the Civil War.

Located at 122nd Street and Riverside Drive—212-666-1640, www.nps.gov/gegr

Solomon R. Guggenheim Museum Uptown "PAY-AS-YOU-WISH" ON FRIDAYS FROM 6 P.M TO 8 P.M. Designed by Frank Lloyd Wright and completed in 1959, the Guggenheim Museum houses a permanent collection of modern art, which ranges from Impressionism to contemporary art, including installations and photography. Throughout the year, the Guggenheim also sponsors several exhibits of modern and contemporary artists.

1071 Fifth Avenue at 89th Street—212-423-3500, www.guggenheim.org

Hall of Fame for Great Americans FREE. Designed by Stanford

White to pay homage to the Pantheon in Rome, this neglected, open-air limestone terrace is situated on the highest natural point in the Bronx. The Hall features over one hundred bronze busts of exceptional American scientists, writers, scholars, educators, military personnel and politicians; the National Sculpture Society once called this the finest collection of its kind in America.

City University of New York, 181st Street and Martin Luther King, Jr. Boulevard, Bronx—718-289-5100, www.bcc.cuny.edu/HallofFame

Harbor Defense Museum of Fort Hamilton FREE. The Harbor Defense Museum's raison d'être is to showcase the importance of the U.S. Army to the New York area. On exhibit are weapons, uniforms, models, dioramas and much more that trace the history of the Army's presence here in New York.

Fort Hamilton Military Community, Building 230, Brooklyn—718-630-4349, www.harbordefensemuseum.com

International Center of Photography FREE FRIDAYS FROM 5 P.M. TO 8 P.M. The ICP is the city's only museum devoted exclusively to photography and is home to several traveling exhibitions throughout the year.

1133 Avenue of the Americas at 43rd Street—212-857-0000, www.icp.org

The Jewish Museum EVERY THURSDAY FROM 5 P.M. TO 8 P.M. IS "PAY-AS-YOU-WISH." Centuries of art from the biblical days to the present illuminate the scope and diversity of Jewish culture and history at the Jewish Museum. Unique interactive displays offer varied perspectives on the Jewish experience: in the Audio Café, visitors can sit in a pre-war era European café and listen to recorded voices speaking about the issues of the day; elsewhere, modern rabbis offer differing views on Talmudic questions via computer touch screens.

1109 Fifth Avenue at 92nd Street—212-423-3200,
www.thejewishmuseum.org

Library for the Performing Arts FREE. Besides being a phenomenal research facility, the Performing Arts Library also hosts frequent exhibits on the lives and work of distinguished actors, choreographers, directors, composers, designers, playwrights, singers, dancers and musicians.

Lincoln Center, 111 Amsterdam Avenue at 66th Street—
212-870-1630, www.nypl.org/research/lpa

Metropolitan Museum of Art EVERY DAY EXCEPT MONDAY IS "PAY-AS-YOU-WISH"—and they really mean it. The Met welcomes more than five million visitors annually, and its unrivalled collections span 5,000 years of art, culture and history from every part of the world. The **BEST BARGAIN** American Wing of the Museum contains the most comprehensive collection of American paintings, sculpture and decorative arts in the world, and the Egyptian and Islamic collections are considered to be among the finest outside their homelands. The Florence and Herbert Irving Galleries for the Arts of South and Southeast Asia contain 1,300 works from India to Indonesia created between the third millennium B.C. and the early 19th century. My favorite part of the museum, the 19th Century European Paintings and Sculpture Galleries, houses the Met's superlative collection of Impressionist paintings. Be sure to check out the mummies and sarcophagi in the Egyptian Galleries, as well as the Temple of Dendur, an ancient temple that the Met rescued from weather, flooding and neglect and moved intact from its original site in Egypt. The Costume Institute, located on the ground floor of the museum, houses tens of thousands of costumes and accessories from the world over, from the 17th century to the present, and offers rotating exhibits. On summer days, the Gerald and Iris B. Cantor Roof Sculpture Garden is a popular place for museumgoers to sunbathe while taking in the art and the breathtaking views of Central Park and the Manhattan skyline. The Met's extensive FREE CONCERT AND LECTURE SERIES (212-570-3949) makes it possible for New Yorkers to "hear great art" throughout the year.

Fifth Avenue and 82nd Street—www.metmuseum.org

Municipal Art Society FREE. Housed in a gorgeous historic building behind St. Patrick's Cathedral, the Society presents exhibitions on urban design, architecture and public art.

457 Madison Avenue between 50th and 51st Street—212-935-3960, www.mas.org

Museum for African Art FREE ON SUNDAYS AFTER 2 P.M. Dedicated to the presentation of African art and culture, the Museum for African Art sponsors two major exhibitions yearly, as well as several smaller shows, each based on a unifying theme. The Museum's collections span many centuries, from ancient to contemporary, and include works by both African and African-American artists.

36-01 43rd Avenue at 36th Street, 3rd Floor, Long Island City, Queens—718-784-7700, www.africanart.org

Museum of American Financial History FREE EXCEPT SUNDAYS AND MONDAYS. An affiliate of the Smithsonian Institution, the Museum of American Financial History was established to extol the American entrepreneurial spirit and democratic free market. Through its exhibitions, the Museum presents the history of Wall Street and the achievements of American businessmen and women, from Alexander Hamilton and J.P. Morgan to present-day dot-com capitalists.

28 Broadway at Exchange Place—212-908-4110, www.financialhistory.org

Museum of American Folk Art FREE ON FRIDAYS FROM 5:30 TO 7:30 P.M. This museum exhibits a wide range of American folk art, from pottery to quilts, carved wood and toys. Periodically, the museum hosts free lectures, demonstrations and performances.

45 West 53rd Street—212-265-1040, www.folkartmuseum.org

Museum of Arts and Design "PAY-AS-YOU-WISH" THURSDAYS FROM 6 P.M. TO 8 P.M. This is the leading art museum for 20th century crafts in glass, metal, fiber, wood and clay. There are large temporary exhibitions that change every three months and smaller shows exhibiting works from the permanent collection.

40 West 53rd Street—212-956-3535, www.americancraftmuseum.org

Museum of Chinese in the Americas "PAY-AS-YOU-WISH." Set in the heart of Chinatown, MoCA traces the complex and diverse history and culture of Chinese in the Western Hemisphere. This small museum's extensive collection of primary resource material on the Chinese American experience includes oral histories, photographs, documents, personal and organizational records, sound recordings, textiles, artifacts, and a library with over 2,000 volumes. The "Mapping Our Heritage" kiosk invites visitors to click on a computerized map of Chinatown for information about the area's historic buildings and their occupants. The Museum also offers walking tours, lectures, book readings, performances and arts workshops.

70 Mulberry Street at Bayard Street, 2nd Floor—212-619-4785, www.moca-nyc.org

Museum of the City of New York EVERY DAY EXCEPT MONDAY IS "PAY-AS-YOU-WISH." All of the objects housed in the Museum of the City of New York relate to the history and traditions of New York City. A toy gallery populated with antique dolls and doll-houses, period rooms from the late 17th to early 20th centuries, and a display of antique fire engines are always on display. The Museum's ongoing show, "Broadway! 125 Years of Musical Theatre," surveys the Great White Way's history through costumes, set models and designs, posters, programs and photographs.

> 1220 Fifth Avenue at 103rd Street—212-534-1672, www.mcny.org

Museum at F.I.T. FREE. This museum presents fun, eclectic exhibits on clothing, costumes and textiles. At the end of each academic year, the Museum showcases the work of its recent graduates.

> Fashion Institute of Technology Campus, Seventh Avenue at
> 27th Street—212-217-7999, www.fitnyc.suny.edu/museum

Museum of Modern Art "PAY-AS-YOU-WISH" ON FRIDAYS FROM 4:00 TO 7:45 P.M. The Museum of Modern Art, which recently reopened after a two-year, $858 million renovation and expansion which nearly doubled its capacity, contains more than 100,000 paintings, drawings, sculptures, works on paper, photographs, films, videos and objects, and houses an unrivalled permanent collection of 20th century art. Monet's "Water Lilies" and the Abby Aldrich Rockefeller Sculpture Garden (a great place to bring a sack lunch and dine al fresco in the spring, summer and fall) are two of MOMA's many highlights.

> 11 West 53rd Street between Fifth and Sixth Avenues—
> 212-708-9400, www.moma.org

National Academy of Design Museum FREE ON FRIDAYS FROM 5 P.M. TO 6 P.M. In 1825, the National Academy of Design was founded to "promote the fine arts through exhibition and instruction." To fulfill its charter, the Academy maintains a permanent collection of some of America's most distinguished design artists, and hosts major exhibitions throughout the year.

1083 Fifth Avenue between 89th and 90th Streets—212-369-4880, www.nationalacademy.org

National Lighthouse Museum "PAY-AS-YOU-WISH"—RESERVATIONS REQUIRED. The 19th century building that houses this museum was originally the United States Lighthouse Depot, the country's main center for the technological development and manufacture of lighthouses. The Museum explores the science and lore of lighthouses.

1 Lighthouse Plaza, St. George, Staten Island—718-556-1681, www.lighthousemuseum.org

National Museum and Archive of Lesbian and Gay History FREE. This museum presents works by lesbian, gay, bisexual and transgendered artists throughout the year. The Archive is open Thursdays from 6 P.M. to 8:30 P.M., or by appointment. Call for exhibit dates.

The Lesbian and Gay Community Services Center, 208 West 13th Street between Seventh and Eighth Avenues— 212-620-7310, www.gaycenter.org

National Museum of the American Indian FREE DAILY 10 A.M. TO 5 P.M., THURSDAYS UNTIL 8 P.M. Housed in the beautiful beaux arts-style 1907 Alexander Hamilton Customs House, the Museum exhibits the finest pieces of the Smithsonian Institution's immense collection of Native American artifacts. The museum also sponsors many public programs including music and dance presentations, films and seminars that explore the lives of the Native American people.

One Bowling Green—212-514-3700, www.americanindian.si.edu

Newhouse Center for Contemporary Art "Pay-As-You-Wish." The Newhouse Center is the main exhibition space at Staten Island's best known art and performance site, the eighty-three-acre Snug Harbor Cultural Center. The Center features exhibitions of contemporary artists and occasionally shows works owned by the Staten Island Institute of Arts and Sciences.

Snug Harbor Cultural Center, 1000 Richmond Terrace at Snug Harbor Road, Staten Island—718-448-2500, ext. 260, www.snug-harbor.org

New Museum of Contemporary Art exhibits the very latest in contemporary art. Half price admission on Thursdays from 6 p.m. to 8 p.m. Not one to shrink from controversy, the Museum, which exhibits the very latest in contemporary art, presents shows that are often gritty, cutting-edge and can sometimes even "frighten the horses." In spite of protests and Cardinal O'Connor's condemnation, it was the New Museum that exhibited André Serano's photographs of bodies in a morgue and a crucifix in a vial of urine. If you want to know what is happening in contemporary art *right now,* this is the place to go.

583 Broadway between Houston and Prince Streets—212-219-1222, www.newmuseum.org

New York City Fire Museum "Pay-As-You-Wish." This tiny museum, set in a former firehouse, displays vintage fire engines and other firefighting paraphernalia from the last century. There is also a moving memorial dedicated to the firefighters who lost their lives in the September 11 attack on the World Trade Center. Along with photos of the lost men are ash-covered artifacts retrieved from the site, and a video and photos chronicling the relief effort.

278 Spring Street at Varick—212-691-1303, www.nycfiremuseum.org

New York City Police Museum "PAY-AS-YOU-WISH." Housed in the former First Precinct station house (built in 1909 and in use until 1973), the Police Museum exhibits detail the history of the NYPD and displays hardware and vehicles used in keeping the peace since the Department's inception. Be sure to see the Hall of Heroes, featuring badges of all those killed in the line of duty since 1854. The exhibit "9/11 Remembered" includes video interviews with police who rushed to the scene of the disaster and a tribute to the twenty-three officers who lost their lives that day.

100 Old Slip—212-480-3100, www.nycpolicemuseum.org

New York Hall of Science FREE ON FRIDAYS FROM 2 P.M. TO 5 P.M. Originally opening during the 1964/65 World's Fair, the Hall of Science has more than 225 hands-on, easy-to-understand exhibits covering everything from the science of light and sound to biochemistry and physics.

47-01 111th Street at 46th Avenue, Flushing Meadows, Queens— 718-699-0005, www.nyhallsci.org

New York Public Library—Humanities and Social Sciences Library FREE. Not only is this the main branch of New York's library system, it is one of the city's architectural gems. Famous the world over for the stone lions Patience and Fortitude posted in front of its gorgeous beaux arts façade, this research-only library presents frequent and well-curated exhibitions. Two of my favorite shows in recent years were a retrospective of the life and works of cartoonist Charles Addams (Creator of the "Addams Family" cartoon), and "Becoming Visible," which chronicled the pre- and post-Stonewall history of the gay and lesbian movement. Be sure to check out the Rose reading room—as ostentatious and awe-inspiring as anything I've ever seen. Free guided tours are conducted at 11 A.M. and 2 P.M. daily.

> 455 Fifth Avenue at 42nd Street—212-869-8089, www.nypl.org

New York Transit Museum—Grand Central Terminal Gallery FREE. This museum contains art, models, transit maps, architectural drawings and exhibits detailing the history of the New York transit system.

> Shuttle Passage-way, Grand Central Train Station, 42nd Street and Lexington Avenue, www.mta.info/mta/museum

Noble Maritime Museum "PAY-AS-YOU-WISH." The Noble Maritime Museum focuses on the writings, photographs, works of art and artifacts of the sailor and artist John Noble. The Museum also presents temporary exhibitions of art and works related to the sea, sailing vessels, and to Noble himself.

> Snug Harbor Cultural Center, 1000 Richmond Terrace at Snug Harbor Road, Staten Island—718-447-6490, www.noblemaritime.org

Pierpont Morgan Library EVERY DAY EXCEPT MONDAY IS "PAY-AS-YOU-WISH." This Renaissance-style former home of financier J. Pierpont Morgan houses a distinguished collection of manuscripts, rare books and drawings detailing the art, history and culture of civilization between the Middle Ages and the 20th century. Treasures from the collection include musical scores, Thoreau's *Journal*, Dickens's *A Christmas Carol* and the only surviving fragment of Milton's *Paradise Lost*. (Note: Closed for renovations until early 2006.)

> 29 East 36th Street at Madison Avenue—212-685-0610,
> www.morganlibrary.org

Queens Museum of Art "PAY-AS-YOU-WISH." Located on the site of the 1964/65 World's Fair (you know, the place with the giant metal globe that you pass on the way to Shea Stadium and LaGuardia Airport), The Queens Museum presents contemporary art exhibitions and is home to a scale model of the entire city of New York. The Museum claims that the model changes and grows as quickly as the city does; I pity the poor fools who are in charge of the Times Square section—they must be losing their minds trying to keep up!

> Flushing Meadows Corona Park, Queens—718-592-9700,
> www.queensmuseum.org

Nicholas Roerich Museum "PAY-AS-YOU-WISH." The Russian-born Nicholas Roerich is world famous as an architect, explorer, artist and philosopher. Through his writings and art, Roerich was a passionate promoter of the value of cultural heritage of all nations and how an appreciation of such can help achieve world peace. The Museum, home to several hundred of Roerich's paintings, pays homage to his life's work, pacifism and spirituality. Especially noteworthy are his paintings from travels in Tibet. This little-known museum is a definite must-see for both the art it houses and the philosophy it espouses.

> 319 West 107th Street at Riverside Drive—212-864-7752,
> www.roerich.org

Rose Museum at Carnegie Hall FREE. This museum houses

some of the world-famous concert hall's most cherished memorabilia in its collections and archives, including photographs, letters, autographs, programs, and other items, all chronicling Carnegie Hall's rich history.

154 West 57th Street near Seventh Avenue—212-903-9600, www.carnegiehall.org

Scandinavia House: The Nordic Center in America "PAY-AS-YOU-WISH." Scandinavia House presents a wide variety of exhibitions covering the life, culture and traditions of the five Nordic countries—Denmark, Finland, Iceland, Norway and Sweden. The exquisite ultra-modern building in which Scandinavia House is located is itself a showcase of Scandinavian design, material and culture. On long-term loan from the National Museums of the five Nordic countries is a selection of modern and contemporary paintings by famous Scandinavian artists.

58 Park Avenue between 37th and 38th Streets—212-879-9779, www.scandinaviahouse.org

Society of Illustrators FREE. This museum presents shows that highlight the evolution of American illustration.

128 East 63rd Street between Park and Lexington Avenues—212-838-2560, www.societyillustrators.org

Staten Island Institute of Arts and Sciences "PAY-AS-YOU-WISH." The Institute has a treasure trove of possessions, from bugs and botanicals to decorative works and paintings by native New York artists and great masters like Chagall, Toulouse-Lautrec and Dürer.

75 Stuyvesant Place, St. George, Staten Island—718-727-1135, www.siiasmuseum.org

Studio Museum in Harlem FIRST SATURDAY OF EACH MONTH IS FREE. Established as the first black fine-arts museum in the U.S. during the height of the civil rights movement, the Studio Museum draws from its permanent collection of photographs, paintings and sculpture by African, African-American and Caribbean artists to present two outstanding exhibitions a year.

144 West 125th Street between Malcolm X and Adam Clayton Powell Boulevards—212-864-4500, www.studiomuseum.org

Whitney Museum of American Art "PAY-AS-YOU-WISH" FRIDAYS FROM 6 P.M. TO 9 P.M. The Whitney contains more than 10,000 works of 20th century American art and actively promotes the work of living artists. Not to be missed is the Whitney's often-controversial Biennial Exhibition, which showcases a diverse collection of contemporary artists.

945 Madison Avenue at 75th Street—212-570-3676, www.whitney.org

Whitney Museum at Philip Morris FREE. This 6,300-square-foot sculpture court and gallery space occupies part of the ground floor of the Philip Morris corporate headquarters and exhibits the work of contemporary American artists in coordination with the Whitney's uptown branch.

120 Park Avenue at 42nd Street—917-663-2453, www.whitney.org

Art Galleries

I once saw a t-shirt that said "So Many Men, So Little Time." That's how I feel about New York's art galleries. There are so damn many of them. Not that that's a bad thing; it's just hard to keep pace. Just when I think I have visited them all, another thirty sprout up in different neighborhoods. Once upon a time, Soho, the upper reaches of Madison Avenue and 57th Street, were the art gallery centers of Manhattan. Now, galleries can be found all over the city—in former warehouses in Chelsea, the meatpacking district, Greenwich Village, the Lower East Side, Tribeca, Williamsburg and DUMBO (Down Under the Manhattan Bridge Overpass) in Brooklyn.

New York's surfeit of galleries has been a windfall for art lovers. They offer an up-to-the-minute education on the most current trends in the art world and exhibit something for every taste—from the archaic to the arcane, from the obtuse to the obscene, from the eclectic to the existential, from the insipid to the inspired—representing all possible mediums. Galleries provide a reason to explore the interesting and diverse neighborhoods where they are located and, best of all, they are free.

A stimulating way to spend the day without spending any money is to do a gallery crawl. Pick a neighborhood where there is a proliferation of galleries and walk. You'll be amazed, awed, sometimes bored, often moved, and perhaps even shocked. And it won't cost you a penny.

For a complete listing of galleries, shows, hours, addresses and phone numbers, pick up a copy of The Gallery Guide, free at any gallery or museum. Extensive gallery information may also be found in the **"Choices" section of the** Village Voice, the **"Art"** sec-

tions of Time Out New York, and New York Magazine, The New Yorker's **"Goings On About Town"** and the **Friday "Weekend" section of** The New York Times.

Viewing Theater

Attending theater in New York City is expensive. Every season ticket prices go up, shutting out the budget conscious from attending. Luckily, there are several ways to beat the high price of theater-going without having to resort to seeing only deconstructed Wedekind plays performed in taxidermists' lofts on the Lower East Side. With a little planning, ingenuity, networking and cunning, you will never have to pay full price for the theater again.

Free Theater

The **Broadway in Bryant Park** series, which plays on several Thursdays in midsummer, presents Broadway and off-Broadway stars performing numbers from their shows. These free lunchtime outdoor concerts begin at 12:30 P.M. and last about an hour and a half.

> Sixth Avenue between 40th and 42nd Streets—212-768-4242, www.bryantpark.org/calendar/broadway.php

Although you won't be able to see an entire show at **Broadway on Broadway**, you will have the privilege of getting a sneak peak of scenes from the season's new productions. This free event, which takes place every year on the first Sunday after Labor Day, happens right in the middle of Broadway and Times Square and draws a huge crowd of theaterphiles, stargazers, Broadway pundits quick to offer their verdicts on the viability of each show, and the merely curious.

> 43rd Street and Broadway—212-768-1560

Another great way to see a show for free is to attend a **final dress rehearsal**. The night before a play's first preview, there is almost always a final dress—the culmination of weeks of rehearsal and the only opportunity to test a show before it plays in front of a paying audience. There are a couple of ways to get in. If you know people involved in the show, let them know you want to be put on the list. If you don't know anyone, go anyway. Since it is not an official performance, most theaters are not real strict about who gets in. They want bodies in the seats to learn from the audience what works and what doesn't. Check the "Guide to the Lively Arts" in *The New York Times* everyday to see what is about to begin previews, then show up at the theater around curtain time the night before that first performance, act like you belong there, walk in confidently and take a seat.

I've seen a lot of theater by going to the final dress. I even saw the final dress of the gonzo hit *The Producers* this way. A friend was given two passes and invited me to be her date. Now that the show has opened to "second-coming" reviews and has received every award known to man, people are clamoring for tickets, the show will probably run for the next millennium, and scalpers are asking for, *and getting,* $500 a ticket. Lucky me.

Every summer, **The New York Shakespeare Festival at the Delacorte Theatre** in Central Park presents two or three free productions of plays by Shakespeare and others under the stars. These productions usually have theater, film and TV names in the leading roles and are often brisk, brazen and fresh interpretations of the classics. Line up on the grass the day of the performance you wish to see. What time you get there should be determined by how popular the show is and who is starring. To insure that you secure a ticket, get there early, and bring a blanket, a book and plenty of water and food. (Meryl Streep and Kevin Kline appeared in *The Cherry Orchard* in 2001; hopeful audience members camped out all night.) Tickets are dispersed at 1 P.M.; two per person. You can hold a place in line for your friends, but they must be there when the tickets are given out. Check listings for performance dates. Enter the park at 79th and Central Park West or 81st and Fifth Avenue. (Note: A limited number of Delacorte Theatre tickets are given out on the day of performance from 1 P.M. to 3 P.M. at the Public Theatre, 425 Lafayette Street between 8th and 9th Streets). On selected dates, tickets are distributed in the other four boroughs; for information call 212-539-8750, or go to the website www.publictheater.org.

A little-known way to see free theater is to become a **Volunteer Usher**. Most off-Broadway (and some Broadway) companies need ushers for every performance, and for about an hour of your time (stuffing programs, learning your assigned seating area and escorting audience members to their seats), you are rewarded with a free place to watch the performance. Besides the free ticket, the other advantage of ushering is, even if the show is a big hit or sold out, you are still guaranteed a seat.

BEST WAY
TO SEE FREE
THEATER

All the following theaters have Volunteer Usher programs; call for details:

- **45 Bleecker**, 45 Bleecker Street between Bowery and Lafayette Streets—212-253-7017, www.45bleecker.com

- **Astor Place Theatre**, 434 Lafayette Street—212-254-4370

- **Atlantic Theatre Company**, 336 West 20th Street between Eighth and Ninth Avenues—212-645-8015, www.atlantictheater.com

- **Bouwerie Lane Theatre/Jean Cocteau Repertory Company**, 330 Bowery at Bond Street—212-677-0060, ext.16, www.jeancocteaurep.org

- **Century Center Theatre**, 111 East 15th Street between Union Square East and Irving Place—212-982-6782, ext. 11

- **Cherry Lane Theatre**, 38 Commerce Street at Grove Street—
  212-989-2020, www.cherrylanetheatre.com

- **City Center Encores Series**, 55th Street between Sixth and Seventh Avenues—212-247-0430, www.citycenter.org/encores

- **Classic Stage Company**, 136 East 13th Street between Third and Fourth Avenues—212-677-4210, ext 56, www.classicstage.org

- **Ensemble Studio Theatre**, 549 West 52nd Street between Tenth and Eleventh Avenues—212-247-4982, www.ensemblestudiotheatre.org

- **Irish Arts Center**, 553 West 51st Street between Tenth and Eleventh Avenues—212-757-3318, www.irishartscenter.org

- **Irish Repertory Theatre**, 132 West 22nd Street between Sixth and Seventh Avenues—212-255-0270, www.irishrepertorytheatre.com

- **Lucille Lortel Theatre**, 121 Christopher Street at Hudson Street—212-924-2817, www.lortel.org

- **Manhattan Ensemble Theater**, 55 Mercer Street between Broome and Grand Streets—212-925-1900, www.met.com

- **Manhattan Theatre Club**, City Center, 130 West 55th Street between Sixth and Seventh Avenues—212-399-3000, www.manhattantheatreclub.com

- **MCC Theater**, 120 West 28th Street between Sixth and Seventh Avenues—212-727-7722, www.mcctheater.org

- **Mint Theater Company**, 311 West 43rd Street at Eighth Avenue, 5th Floor—212-315-9434, www.minttheater.org

- **New Group**, 410 West 42nd Street—212-244-3380, ext. 308, www.thenewgroup.org

- **New York Theatre Workshop**, 79 East 4th Street between Bowery and Second Avenue—212-780-9037, www.nytw.org

- **Pearl Theatre Company**, 80 St. Mark's Place between First and Second Avenues—212-598-9802, www.pearltheatre.org

- **Performance Space 122**, 150 First Avenue at 9th Street—212-477-5829, ext. 5288, www.ps122.org. (Ask for ext. 304.)

- **Performing Garage**, 33 Wooster Street between Broome and Grand Streets—212-966-3651, www.thewoostergroup.org

- **Playhouse 91**, 316 East 91st Street between First and Second Avenues—212-831-2001

- **Playwrights Horizons**, 416 West 42nd Street between Ninth and Tenth Avenues—212-564-1235, www.playwrightshorizons.org

- **Rattlestick Theater**, 224 Waverly Place at Seventh Avenue and 11th Street—212-627-2556, www.rattlestick.org

- **Roundabout Theatre Company**, The American Airlines Theatre, 227 West 42nd Street—212-719-9393, www.roundabouttheatre.org. (Go by the theater Box Office between 10 A.M. and 6 P.M. and sign up for the date you'd like to work.)

- **Second Stage Theatre**, 307 West 43rd Street at Eighth Avenue—212-787-8302, ext 307, www.secondstagetheatre.com

- **Signature Theatre Company**, 555 West 42nd Street between Tenth and Eleventh Avenues—212-244-7529, www.signaturetheatre.org

- **Soho Playhouse**, 15 Vandam Street between Spring and Prince Streets—212-691-1555

- **Soho Repertory Theatre**, 46 Walker Street—212-941-8632, www.sohorep.org

- **Theatre for the New City**, 155 First Avenue at 9th Street—212-254-1109, www.theatreforthenewcity.net

- **Vineyard Theatre**, 108 East 15th Street at Union Square East—212-353-3366, ext.226, www.vineyardtheatre.org

- **York Theatre Company**, St. Peter's Church, 619 Lexington Avenue at 54th Street—212-935-5824, ext. 19, www.yorktheatre.org

Inexpensive Theater

Okay, so you're too scrupled to sneak into a dress rehearsal; you have an aversion to escorting hordes of people to their seats; you refuse to see any theater that is presented in a former meat locker; and you hate the great outdoors. Well, you probably won't be seeing much *free* theater. Never mind—there are still several ways you can attend shows at greatly reduced rates. Call, e-mail or send a letter to the organizations suggested below for further details:

Audience Extras handles leftover tickets, often for coveted house seats, to plays, musicals, concerts and dance performances. Membership is a yearly fee of $85, but after that, you can receive up to two tickets for a service charge of only $3.00. Most tickets are sold on the day of performance.

212-686-1966, www.audienceextras.com

There is always someone standing in front of a theater **hawking tickets**. You've seen them: the little lady with blue hair at the matinee whose friend Selma suddenly got sick; the pinstriped stockbroker whose date stood him up; the sad-sack suburban housewife whose husband just remembered there was a playoff game on TV. In hopes of getting their money back on these nonrefundable tickets, they half-heartedly wave them in the air, hoping for a taker. This is where your charm and a little of the "lean and hungry look" will come in handy.

Approach the person and ask how much they are asking for the ticket. They will tell you the full price. In as sweet a way as you can muster, say that you cannot afford to pay that much because you came to the theater with the intention of buying a $15 Standing Room ticket and that's all the money you've got. Suggest to the seller that *if they do not sell the ticket by curtain time,* you would buy it from them for the price you would have paid for S.R.O. They will almost immediately say, "No, I need to get full price for the ticket." State that you understand completely, but just in case they cannot sell it, you will wait. Inevitably, they will give you a condescending smile (they always do), as if to say "Of course I'll sell this ticket." Smile back, walk away, but stand in a place where they can see you.

The closer it gets to curtain time, the more desperate they will become—and the less successful. At a minute or so before curtain, approach them again and say something to the effect that $15 is better than nothing. At this point, they will almost always perform the transaction, grateful to have made anything at all on the ticket.

This is a trick an actor friend taught me in my early days in New York and it has never failed me. It is very hard to sell a single ticket at the last minute, even for a Broadway blockbuster. And, human nature being what it is, the seller will ultimately always want to make something on the ticket instead of swallowing the full amount. For your part, it takes a total lack of modesty as well as some tenacity and courage to pull this off successfully. Don't forget, you're going to be sitting next to the seller who will be stewing over his/her inability to get more than a fifth of the ticket's value. (Note: Do yourself a favor and don't go to the theater with $100 bills and ask the seller to make change; this is a sure way to guarantee the transaction will founder.)

The **Hit Show Club** service distributes free coupons redeemable at participating box offices for anywhere from a third to a half off regular ticket prices of the large, long-running Broadway block-busters. Hit Show Club coupons can be found at libraries, book-stores, visitor centers, at the club office or via mail. Each coupon may be exchanged for up to four reserved seats at least one hour before the performance, or can be mailed to the theater, giving a date and alternate date with payment. The coupon is usually not valid for the first eleven rows of the orchestra, and availability is subject to prior sale. No refunds, no exchanges.

630 Ninth Avenue between 44th and 45th Streets, 8th Floor—
212-581-4211, www.hitshowclub.com

The **International Fringe Festival,** which takes place in several locations on the Lower East Side over two weeks in August, presents a variety of theater companies and performers from around the world. As the name of the festival implies, most of the companies featured are of an experimental or avant-garde bent. Tickets for all events are a reasonable $15 for adults, $8 for seniors and kids under 12; you may purchase a pass for five performances for $65 or ten for $110.

212-429-8877, www.fringenyc.org

New York Theatre Workshop, whom I feel does some of the most interesting and cutting-edge work in town, has a terrific general discount ticket policy: every Sunday evening at 7:00 P.M. all tickets are only $20. These tickets must be purchased in person at the box office but may be bought in advance for any Sunday evening performance during the course of a play's run.

79 East 4th Street between Second and Third Avenues—
212-460-5475, www.nytw.org

The **Joseph Papp Public Theatre** offers tickets for $15 cash if there are any left thirty minutes before show time.

425 Lafayette Street between 8th and 9th Streets—
212-260-2400, www.publictheatre.org

When producers need to "paper" a house for certain performances (such as opening nights, when critics are in the house, special events and benefits) with discreet, courteous and well-groomed individuals, they donate tickets to **Play by Play**. Play by Play then offers them to its members. You think you're discerning, friendly, and can clean up on occasion? If so, you're an ideal candidate for Play by Play membership. To join, pay a yearly fee of $99 and a service charge of $3 per ticket (you are entitled to two tickets per each available event). A couple of shows and your membership has practically paid for itself. Occasionally producers will want to gauge audience response to their show and will ask Play by Play members to complete a survey and score sheet. You're thinking "some nerve"—they make you dress up nice and pretend like you paid a fortune for these tickets, and now you have to fill out a damn survey? Don't worry, they are easy to complete, consisting primarily of multiple choice and numerical scoring. Trust me, it's worth it... the seats the producers provide are very good and the events that they are "papering" are almost always special performances. Tickets to events are listed through a telephone hotline and can be ordered Monday through Friday from 2 P.M. to 5 P.M. Tickets are offered for performances any time from the day of the listing up to seventy-two hours in advance.

165 West 46th Street, Suite 412, New York, NY 10036—
212-868-7052, www.play-by-play.com

For about $20 and a valid student ID, you can purchase a **Student Rush** ticket. Many, but not all, of the theaters offer Rush seats, although no two theaters have the same distribution policy; some disburse them in the morning, others only make them available thirty minutes before show time. Go by the theater and inquire if they have Student Rush and what time those tickets are given out. Line up early, as Rush tickets are limited and popular.

Standing Room Only tickets, which range from $15 to $20, are sold on the day of performance and usually only if the show is sold out. Since not all theaters can accommodate standing room, go by the theater and inquire if they have S.R.O. The wonderful thing about "Standing Room" is that you are above the heads of the audience. Although your feet and legs may get a little tired, you have a great view of the stage ... and every seat in the orchestra section. During the first act, scope out where the empty seats are; there are always a few, even for the biggest hits. As soon as the lights come up at the intermission, walk quickly to that seat and sit. It is now yours. I've done this numerous times and have seen some of Broadway's greatest plays this way—Lily Tomlin's *The Search for Signs of Intelligent Life in the Universe, Dreamgirls, The Beauty Queen of Leenane, The King and I, Hairspray, Mamma Mia, Les Liaisons Dangereuses* (ten times ... I liked the play). Not once was I hassled or asked to leave the seat.

Something I've never done but that comes highly recommended is to **surf the websites of the city's theater companies** (e.g. Roundabout, Manhattan Theatre Club, New York Theatre Workshop, et al.) and get on their e-mail lists. If these companies need to fill empty seats at the last minute, they will contact everyone on their list and offer tickets at a huge savings. The friends who have done this say they have never paid more than $20 and almost always have been placed in house seats.

Committed to building audiences and supporting the performing arts in New York City, the **Theatre Development Fund (TDF)**

oversees three different discount ticket programs. The most famous of these is the **TKTS Booth**, located in the center
of the theater district in Duffy Square. TKTS sells
tickets at a 25 to 50 percent savings (with a $2.50 ser-
vice charge per ticket) for most Broadway and off-
Broadway offerings. The lines form a couple of hours
before the booth opens and can look intimidating.
Don't fret though, they move quickly. A secret I learned years ago
is to go much later, after 6:30 or 7 P.M., when the lines have sub-
sided, because later in the day the booth actually offers a better selection of shows and seats. Why? Hoping to sell them at full price,
most theaters hold on to their best seats until the last minute and
transfer them to TKTS close to curtain time if they haven't been
sold. A second TKTS booth is located at the South Street Seaport.
This outpost is not nearly as busy as the Duffy Square facility,
which means shorter lines and less of a wait. Other conveniences of
this facility include earlier opening hours, and matinee tickets may
be purchased here the day before a show.

TDF's second program involves its mailing list of over 80,000
members to whom it offers discounted tickets via snail and/or e-
mail on a rotating basis. The discounts under this program are
tremendous—as much as 75 percent or more for both Broadway
and off-Broadway shows. The caveat? To be eligible for membership, you must be one of the following: student, teacher, union
member, retired person, performing arts professional, clergy, or
member of the armed forces. Eligible applicants may write to TDF
(enclosing a self-addressed stamped envelope) for an application
form. You may also download and fill out the form online. Either
way, you must provide proof of eligibility and pay an annual processing fee of $22.50 (only $15 for members of the acting unions
during their first year on the mailing list).

Thirdly, TDF offers a **Voucher Program**, which is a book of four
passes for $28 to cutting-edge, off-off-Broadway theater as well as

BEST BARGAIN

to unconventional music and dance events. Each voucher is good for one admission within a year from the date of purchase. Vouchers are only available to those on the TDF mailing list.

Along with its great services, TDF sends quarterly newsletters and periodic e-mail updates of available shows, also maintains a website where you can find everything you need to know about its programs, and provides information by phone on all theater, dance and music events in the city (212-768-1818). Join the mailing list, take advantage of the TKTS booth, and enjoy the savings TDF extends to you.

- **TKTS Duffy Square**, 47th Street at Broadway—212-221-0013. For evening performances, TKTS is open Monday to Saturday 3 P.M. to 8 P.M.; Sunday 11 A.M. to 7 P.M. For matinee tickets, TKTS is open Wednesday and Saturday 10 A.M. to 2 P.M.; Sunday 11 A.M. to 2 P.M. Cash or traveler's checks only.

- **TKTS South Street Seaport,** 199 Water Street between Front and John Streets, at the southeast corner of the Resnick-Prudential Building. Open Monday to Friday 11 a.m. to 5:30 p.m.; Saturday 11 a.m. to 3:30 p.m.

- **TDF Mailing List,** 1501 Broadway, New York, NY 10036—212-221-0013), www.tdf.org

The **theater-related websites** www.playbill.com, www.broadwaybox.com, www.hotnycdeals.com, www.smartix.com and www.theatremania.com, periodically offer substantially discounted tickets (up to 50 percent off) to a number of Broadway, off-Broadway and off-off-Broadway shows. Check these sites often as ticket availability changes daily.

Twofers are free vouchers that work much the same way as the Hit Show Club coupons. These vouchers may be found in hotels,

libraries, bookstores, visitor centers, etc., and allow you to buy
two tickets for slightly more than the price of one. Like the Hit
Show Club coupons, Twofers are mostly for the large, long-running Broadway standards.

At the **Vineyard Theatre**, professional performing artists who
show a paid-up union card may, at the beginning of the theatre's
season (usually early fall), purchase a membership for only $15
and then pay just $10 per show for the entire season.

108 East 15th Street—212-353-0303, www.vineyardtheatre.org

For just $99 (and a $4.50 processing fee per ticket), you can join
TheatreMania's "Gold Club," a theater club that provides
members with a full year's access of complimentary tickets for
two to participating shows. Offerings include Broadway, off-
Broadway, off-off-Broadway, Long Island shows, comedy, dance
and music. "Gold Club" members also receive a free subscription
to the bi-weekly "TM Insider" newsletter, which contains the latest information on what's happening in the theater as well as exclusive discount offers. Once a member, you may access the Gold
Club's complimentary show database (check often as it is updated
throughout the day) and make reservations on a first come/first
reserved basis.

Viewing Film

I love bringing out-of-towners to the movies in Manhattan. I love seeing their dumbstruck reactions when they learn it costs $10 (or more!) to see a movie.

I remember years ago when ticket prices edged up to $7.50. Then Mayor Ed Koch was indignant and suggested in an interview that all New Yorkers boycott the movies. Koch rallied the troops... we were all filled with ire and high dudgeon, ready to sacrifice our film watching needs on principle. Come the following weekend, however, the withdrawal was too much and we headed in droves to the multiplexes, begrudgingly plunking down $7.50 for our film fixes.

Today, it is no different. Although resentful, we shell out $10 for the visual, aural and emotional thrill we get in the dark. We'd probably do the same tomorrow if tickets jumped to $20. Going to the movies is just too important and desirable an activity. Movies are what New Yorkers do. I am happy to report that there are several ways that we lemmings can beat the high cost of film-going.

Free Film

The **AMC Chain of Theaters** offers filmgoers its **Movie Watcher's Frequent User Card**. Each time you purchase a movie ticket at AMC, present your Movie Watcher's Card at the Box Office. Once you've bought ten tickets, AMC will give you one free pass to view a film of your choice in any of their theaters. Your

Movie Watcher Card also accrues points toward free concessions items and entitles you to free popcorn on Wednesdays.

42nd Street just east of Eighth Avenue, and 34th Street west of Eighth—www.moviewatcher.com

The **Brooklyn Bridge Park Summer Film Series**, sponsored by the Brooklyn Bridge Park Coalition, shows free movies in Empire-Fulton Ferry State Park on the waterfront between the Brooklyn and Manhattan Bridges. The series is held on Thursdays in July and August and begins promptly at 8:45 P.M. If you're not into the film, the dramatic views of the bridges and the lower Manhattan skyline will more than capture your attention.

718-802-0603, www.bbpc.net

One of the things that I think makes this city great is the **Bryant Park Film Festival** (www.bryantpark.org/calendar/film-festival.php). Running on Monday nights (rain date on Tuesdays) from June to August, this free festival features film classics such as *Sorry, Wrong Number*, *Mildred Pierce*, *Auntie Mame*, *Breakfast at Tiffany's* and *War of the Worlds*. There is nothing quite like the sight of thousands of New Yorkers of all ages, races, persuasions and sizes merrily cavorting on the lawn before and during the show. Everywhere you look, you can see people talking, laughing, sharing food. The roar of excitement that the crowd lets loose at the beginning of the prefilm cartoon can be heard down to the Battery, and the happiness continues throughout the evening. It is a decidedly festive atmosphere and makes you almost forget you live in the most jaded city in the world. Disney has nothing on this place—Bryant Park on a Monday night in summer is the happiest place on earth. (Note: Screenings begin at sunset, but arrive early to secure a place on the lawn.)

BEST FREE
MOVIE OUTING

In the summer months, **Celebrate Brooklyn** sponsors a free film festival under the stars every Thursday evening at dusk at the Prospect Park Bandshell. The films are usually classics like *Rebel Without a Cause* and *Around the World in 80 Days* and are preceded by live music or storytellers. Call Brooklyn Information and Culture (718-855-7882) for a full schedule of screenings or visit their website at www.celebratebrooklyn.org.

The Media Center at the **Donnell Library** has an extensive library of film and video. You may view any of these at the library for free if you make an appointment twenty-four to forty-eight hours in advance. The library's immense catalog of titles will amaze you. The Media Center also sponsors film screenings every Wednesday and Thursday in the fall, winter and spring, and Wednesdays in the summer.

20 West 53rd Street between Fifth and Sixth Avenues— 212-621-0618, www.nypl.org

During the summer months, the **Duke Ellington Boulevard Neighborhood Association (DEBNA)** presents free movies under the stars at La Perla Garden on Wednesdays, beginning at dusk. Bring chairs, blankets and the kids, as most screenings have an emphasis on children's films.

West 105th Street between Manhattan and Columbus Avenues—212-340-8067, www.debna.org

On Fridays, the **Film and Media Program of the Museum of Modern Art** presents screenings of films chosen from its vast library (19,000 and counting). The screenings are often retrospectives of a particular filmmaker's work or are themed (e.g. the films of a select country) and are drawn from a variety of genres including classic, contemporary, international and independent works.

The beautiful thing about the Friday screenings is that they are free to all with a paid admission to the museum, which is "Pay-As-You-Wish" from 4:00 P.M. to 7:45 P.M. For a screening schedule, visit the MOMA Film and Media website.

> 11 West 53rd Street between Fifth and Sixth Avenues—
> 212-708-9480, www.moma.org/film

Most of the other **New York City Libraries** (see chapter on "Books") show free films and documentaries sporadically throughout the year. For more information and a schedule of screenings, contact your local library, pick up the monthly "events" booklet or go to the New York Public Library website at www.nypl.org and click on "Events," then search by borough or library.

If you can't bear all that happiness in Bryant Park (or all those people) but still want to see a movie in the great outdoors, head to the Hudson River—Piers 25 and 54 to be exact. In the summer, the Hudson River Park Trust presents **Riverflicks**, a series of free movies that play a couple of times each week (Wednesdays at Pier 54, Fridays at Pier 25). Unlike Bryant Park, they throw in free popcorn as well. All films at Pier 25 are rated G or PG. Call or go online for a weekly schedule of screenings, locations and directions.

> Piers 25 and 54—212-533-PARK, www.hudsonriverpark.org

Each Wednesday evening in July and August, the **Socrates Sculpture Park**, in collaboration with the Museum of the Moving Image and the Partnership for Parks, presents an outdoor festival of international film. Admission is free and all films begin at sunset. Festival sponsored prescreening music and dance performances begin at 7 P.M.

> Broadway at Vernon Boulevard, Long Island City, Queens—
> 718-956-1819, www.socratessculpturepark.org

Sony's Wonder and Technology Lab offers free summer movie screenings at 6 P.M. on Thursday evenings. Ostensibly, the films they show are kid's flicks, but who died and made *Dr. Strangelove, Big Fish, Mr. Deeds* and *Labyrinth* children's films? Although the films are free, you must call to make reservations in the week of the screening that you would like to attend.

550 Madison Avenue between 55th and 56th Streets—
212-833-7620, www.sonywondertechlab.com

Inexpensive Film

At the **Brooklyn Heights Pavilion**, the first show of the day costs only $4. In addition, a "Bargain Day" special on Mondays and Tuesdays makes all screenings $4.

70 Henry Street, Brooklyn—718-596-7070

Cinema Classics Screening Room, deep in the heart of the East Village, is hands down the least glamorous place to view film in the city. Badly framed movie posters hang haphazardly on graceless brick walls; the theater only has sixty seats. But it's appeal, besides the low ticket price of just $6.00, is its eclectic programming; the films screened here are drawn from art-house, classic, contemporary independent and foreign genres and are almost always engaging. Call or visit the website for a schedule.

332 East 11th Street between First and Second Avenues—
212-677-5368, www.cinemaclassics.com

The **Cobble Hill Cinema** is a first-run, five-screen movieplex that has bargain showings throughout the week. Monday through Friday, all shows before 5 P.M. are only $5; tickets all day and evening Tuesdays and Thursdays are only $5; and Saturday and Sunday matinees before 2 P.M. are $5.

265 Court Street, Brooklyn—718-596-9113

Probably due to the glut of new state-of-the-art, stadium-seating film palaces just blocks away, the multiscreen **State Theatre** inside the Virgin Record Store has recently become a discount movie house. For just $4.95, you can see either first-run films that have exhausted their stay at other venues or Indian "Bollywood" features.

1540 Broadway between 45th and 46th Streets

Viewing Live Television

Several television talk and variety shows are shot daily right here in the Big Apple, and every one of these need a live studio audience. It's free to see any of these tapings, but the waiting period for many of the more popular shows like *Late Show with David Letterman* and *Saturday Night Live* can be as long as a year. For tickets, call or send a postcard with your name, address, dates you would like to attend, and day and evening phone numbers, to the attention of the show's name, plus "Tickets."

The Caroline Rhea Show has standby tickets available at 7:30 A.M. on tape days—Monday through Wednesday at 10 A.M., and Thursday at 10 A.M. and 2 P.M. (NBC Tickets, 30 Rockefeller Plaza, New York, NY 10012—212-664-3056, ext.3, carolinerhea@nbc.com)

The Daily Show with Jon Stewart tapes every Monday through Thursday at the show's studios, located at 513 West 54th Street near Tenth Avenue. Doors open at 5:45 P.M. You must be 18 or over to attend. Write a month in advance of when you would like to see a taping. (1775 Broadway, 9th Floor, New York, NY 10019)

DaySide with Linda Vester—You must arrive at the studio no later than 11:30 A.M. for a 1 P.M. to 2 P.M. live broadcast. (1211 Avenue of the Americas, New York, NY 10019—877-369-8587)

Emeril Live—This very popular show tapes two or three shows a day in a one-week period, three times a year. For tickets, visit the Food Network website at www.foodtv.com. (733 Eleventh Avenue, New York, NY 10019)

Judge Hatchett—Contact the show about a month in advance of when you want to see the taping. Shoots Tuesday, Wednesday and Thursday at 10:30 A.M. and 1 P.M. (440 West 42nd Street, New York, New York 10036—212-352-8600)

The Graham Norton Effect—Send your ticket request via e-mail a couple of months in advance of when you want to see a taping. Shoots on Tuesdays at 7:30 P.M. (grahamnortonny@broadwayvideo.com)

Last Call with Carson Daly—(30 Rockefeller Plaza, New York, NY 10012—212-664-3056)

Late Night with Conan O'Brien—Call or write a month in advance of the tape date you desire. You may reserve up to five tickets. Standby tickets are also available on tape days, Tuesday through Friday at 9 A.M. at the 49th Street entrance of 30 Rockefeller Plaza, but you have to return at 4:15 P.M. to see if there is indeed room. (NBC Tickets, 30 Rockefeller Plaza, New York, NY 10012—212-664-3056, ext. 1)

Late Show with David Letterman—Write or call to order tickets well in advance of when you want to see the taping (as much as a year in advance!). For standby tickets *on the day* of the show, call 212-247-6497 at 11 A.M. The Late Show tapes Monday through Thursday. (Late Show Tickets, Ed Sullivan Theatre, 1697 Broadway, New York, NY 10019—212-975-1003)

Live with Regis and Kelly—Send a postcard at least a year in advance of when you want to see a taping. You are allowed up to four tickets. For standby tickets, line up at the corner of 67th Street and Columbus no later than 7 A.M. on weekdays. (Ansonia Station, P.O. Box 230-777, New York, NY 10023—212-456-3537)

Living It Up with Ali and Jack—Tapes live every Monday through Thursday from 9 A.M. to 10 A.M. A second show shoots Thursday afternoon at 1 P.M. Arrival time for the morning shows is 7:15 A.M. for the 9 A.M. show. Arrival time for the Thursday afternoon show is 11:30 A.M. for the 1 P.M. show. (CBS Broadcast Center, 524 West 57th Street, New York, NY 10019-2985—866-454-8686)

Maury Povich Show tapes Tuesday through Thursday at 10:30 A.M. and 1 P.M. at the USA Studios. On average, the show is booked about three weeks ahead of taping. When sending your request, make sure to include the number of tickets you would like. (Studios USA, 15 Penn Plaza/Grand Ballroom, New York, NY 10001)

Montel Williams Show—Request tickets two weeks ahead of taping. Tape dates are Tuesday through Thursday at 10 A.M., 1 P.M. and 4 P.M. You are allowed up to four tickets. (433 W 53rd Street, New York, NY 10019)

The People's Court—Call or write several weeks in advance of when you would like to see a taping. The show tapes Tuesday and Wednesday, in the morning and afternoon. Taping times will be confirmed with your ticket request. (401 Fifth Avenue, New York, NY 10016—888-780-8587)

Ricki Lake Show—Tapings for this show are on Wednesdays and Thursdays at 3 P.M. and 5 P.M., and Fridays at 1 P.M. and

3 P.M. Write or call for tickets, or go in person at least an hour before taping. (221 West 26th Street, New York, NY 10112—212-352-8600)

Saturday Night Live—Only accepts requests for tickets in August; you may not ask for a particular date or quantity of tickets. There are standby tickets, but these are nearly impossible to score. Try your luck: get on the standby line on the mezzanine level of Rockefeller Center (at 49th Street) by 9 A.M. the morning of the taping. (NBC Tickets, 30 Rockefeller Plaza, New York, NY 10012—212-664-3056, ext.4)

Total Request Live—For tickets, call 212-398-8549 a month before you would like to attend. TRL airs live Monday through Friday at 4 P.M. There is a slim chance that you can secure a standby ticket; arrive at least two hours before the show begins. You must be between 16 and 24 years old to gain admittance. (MTV Studios, 1515 Broadway at 45th Street, New York, NY 10019)

Tough Crowd with Colin Quinn—For free tickets, call 212-560-2663 or e-mail tickets@toughcrowdtv.com. Tapes Monday through Thursday at 6 P.M. You must be 18 or over to attend. (Sony Studios, 447 West 53rd Street, New York, NY 10019—212-560-2663)

The View—Send your request two to three months prior to when you would like to see a taping. Standby tickets are available on tape days; arrive by 9 A.M. (Ticket Coordinator, The View, 320 West 66th Street, New York, NY 10023)

The **John Walsh Show** tapes daily at 11:30 A.M. and 2:30 P.M. (30 Rockefeller Plaza, New York, NY 10012—800-551-6261)

Who Wants to be a Millionaire? tapes Monday, Tuesday and Thursday at 4 P.M., and Wednesday at 12:30 P.M. and 4 P.M. Write in with a request for tickets (only four per household) two months prior to your desired tape date. (Columbia University Station, P.O. Box 250225, New York, NY 10025)

The website **www.nytix.com** offers a constantly updated listing of all the television shows shot in New York, as well as information on obtaining tickets. It also offers a $1.99-a-minute phone service you can call to find out about the availability of standby tickets for each show.

Listening to Music

Besides being the art, dance, theater, business, fashion, retail and museum capital of the world (not that I am at all jingoistic), New York is also the greatest city in the world for music. On any given day or night, live music is everywhere throughout Gotham—concert halls, Broadway and off-Broadway theaters, bars, clubs, restaurants, parks, museums, street corners; even the subway platforms serve as impromptu stages for a variety of musical offerings. There is something in New York for every musical taste. When it comes to classical music, we have one of the best and oldest American symphony orchestras, the New York Philharmonic, and the most famous concert venue, Carnegie Hall, which plays host to the world's great orchestras and singers. Two of the most famous opera companies, the Metropolitan and the New York City Opera, reside here. And the city has more outlets that present chamber music, soloists and orchestras than do some entire countries.

Nowhere in the world, except perhaps New Orleans and Newport during their annual festivals, has more jazz offerings. As for rock, blues, punk, world, experimental and progressive, the best way to gauge just how much of it is out there is to open the *Village Voice* music section each week. The number of pages (thirty-two in the *Voice* as I write), ads and listings devoted to music is astounding.

For the budget-conscious, several places in New York offer music at little or no cost:

Free Music

For some real get-down, hand-clapping, foot-stomping gospel, there's no better place on the planet than **Abyssinian Baptist**

Church on a Sunday morning. Abyssinian's raucous, spine-tingling gospel choir performs during the 9 A.M. and 11 A.M. services; a large area of the church has been designated for tourists and aficionados. Arrive early as the line to get in goes around the block; more than once I've been turned away. The cost for this uplifting experience is just a dollar. Of course, if the spirit moves you, you may always give more.

132 West 138th Street—212-862-7474, www.abyssinian.org

The **Bronx Symphony Orchestra**, composed of professional and serious nonprofessional musicians, presents free symphonic concerts throughout the year.

2141 Muliner Avenue, Bronx—718-601-9151, www.bronxsymphony.org

The **Brooklyn Academy of Music** sponsors three different free concert series during the summer months. The **BAM Free Concerts in Brooklyn Parks** (212-360-8290) series offers over a dozen evening concerts in parks throughout the borough, featuring R&B, jazz, funk, blues, reggae and salsa. **BAM Outside** (718-636-4100) presents free noonday concerts of popular music at nearby MetroTech Center (Flatbush Avenue and Myrtle Avenues). **BAM Rhythm and Blues Festival at MetroTech** presents free R&B concerts at noon on Thursdays in July and August.

30 Lafayette Avenue, Brooklyn—718-636-4100, www.bam.org

The **Brooklyn Symphony Orchestra**, a community ensemble composed of amateur, student, semi-professional and professional musicians, presents several concerts of classical, romantic and 20th century works at various Brooklyn venues from September to May. Admission to the BSO's concerts is always free with a suggested contribution of $10. For a concert schedule and location information, call or visit the BSO website.

> 718-499-2025, www.brooklynsymphonyorchestra.org

Bryant Park presents free classical music and jazz in the open air throughout the summer months.

> Sixth Avenue at 42nd Street—212-768-4242, www.bryantpark.org

The **Carnegie Hall Neighborhood Concert Series** presents a number of free jazz, pop, classical and folk concerts in neighborhoods throughout all five city boroughs. The concerts are held in a variety of locations, including libraries, shelters and community, cultural, and religious centers. For kids, the Neighborhood Concert Series hosts workshops for children between the ages of 7 and 14, and presents special concerts for those that are in nursery school.

> 212-903-9670, www.carnegiehall.org

Castle Clinton presents free Thursday evening concerts in July and early August. The roster of performers varies from rock, blues, jazz and gospel and has featured such groups as The Crash Test Dummies, The Blind Boys of Alabama and jazzman John Scofield. Seating is very limited and on a first come/first served basis; concerts are at 7 P.M. with access to the venue beginning at 5 P.M.

> Battery Place at State Street—212-835-2789, www.nps.gov/cacl

During the summer months, **Celebrate Brooklyn** stages free world-class music concerts al fresco at the beautiful Prospect Park Bandshell. The music is performed by some of the world's leading groups and individuals—anything from reggae to classical, world, pop, hip-hop, Latin, Celtic, ethno-techno, salsa, funk, rock, jazz, blues, bossa nova, electronica, dub, Sufi-rock, avant-garde, rap, zydeco, Zulu, Afro-Caribbean and Rai.

Prospect Park Bandshell, 9th Street and Prospect Park West, Brooklyn—718-855-7882, www.celebratebrooklyn.org

From mid-June to late August, **Central Park Summerstage** hosts an astounding line-up of world famous and almost-famous groups. The musical offerings span all genres with something for everyone: all concerts (with a few exceptions) are free.

Rumsey Playfield, 72nd Street near Fifth Avenue in Central Park—212-360-2777/212-360-2756, www.summerstage.com

Through its **Concerts in the Parks** series, the **New York Philharmonic** presents free outdoor summer concerts in city parks in all five boroughs. Concerts begin at 8 P.M. and finish with a flourish of fireworks.

212-875-5709, www.nyphil.org

The **Continental Center** in the Financial District presents the free Juilliard Artists in Concert series every Tuesday afternoon at lunchtime.

180 Maiden Lane at Front Street—212-799-5000, www.juilliard.edu

Every Friday evening from late June through July, the **Cooper-Hewitt Museum** hosts its free Cross-Currents concert series, which presents a wide spectrum of musical genres appealing to most every taste.

2 East 91st Street at Fifth Avenue—212-849-8400, www.ndm.si.edu

Call or write in advance for tickets to great free classical music concerts held at **The Frick Collection** from September to May.

(Note: You can also show up an hour before a concert and try to secure a "no-show" seat.)

> 1 East 70th Street at Fifth Avenue—212-288-0700, www.frick.org

The **Harlem Meer Performance Festival**, located at the Charles A. Dana Discovery Center in Central Park, presents free music concerts that reflect the city's cultural heritage and ethnic diversity. Performances, ranging from modern jazz to salsa and gospel, are held on Sundays at 4:00 P.M. from June through August.

> 110th Street and Central Park North—212-860-1370,
> www.centralpark2000.com/database/jazz_hm.html

Harlem Week, the world's largest black and Latino festival, features art exhibitions, music, film, and dance presentations and a huge festival on Fifth Avenue from 125th to 135th Streets in early to mid-August. Music performances include jazz, gospel and R&B.

> 212-862-8477, www.harlemdiscover.com/harlemweek

The ten-week **Hudson River Festival**, held in the summer months, presents free music, dance, theater and storytelling events as well as art exhibitions. The festival is held at several riverside venues including Battery Park, the Winter Garden of the World Financial Center, Castle Clinton and the Battery Park Esplanade. Call or go to the website for a complete schedule.

> 212-945-0505/212-528-2733, www.hudsonriverfestival.com

Dedicated to the presentation, preservation and propagation of jazz, 'America's Classical Music,' the **Jazzmobile** presents free mobile concerts, festivals and special events throughout New York's five boroughs. Since its inception over forty years ago, this multiple award-winning organization's roster of performers has been a Who's Who of jazz greats. Besides music concerts, Jazzmobile presents free workshops, master classes, lecture demonstrations and enrichment programs that are conducted by many of the jazz legends that grace its stages.

212-866-4900/212-860-3616, www.jazzmobile.org

The **Martin Luther King, Jr., Concert Series**, at Wingate Field on Kingston Avenue across from Kings County Hospital in Brooklyn, presents free concerts of jazz, R&B, oldies, gospel and Caribbean music on Mondays at 7:30 P.M. in July and August.

718-469-1912, www.brooklynconcerts.com

The **Library for the Performing Arts** at Lincoln Center periodically presents free classical and Broadway music concerts.

111 Amsterdam Avenue at 66th Street—212-870-1630, www.nypl.org/research/lpa

The **Lincoln Center Out-of-Doors Festival** offers a spectacular daily roster of free music concerts and dance events (featuring the great and nearly-great) for three weeks in August.

Lincoln Center and Damrosch Park, 64th Street at Columbus Avenue—212-875-5456, www.lincolncenter.org

The music, mostly rock, at **Luna Lounge** on the Lower East Side is always free. The performance space in the rear of the bar is comfy and the drinks here are inexpensive. As the music is free, the quality varies widely.

171 Ludlow Street between Houston and Stanton Streets— 212-260-2323, www.lunalounge.com

From September to June, the **Metropolitan Museum of Art**

hosts a staggering number of free concerts of music from around the world. Moreover, the Met presents chamber music in the bar and piano music in the cafeteria on Friday and Saturday evenings, making it one of the best "cheap date" spots in New York.

1000 Fifth Avenue at 82nd Street—212-570-3949, www.metmuseum.org

An ideal way to experience great music and hear excellent up-and-coming performers and composers, all at no cost, is to attend a concert at one of New York's exceptional **music schools**. Call any or all for their complete concert schedules:

- **Bloomingdale School of Music**, 323 West 108th Street— 212-663-6021, www.bsmny.org

- **Brooklyn Conservatory of Music**, 58 Seventh Avenue at Lincoln Place, Park Slope, Brooklyn—718-622-3300, www.brooklynconservatory.com

- **Juilliard School of Music**, Lincoln Center, 60 Lincoln Center at 66th Street—212-769-7406, www.juilliard.edu. Throughout the school year, September to May, Juilliard presents almost daily student recitals at its Paul Recital Hall; larger events take place most Wednesdays at 1 p.m. at Alice Tully Hall.

- **Manhattan School of Music**, 120 Claremont Avenue at Broad-way—212-749-2802, www.msmnyc.edu

- **Mannes College of Music**, 150 West 85th Street between Columbus and Amsterdam Avenues—212-580-0210, www.mannes.edu

From the end of June to early August, the **Naumburg Bandshell** in Central Park plays host to a series of free concerts of classical and semi-classical music. Performances are on Tuesday evenings at 7:30 P.M. For information and a concert schedule, call or go to the Naumburg Orchestral Concerts website.

Mid-park just south of the 72nd Street cross-drive near Fifth Avenue—212-262-6927, www.naumburgconcerts.org

For the consummate Irish experience, nothing in New York beats **Paddy Reilly's Music Bar** for its authentic pub décor, all draft Guinness bar, the lilting Erin accents of a majority of its patrons, and especially the music it presents. Voted "Best Irish Music Bar" by the *Village Voice* in 1999, Paddy's features a variety of live Irish music concerts seven nights a week. On five of those nights you may partake of the charms of this bar without paying a penny, as there is no cover or drink minimum Sunday through Thursday.

519 Second Avenue at 29th Street—212-686-1210, www.padddyreillys.com

From May to September, the **River to River Festival** (www.rivertorivernyc.com) presents hundreds of free music concerts and cultural events at venues all over Lower Manhattan. Performers include everyone from the new and unknown to the world-renowned.

Rodeo Bar, which bills itself as the city's "premier Southern Roadhouse," serves up live Country & Western music seven nights a week starting at 10 P.M., and never charges a cover. I have it on good authority that the shows at Rodeo Bar (which was dubbed "The Best Club to Kick Some Shit" in the *Village Voices's* 2002 "Best of New York" issue) are consistently good and lively and the drinks are consistently strong and cheap.

375 Third Avenue at 27th Street—212-683-6500

St. Paul's Chapel offers free lunchtime concerts of mostly classical music every Monday from 1 P.M. to 2 P.M. throughout the year.

> 211 Broadway at Fulton Street—212-602-0874,
> www.saintpaulschapel.org

The **Seaside Summer Concert Series** in Asser Levy Park in Brooklyn offers free concerts of rock, disco, Latin and contemporary music on Thursdays in July and August beginning at 7:30 P.M.

> 718-469-1912, www.brooklynconcerts.com/seaside.html

In the summer months, **South Street Seaport Concerts** presents several free concerts throughout the week: Latin jazz and salsa concerts on Wednesdays, the "Sam Goody Home Before Midnight" showcase of new bands on Thursdays. During the Christmas holidays, the chorus of St. Cecilia's performs traditional and international carols on choir risers that are configured into the shape of a giant Christmas tree. In the spring and fall, there are free midweek dinnertime jazz concerts, often featuring some of the genre's greatest performers.

> Pier 17, Fulton Street at South Street on the East River—
> 212-732-8257, www.southstreetseaport.com

Trinity Church, one of the oldest and most beautiful churches in New York, offers free year-round concerts every Thursday at 1 P.M. Chamber groups, choruses and soloists are among the performers heard here.

> 74 Trinity Place—212-602-0747, www.trinitywallstreet.org

Every Tuesday at 8 P.M. in July, the **Washington Square Music**

Festival features outdoor concerts of mostly chamber orchestra and big band music.

> Washington Square Park, LaGuardia Place at West 4th Street—
> 212-252-3621, www.washingtonsquaremusicfestival.org

At lunchtime or after work, catch free concerts in all musical genres at the **World Financial Center Winter Garden**.

> West Street between Liberty and Vesey Streets—212-945-0505,
> www.worldfinancialcenter.com

Inexpensive Music

At the intimate Lower East Side club **Arlene Grocery**, three to eight local bands are featured nightly. The talent here can sometimes be hit or miss, but with the low cover charge and cheap drinks, it is worth the risk—you may go on a night when tomorrow's superstars are performing.

> 95 Stanton Street between Ludlow and Orchard Streets—
> 212-358-1633, www.arlene-grocery.com

At **Arthur's Tavern**, there is never a cover charge to hear a continuous stream of jazz and blues from 9 P.M. to 3 A.M., although they have a two-drink minimum on weekends and one-drink minimum on weeknights.

> 57 Grove Street near Bleecker Street—212-675-6879,
> www.arthurstavernnyc.com

Classic rock, jazz and blues are what you'll hear on the intimate stage at **The Back Fence**. There is a $5 cover on Saturdays with a two-drink minimum; no cover all other nights. Performances begin at 6 P.M. to appease both hardcore music junkies and those who go to bed early.

> 155 Bleecker Street at Thompson Street—212-475-9221, www.thebackfenceonline.com

The **Baggot Inn**, an Irish pub that features music nightly, charges between $5 and $10 Thursday through Saturday, but Sundays through Wednesdays are free. Music ranges from Celtic to Irish rock, funk and blues, as well as open mic nights when the uninhibited have the opportunity to showcase their hidden talents. Drink prices here are also cheap.

> 82 West 3rd Street between Thompson and Sullivan Streets— 212-477-0622, www.baggotinn.com

The **Bitter End** has been the springboard for the careers of countless bands and vocalists since 1961, and still presents talent it believes will be tomorrow's superstars. On any given night, you can hear several up-and-coming groups as well as an occasional headliner, for a reasonable $5 to $10.

> 147 Bleecker Street between Thompson Street and LaGuardia Place—212-673-7030, www.bitterend.com

The **Blue Note**, considered the "Jazz capital of the world," is the city's most famous jazz venue and with a roster of performers that reads like a Who's Who of jazz greats, it is also one of the city's most expensive. But you can hear music here inexpensively: on Fridays and Saturdays from 2 to 4 A.M., you can catch a jam session for a paltry $8. On Sundays, you get music with the Blue Note's reasonably priced jazz brunch for $19.50. Brunch reservations required.

> 131 West 3rd Street between MacDougal Street and Sixth Avenue—212-475-8592, www.bluenote.net

Bronx Arts Ensemble presents a variety of concerts in differing venues throughout the borough. Tickets are usually between $10 and $20. although many summer performances are free.

> Golf House, Van Cortlandt Park, Bronx—718-601-7399, www.bxartsensemble.org

Carnegie Hall has $10 student rush tickets for certain performances.

> 881 Seventh Avenue at 57th Street—212-247-7800, www.carnegiehall.org

If loud, unruly music is your thing, then **CBGB** is the place for you. Considered the venue that introduced punk music to the world, CBGB presents a variety of mostly "underground" bands nightly for a cover charge of $7 to $15. You must be 16 with a valid I.D. to enter and 21 to drink. If, on the other hand, you like your music a little more tame, go next door to **CB's 313 Gallery** for softer, more acoustic offerings and a cover price between $5 and $8.

- **CBGB**, 315 Bowery at Bleecker Street—212-982-4052, www.cbgb.com

- **CB's 313 Gallery**, 313 Bowery—212-677-0455

The jazz club, **Cleopatra's Needle**, charges no cover to hear music but stipulates a $10 food or drink minimum per set at each table.

> 2485 Broadway between 92nd and 93rd Streets—212-769-6969, www.cleopatrasneedleny.com

The **C-Note** offers multiple live music acts seven nights a week. The kinds of stuff you'll hear include jazz, acoustic, indie, rock and country. The C-Note also hosts "Open Mic" events and a weekly Blues jam in which anyone may participate. There is a one-drink minimum that is rarely enforced and almost never a cover.

157 Avenue C at 10th Street—212-677-8142, www.thecnote.com

The punk palace **Continental** features hardcore punk and rock groups nightly, with occasional surprise superstars like Iggy Pop and Deborah Harry dropping in to do a song or two. Admission is free Sunday through Tuesday, and Thursday. There is a $5 cover charge on Wednesday; between $5 and $10 on Friday and Saturday.

25 Third Avenue between St. Mark's Place and Stuyvesant Street—212-529-6924, www.continentalnyc.com

There is never a cover (but there is a two-drink minimum) to hear jazz at **Detour**, which showcases New York's new and rising combos nightly. Besides the free admission, drinks at this venue are inexpensively priced, with $3 happy hour drinks Monday through Friday from 4 P.M. to 7 P.M.

349 East 13th Street between First and Second Avenues—212-533-6212, www.jazzatdetour.com

If you want to hear the music that the music cognoscenti go to listen to, check out one of the **Jupiter Symphony Chamber Players** concerts held on Mondays at 2 P.M. and 7:30 P.M. from September through May. The Jupiter Symphony presents what many feel are the most adventurous concert programs in New York. At any given concert, you'll hear music from both the standard repertoire as well as that of the more obscure and rarely performed. Jupiter concerts also often feature world-class soloist players and singers. For each concert, there are a slew of $10 and $15 tickets, which is remarkable given the outstanding quality and variety of the performances. All concerts, except where otherwise noted, are held at Good Shepherd Presbyterian Church.

152 West 66th Street, west of Broadway—212-799-1259, www.jupitersymphony.com

The Knitting Factory's huge array of music performances varies in price from $5 to $25.

74 Leonard Street between Broadway and Church Streets— 212-219-3006, www.knittingfactory.com

The Living Room, an intimate and always packed venue for a diverse array of acoustic and indie music, never charges a cover (there is, however, a one-drink minimum). The appeal of this tiny, no-frills singer showcase space is the audience it attracts...bona fide music lovers who are reverent yet relaxed.

84 Stanton Street at Allen Street—212-533-7235, www.livingroomny.com

Merkin Concert Hall offers probably the most eclectic program of concerts in the city. Performances scheduled cover the musical spectrum from ethnic to classical, jazz and experimental. Tickets are as low as $10.

129 West 67th Street between Broadway and Amsterdam Avenue—212-501-3330, www.ekcc.org

The **Mostly Mozart** summer festival of concerts at Alice Tully and Avery Fisher Halls at Lincoln Center does include a few free performances as well as offering $20 student tickets (available on the day of the event).

212-875-5456, www.lincolncenter.org

To hear the great **New York Philharmonic Orchestra** is not a cheap proposition as ticket prices can go as high as $300. To attend a performance at reduced rates look for:

- $10 Student Rush tickets are available on weeknights. Call 212-875-5030 at 10:30 A.M. on the day of the concert for availability.

- Friday matinee concert seats for as little as $22.

- Discount seats for several Saturday matinees; reduced rates vary by performance.

- Open Rehearsals are just $14. Most rehearsals are held on Thursday mornings, with a handful taking place on other weekday mornings; consult the website for a schedule.

Call for more information regarding discounts and a full schedule of concerts.

Avery Fisher Hall, 10 Lincoln Center at Columbus Avenue and 65th Street—212-875-5030, www.nyphilharmonic.org

Founded at the turn of the last century by a student who wanted to make music accessible to the masses, the **People's Symphony Concerts** offers great orchestral music performed by the city's top musicians for just $7.50, and their Artists' Series and Chamber Series (six concerts per series) is $23. Concerts are held at the Washington Irving High School auditorium (40 Irving Place at 16th Street) and at Town Hall (123 West 43rd Street at Sixth Avenue).

201 West 54th Street—212-586-4680, www.pscny.org

Roulette presents a concert series of adventurous music by internationally famous music "experimentalists." Tickets are usually between $12 and $20.

228 West Broadway between White and North Moore Streets, 2nd Floor—212-219-8242, www.roulette.org

Smoke is free Sunday to Thursday (there is, however, a two-drink minimum). The cover charge on Friday and Saturday ranges between $20 and $30, depending on the act. Smoke hosts a rotation of great jazz bands, and there is always a jazz headliner dropping in to jam.

2751 Broadway between 105th and 106th Streets—212-864-6662, www.smokejazz.com

Symphony Space on the Upper West Side programs an always interesting and eclectic array of free and reasonably priced musical performances throughout the year. Ticket prices average $20.

2537 Broadway at 95th Street—212-864-5400, www.symphonyspace.org

Town Hall, the original "Tammany Hall," is a great concert venue that hosts a variety of musical performances ranging from classical to jazz, rock, popular, big band and world music. Town Hall presents several free concerts, and cheap seats go for as little as $10. It also offers discount ticket books for even greater savings.

123 West 43rd Street at Sixth Avenue—212-840-2824, www.the-townhall-nyc.org

Alice Tully Hall concerts sometimes have student rush seats available. Call around 11:30 A.M. on the day of the performance.

Lincoln Center at Broadway and 66th Street—212-875-5050, www.lincolncenter.org

Wave Hill has a concert series from fall to spring, bringing audiences to its Armor Hall for a variety of classical music and jazz performances.

> 675 West 252nd Street, Riverdale—718-549-3200,
> www.wavehill.org

Zinc Bar charges only $5 nightly with a drink minimum to hear great world music, including African, Brazilian, flamenco, jazz, Latin and samba.

> 90 West Houston Street between LaGuardia Place and Thompson Street—212-477-8337, www.zincbar.com

Viewing Opera

Who would have thought that opera could thrive on the seedy Bowery in the East Village? Anthony and Sally Amato, that's who. In 1948, they founded the **Amato Opera Theatre** that in the years since has presented thousands of performances of over forty of the world's great repertory operas, as well as rarely performed works and world premieres. The Amato Opera productions are all fully realized and the casts are comprised of many well-known and aspiring singers and artists. You won't need opera glasses at the Amato…the auditorium is tiny enough—only one hundred seven seats—that you will have a very clear view of the tenor's tonsils and the spinto's spit. Amato stages six productions throughout the year. Tickets are $30, $25 for seniors and students. One caveat: Because part of the Amato's mission is to provide a testing ground for young singers seeking training and experience in opera performance, the casting can sometimes be weak.

319 Bowery at Bleecker Street—212-228-8200, www.amato.org

The not-for-profit **American Opera Projects, Inc.** develops, nurtures and produces new American operas and innovative opera projects and gives performances at several venues around the city. American Opera Projects commissions new works primarily from American librettists and composers and presents them in workshop performances. The musical styles and themes of this company's work are diverse, reflecting the vast range of contemporary American culture. AOP's works are top rate, the opera stories are fascinating (I especially loved their production of *Fireworks*, an opera about a sweet alien who is sent to earth to find out why colored lights are shot into the sky the same time each year), and the singers are culled from pros and up-and-comers. Tickets to most performances are as low as $12, $10 for students and seniors.

138 South Oxford Street, Brooklyn—718-398-4024, www.aopinc.org

Established in 1967 to provide a platform for aspiring singers, the **Bronx Opera** presents one known and one rarely performed opera each season. All Bronx Opera productions are sung in English, with a full chorus and orchestra, and are performed in the Bronx's Lehman College Lovinger Theatre, in Manhattan's Danny Kaye Playhouse at Hunter College, and Long Island's John Cranford Adams Playhouse at Hofstra University. Ticket prices are between $15 and $30 for performances in the Bronx and between $30 and $35 elsewhere.

718-365-4209, www.bronxopera.org

The **Center for Contemporary Opera**, dedicated to the creation and performance of contemporary American opera and opera in English, presents four fully mounted productions per season. Many of the works, which are presented in venues throughout the city, are either New York City or world premieres. For most performances, ticket prices start at around $25.

212-758-2757, www.conopera.org

BEST BARGAIN

People pay upwards of $250 for a single ticket to see the **Metropolitan Opera**. That's right, $250! You don't have to. Standing Room tickets to the Met are available for $12 in the Family Circle and $16 in the orchestra, Monday through Friday, and $15 and $20, respectfully, on Saturday. Then, you can often slide into an unoccupied seat (the ones that go for $250) once the performance begins—just keep an eye out for the overly efficient and often surly ushers who patrol the Standing Room section during the first several minutes of the performance. If you are too timid to steal a seat, you can always purchase one up in the "nosebleed" section (known formally as the Family Circle) for $20 weeknights and $25 on Saturdays, but leave the opera glasses at home and bring a telescope. In the summer, the Metropolitan Opera also offers a series of free concerts in parks throughout the city.

30 Lincoln Center Plaza—212-362-6000, www.metopera.org

The **New York City Opera**, which in the last few years has had a resurgence as one of the city's preeminent cultural institutions, provides audiences three ways to save at the box office:

Custom Subscription Plan lets you create your own series of four to six performances of the productions you want to see, when you want to see them. This plan also entitles you to exchange privileges and preferred seating. Ticket prices under this plan start as low as $23 per performance on a weeknight; $26.50 for weekend nights.

Discovery Series lets you create your own flexible and convenient series of three operas with the benefit of exchange privileges and preferred seating. Tickets for each performance in this plan start at around $26 on a weeknight and $30 for the weekend.

Individual Tickets—If you order tickets prior to the season, you can get the best seats available and pay a lower advance purchase ticket price. If purchased early, Individual Tickets start at around $25 for weeknights, $30 for weekends.

(Note: The ticket prices I quote are for the back rows of the

Fourth Ring—the seats furthest from the stage. However, at the New York City Opera, you can always move to better seats after the intermission.) The New York City Opera does offer $10 **Rush Seats** for seniors and students that may be purchased on the day of performance, and $12 **Standing Room** tickets. The old trick of standees grabbing seats soon after the performance begins works as well here as it does at the Met.

New York State Theatre, 20 Lincoln Center—212-496-0600, www.nycopera.com

New York Grand Opera offers free, fully mounted opera performances under the stars at the **Central Park Summerstage** (Rumsey Playfield, Central Park at 72nd Street and Fifth Avenue) every Wednesday night in July. They do not have a roster of international divas and divos (what do you expect for free?) but the singers are very good and don't get in the way of the music.

212-245-8837, www.newyorkgrandopera.org

Opera Company of Brooklyn presents performances at various locations throughout Brooklyn of affordable, high quality opera in intimate and innovative productions. Opera Company of Brooklyn's repertoire is drawn mostly from popular fare like *Madame Butterfly*, *The Elixir of Love*, and *Amahl and the Night Visitors*, and features established singers as well as promising young talent. Individual tickets range from $15 to $20; low-price subscriptions are available.

212-567-3283, www.operabrooklyn.com

The **Regina Opera** has been presenting operatic productions and concerts in Brooklyn since 1970. What is astounding about this company is that they charge so little for so much. Each opera is fully staged, designed and costumed, and is accompanied by a thirty-five-piece orchestra. Casts are a mix of professionals and student singers. You get all this for $15. Amazing. Better still, seniors only pay $10, high school and middle school students pay $5, and children under 12 are free. The Regina presents three operatic productions of four performances each and five operatic and popular music concerts yearly. Admission for the concerts is $8 for adults, $5 for students and again, children are free.

1251 Tabor Court, Brooklyn—718-232-3555, www.reginaopera.org

Viewing Dance

Free Dance

Bryant Park presents free dance performances in the open air throughout the summer months. Performers and times vary.

Sixth Avenue at 42nd Street—212-768-4242, www.bryantpark.org

Throughout the summer months, **Celebrate Brooklyn** presents free dance performances, generally on Friday evenings, by some of the metropolitan area's leading companies like Mark Morris Dance Group, Ben Munisteri Dance Company and RhythMEK.

Prospect Park Bandshell, 9th Street and Prospect Park West, Brooklyn—718-855-7882, www.celebratebrooklyn.org

On select Fridays in July and August, **Central Park Summerstage** features free outdoor dance concerts of new works by emerging choreographers and companies.

Rumsey Playfield, Central Park at 72nd Street and Fifth Avenue—212-360-2777, www.summerstage.com

Dance Theatre Workshop is probably New York's primary presenter of "the next big thing" in dance. Many of the choreographers and dancers seen here today are emerging artists who hope to use their Dance Theatre Workshop performances as a springboard to becoming tomorrow's stars. The Workshop's very full roster of work is always innovative, experimental and provocative and there is something here for every taste and temperament. Tickets are between $20 and $25; a 40 percent discount is offered to students and seniors. Volunteer for their usher program (ext. 214), where for a couple of hours of your time folding programs and seating the audience, you will be given a free seat.

219 West 19th Street between Seventh and Eighth Avenues—
212-691-6500, www.dtw.org

For twenty years, the **Downtown Dance Festival** has held free afternoon dance performances on the Great Lawn in Battery Park during the last week in August. These recitals begin at noon and feature a mix of styles, including modern, ethnic, youth groups and even Morris dancers.

380 Broadway, 5th Floor—212-219-3910, www.batterydanceco.com

Harlem Week includes presentations during its large black and Latino festival that offers art exhibitions, music, film, and a huge festival on Fifth Avenue from 125th to 135th Streets in early to mid-August.

212-862-8477, www.harlemdiscover.com/harlemweek

The ten-week **Hudson River Festival**, held in the summer months, presents dance as well as free music, theater and story-telling events and art exhibitions. Events take place at several riverside venues including Battery Park, the Winter Garden of the World Financial Center, Castle Clinton and the Battery Park Esplanade.

212-945-0505/212-528-2733, www.hudsonriverfestival.com

The **Joyce Theatre**, once a movie theater, is now the premier presenter of contemporary dance in the city. Throughout the year, the Joyce hosts several renowned companies, like Eliot Feld's Ballet Tech, Compagnie Maguy Marin, Stephen Petronio Company,

Philadanco and Pilobolus Dance Theatre. You can purchase Standing Room tickets if all seats are sold. The Joyce is one of the few theaters featuring dance that still has a volunteer usher program. To become a volunteer usher, call 212-691-9740 and ask for the Volunteer Usher Services.

> 175 Eighth Avenue at 19th Street—212-242-0800, www.joyce.org

The **Lincoln Center Out-of-Doors Festival** offers a spectacular roster of free daily dance events and music concerts (featuring the great and nearly-great) for three weeks in August.

> Lincoln Center, Damrosch Park, 64th Street at Columbus Avenue—212-875-5456, www.lincolncenter.org

Continuing a tradition that first began in the 1960s, **Movement Research at Judson Church** presents free Monday evening performances from September through June each year (doors open at 7:45; for a good seat, arrive early). The Judson Church concerts feature the work of both emerging and established choreographers.

> 55 Washington Square South at Thompson Street—212-477-0351, www.movementresearch.org, www.judson.org

From May to September, the **River to River Festival** (www.rivertorivernyc.com) presents hundreds of free dance offerings and cultural events at venues all over Lower Manhattan. Performers range from the new and unknown to the world-renowned.

Inexpensive Dance

The **Brooklyn Arts Exchange** programs various dance performances by emerging choreographers and dancers. Tickets for these concerts range from $8 to $15.

421 Fifth Avenue at 8th Street, Park Slope, Brooklyn—
718-832-0018, www.bax.org

At one of New York's largest and most reputed dance training centers, **Dance Space Center** in Soho, which provides quality dance education through a wide variety of classes, workshops and performance programs, you may attend student performances and concerts by a variety of local dance companies in their black box theater. Also presented is a "Works in Progress" series (a bi-monthly showcase of informal performances by new and experienced artists looking for feedback to help facilitate the development of their work) and "Raw Material" showcases that enable emerging artists to affordably perform their work in a professionally produced concert. Prices for these performances are never more than $15 and many of them are free or "Pay-As-You-Wish."

451 Broadway between Grand and Howard Streets, 2nd Floor—
212-625-8369, www.dancespace.com

Danspace Project at St. Mark's Church in the Bowery provides a lofty home for downtown dance. Besides hosting dance concerts throughout the year, Danspace Project's special programs include "Global Exchange," presenting the work of international artists and choreographers and "City/Dans," highlighting the work of homegrown choreographers. Danspace Project tickets cost between $10 and $20 with several free performances.

Second Avenue at 10th Street—212-674-8194,
www.danspaceproject.org

Myriad dance companies from around the world perform in the **International Fringe Festival**, which takes place in several locations on the Lower East Side over two weeks in August. As the name of the festival implies, most of the companies featured are of an experimental or avant-garde bent. Pay a reasonable $15 for all events ($8 for seniors and kids under 12), or purchase a pass for five performances at $65 or a ten-performance pass for $110.

> 212-429-8877, www.fringenyc.org

The **Merce Cunningham Studio** in the Westbeth complex is the rehearsal space for Merce Cunningham's company by day; but at night, young choreographers and dancers utilize it to showcase their work. Since anyone who can afford to rent this space has access to it, the work can be real hit-or-miss. A miss is not so bad however when you are paying between $5 and $10, the average cost of tickets at this venue.

> 55 Bethune Street, 11th Floor, between Washington and West Streets—212-691-9751, www.merce.org

The **Metropolitan Opera House**, home to the American Ballet Theatre (www.abt.org) in the spring, hosts several international dance companies throughout the year. Tickets here for dance are not as high as they are for opera, but they're still pricey, topping over $150. To save money, do the same thing I suggested for the opera: buy a Standing Room ticket for between $12 and $20. As soon as the performance begins, look for an empty seat and stake your claim to it. Once the ushers who patrol the Standing Room area leave (about ten minutes into the performance), quietly and unobtrusively, take your seat.

> Lincoln Center, Columbus Avenue at 65th Street—212-362-6000, www.lincolncenter.org

Unfortunately the **New Victory Theatre** only infrequently hosts dance, but when it does, the work, the companies and the choreographers are always first-rate. In the past, such dance luminaries as Mark Morris, Suzanne Farrell and Mikhail Baryshnikov have performed here. With the cheapest seats costing only $10 for the upper balcony, and because this house is rather intimate, you will have an excellent view of the stage and it won't cost a fortune.

209 West 42nd Street between Seventh and Eighth Avenues— 646-223-3020, www.newvictory.org

With a company of ninety dancers and an active repertory of over one hundred fifty works, the **New York City Ballet** is one of the foremost ballet companies in the world. Happily, this company makes its repertory available to everyone through its many low-priced ticket programs. These programs include:

Individual Tickets start at $16 for the back rows of the fourth ring, but you can always move to better seats after the intermission (just make sure they have been vacated).

$10 Student Rush Tickets—Any high school or university student with valid student ID may purchase one ticket either online through NYCB's website or in person at the New York State Box Office window. Student Rush is not available for every performance. Availability is posted weekly and can be checked at NYCB's website or by telephoning the Student Rush Ticket Hotline at 212-870-7766. Student Rush tickets must be purchased on the day of performance. For weekday and evening performances, online ticket orders must be placed by 3 P.M.; for weekend matinees, by 11 A.M. These tickets depend on availability, with seating locations assigned by the Box Office.

Fourth Ring Society—For a $15 fee, you are entitled to purchase tickets in the Fourth Ring for $12 (usually priced at $32). As a member of the Fourth Ring Society, you may go as often as you like; buy your tickets in advance for any performance; attend pre-show lectures; and are given Thank You gifts like free cappuccino at each performance, an NYCB t-shirt and discount coupons for area restaurants.

Standing Room Tickets cost $12. (Use the old trick of sliding into seats soon after the performance begins.)

New York State Theatre, Columbus Avenue and 65th Street— 212-870-5660, www.nycballet.com

P.S. 122 presents all kinds of dance performances, from the avant-garde to the outrageous. Most of the work here is new, created and performed by emerging dance professionals. Ticket prices to see dance at P.S. 122 are very inexpensive, between $10 and $20; seniors and students with a valid ID receive $3 off the ticket price.

150 First Avenue at 9th Street—212-477-5829, www.ps122.org

New York City Information Outlets

311

A recent expansion of the New York City telephone hotline, 311, now provides information about a plethora of cultural events, including concerts, museum exhibits, restaurants and theater.

Alliance for Downtown New York

City Hall Park (at Park Row and Broadway)—212-566-6700, www.downtownny.com

Fashion Center Information Kiosk

555 Seventh Avenue at 39th Street—212-398-7943, www.fashioncenter.com

NYC & Company / I ♥ NY

Convention and Visitors Bureau Visitors Information Center, 810 Seventh Avenue (between 52nd and 53rd Streets)—212-484-1222, www.nycvisit.com

Times Square Visitors Center

1560 Broadway between 46th and 47th Streets—212-869-1890, www.timessquarebid.org

Cultural Listings

There is a plethora of listings available, both in periodicals and on the internet, detailing the events and attractions of any given week in the city. Most contain information on music, dance, theater, museums, parks, film, art galleries, walking tours, events for children, entertainment venues, monuments, historical buildings, political meetings, shopping, nightlife, fashion, book signings, lectures, restaurants and much more. Most of these listings include hours and admissions, maps and event calendars.

Newspapers and Magazines

The **"Around Town" section of** *Time Out New York* (www.timeoutny.com) offers a comprehensive list of happenings in and around New York every week. Many if not most of these events are free and range from political debates and rallies, to celebrity sports tournaments, music boat cruises, bicycle tours, Revolutionary War reenactments (yeah, the British invaded Staten Island), seminars, book readings, workshops, career fairs, cultural arts festivals, crafts fairs, as well as concerts, walking tours, museum, gallery, performing arts, film, and street fair listings.

In the "Weekend Fine Arts/Leisure" section of the Friday edition of *The New York Times* (www.nytimes.com), there is always an extensive listing of the coming weekend's free and inexpensive city activities. The column titled "Spare Times" lists everything from museum shows to walking tours, street fairs, free films, neighborhood festivals, fun runs and bicycle tours, as well as lots of stuff to do with kids. The pages also carry informative articles and full-length and capsule reviews of gallery and museum exhibitions. It's a very handy guide to turn to, especially on those Fridays when you're whining in your apartment about not having anything to do over the weekend.

The **"Arts and Leisure" section of the Sunday *New York Times*** carries reviews and articles on the current cultural scene, as well as pieces detailing upcoming events and an exhaustive listing of all the arts.

An invaluable resource to enjoying New York's museums is the magazine ***Museums New York***, which is published monthly and can be purchased at museum shops and newsstands. In *Museums New York* you'll find a comprehensive guide to all the city's museums, with opening and closing times, articles about current exhibitions and a list of most of the galleries.

Created for budget-conscious New Yorkers, ***Club freeTime Magazine***, sold by subscription and at select newsstands throughout the city, lists free and discounted cultural events and educational offerings such as concerts and performances, lectures, walking tours, film screenings, readings, street fairs and festivals, singles gatherings and workshops in Manhattan. To subscribe or to find a newsstand nearest you that carries *Club freeTime*, contact their office at 20 Waterside Plaza, Suite 6F, New York City, NY 10010—212-545-8900 or visit their website at www.clubfreetime.com. For members only, the *Club freeTime* website also lists countless free events. Cost to join is $2.95 per month, $7.95 for three months and $19.95 per year.

And, of course, ***New York Magazine*** (www.newyorkmag.com), the ***Village Voice*** *(www.villagevoice.com)*, ***The New York Post*** (www.newyorkpost.com), ***New York Press*** (www.nypress.com),

The Daily News (www.nydailynews.com), and *The New Yorker* (www.newyorker.com) carry in-depth listings, articles and reviews of all things cultural that are happening in the city.

Cultural Websites

www.aislesay.com

www.allianceforarts.org

www.allny.com

www.americantheaterweb.com

www.broadway.com

www.broadwaybeat.com

www.broadwaystars.com

www.broadwayworld.com

www.curtainup.com

www.entertainment-link.com

www.fandango.com

www.ilovenytheatre.com

www.livebroadway.com

www.moviefone.com

www.musicalheaven.com

www.newyork.citysearch.com

www.newyorkmag.com

www.notfortourists.com

www.ny.com

www.nyc.com

www.nyc.gov

www.nycpulse.com

www.nyctourist.com

www.nycvisit.com (New York Convention and Visitor's Bureau)

www.nytheatre.com

www.nytheatre-wire.com

www.nytimes.com

www.offbroadway.com

www.oobr.com (Off-Off-Broadway Reviews)

www.papermag.com

www.playbill.com

www.readio.com

www.showpeople.com

www.stagebill.com

www.talkinbroadway.com

www.talkentertainment.com

www.tcg.org (Theatre Communications Group)

www.tdf.org (Theatre Development Fund)

www.theatermania.com

www.theatrereviews.com

www.theinsider.com/nyc

www.things2doinnewyork.com

www.timeoutny.com

www.timessquarebid.org (Times Square Visitor's Center)

www.tonyawards.com

www.totaltheater.com

www.variety.com

www.villagevoice.com

Contact Me

Do you have a favorite low-priced haunt that I haven't included here? Know another way to save money or get the best for less? If so, forward your ideas to me. I'll follow up on all suggestions, and those I deem eligible will be included in the next edition of this book.

Write to:
Craig Wroe/*Living Smart—New York City*
c/o Amadeus Press/Limelight Editions
512 Newark Pompton Turnpike
Pompton Plains, NJ 07444
www.limelighteditions.com
info@limelighteditions.com

CRAIG WROE is an actor, writer and teacher, and has lived in New York City since 1984. His acting credits include appearances on London's West End and the Bristol Old Vic, off- and off-off-Broadway, film, television, commercials, industrials and several leading regional theaters. As a teacher, Craig lectures on acting and "the business" at colleges and universities throughout the country and is on the faculty of New York's School for Film and Television. As author of *An Actor Prepares ... to Live in New York City* (Limelight Editions, 2003) and *An Actor Prepares ... to Work in New York City* (Limelight Editions, 2004), Craig has conducted seminars on "Living the Good Life in the Big Apple" for the Learning Annex, and has appeared on NBC's *Weekend Today in New York*.